real food for everyone

Real Food for Everyone

vegan-friendly meals for meat-lovers, vegetarians, and vegans

Ann Gentry

Photography by Sara Remington

Andrews McMeel
Publishing

Kansas City · Sydney · London

real food for everyone

Andrews McMeel Publishing, LLC
an Andrews McMeel Universal company
1130 Walnut Street, Kansas City, Missouri 64106

www.andrewsmcmeel.com

15 16 17 18 19 SDB 10 9 8 7 6 5 4 3 2 1

ISBN: 978-1-4494-6653-4

Library of Congress Control Number: 2014948819

Design: Diane Marsh
Photography: Sara Remington
Food Stylist: Robyn Valarik
Food Stylist Assistant: Mara Dockery
Prop Stylist: Dani Fisher
Prop Stylist Assistant: Bella Foster
Camera Assistant: Shawn Corrigan
Editor: Jean Z. Lucas
Art director: Julie Barnes
Production editor: Maureen Sullivan
Production manager: Carol Coe
Demand planner: Sue Eikos

Photography on pages 28, 216, 220, 228, 232 courtesy of iStockphoto.com

www.realfood.com

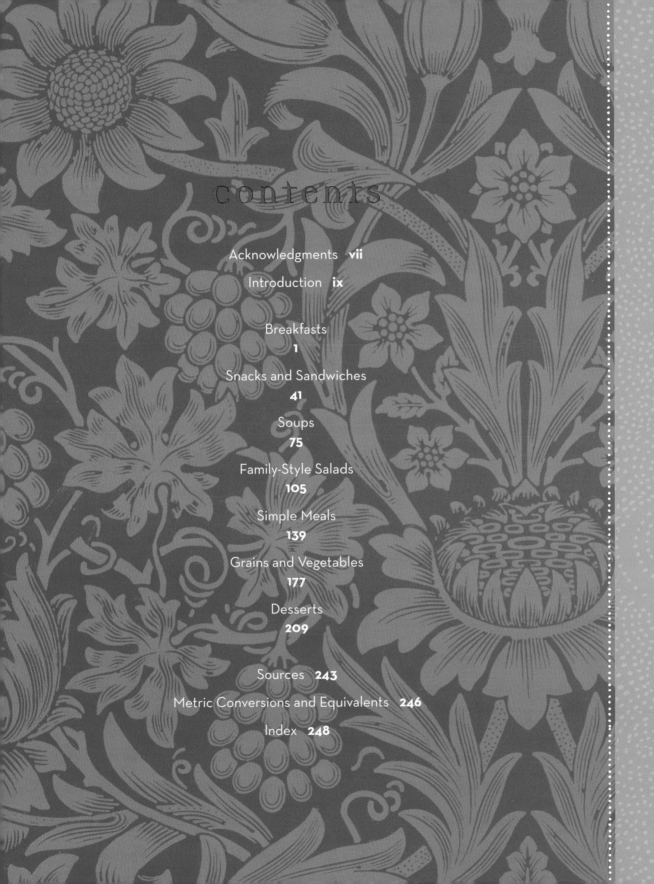

contents

*I*t takes a village to raise a cookbook. I have much gratitude to *my village*: my immediate family, friends, business associates, employees, and guests at Real Food Daily who contributed to the raising of this book.

many thanks,

To Rochelle Palermo, my recipe editor and tester for both my cookbooks, who transformed my culinary ideas into coherent, executable recipes for all to enjoy.

To writer Laura Samuel Meyn, who came through at every juncture in this

acknowledgments

process with laserlike attention to detail and made sense of my half-baked or sometimes overcooked words and ideas.

To Sara Remington and team—you can come over to my house any time to prep, cook, style, shoot, and make magic turning my recipes into beautiful photographs.

To the team at Andrews McMeel, starting with publisher Kirsty Melville, who once again opened a door for me; Jean Lucas, my editor, who was always available and kept me on point; and Julie Barnes and Diane Marsh, the fantastic design team who created the right frame for my recipes and Sara's photographs.

To my Real Food team, Kacy Hulme and Beth Griffiths, my assistants who held my work space together—thank you both for the support you gave me in writing this book. And to my chefs, Shelly, Ivy and Romualdo—thanks for answering all my persnickety questions.

To Robert Jacobs, my husband, for his unwavering support and belief in what I do.

And to our children, Halle and Walker, who are the future faces of a world where more people will eat delicious, balanced, organically grown "real food."

INTRODUCTION

Want your family to enjoy delicious, healthful meals and snacks? Feel and look their best? Improve their long-term health? Help the environment? Vegan food makes an incredible difference, for our bodies and for the world around us. I've been experimenting with various vegetarian and vegan cuisines for three decades, starting as a young actress struggling with my weight and appearance, and today as a working mother with two children and the proprietress of America's leading organic vegan restaurants, Real Food Daily. I've learned in order to stick with a plant-based diet, one must cook at home, with simple recipes. This book is filled with flavorful and satisfying recipes that support everyone's health, personal ethics, and the environment that we all share.

IT'S NOT NECESSARY TO BECOME VEGAN OR VEGETARIAN TO ENJOY THE BENEFITS OF EATING PLANT-BASED MEALS. Don't let an all-or-nothing attitude turn you off: It's well worth the effort to consume less meat and dairy even if you don't eliminate it entirely. In fact, my own diet is just shy of 100 percent vegan. On occasion, I eat a small amount of fish and dairy.

After a childhood spent eating a typical American diet, Southern-style, and later surviving on sweets and cigarettes in college, my life took a profound turn in my twenties. I was an aspiring actress in New York City, waiting tables at a vegetarian restaurant in Greenwich Village. Whole Wheat 'n' Wild Berrys was a place percolating with energy and information about how to eat differently. I quickly eliminated meat and dairy from my diet.

Inspired by the budding natural foods movement, I experimented with fasting, juicing, and megavitamins. But conflicting information and impractical dietary regimes left me feeling lost and confused. After wading through most of the natural foods store's offerings, I found macrobiotics, a diet based on whole grains and vegetables, to be the most sensible and balanced. Macrobiotics taught me how to eat, and how to cook. Most important, macrobiotics taught me the connection between diet and health. (For more on macrobiotics, turn to page 202.) Later, when I moved to California, my newfound proximity to local organic farmers and outdoor markets was another great inspiration.

Over the years, I've explored the many permutations of a plant-based diet. I spent years as a strict vegan and a macrobiotic, and I experimented with raw foods, food combining, wheat- and gluten-free eating, and other dietary regimes. Today, I know what makes me feel best—a mostly vegan diet.

IT'S a GOOD TIME TO BE VEGAN OR VEGETARIAN.
In the 1970s natural foods was a fringe movement, but today it is mainstream. Being vegan is actually cool. When I began changing my diet, many vegetarian products and ingredients were only available at a few independent natural foods stores. Today, vegetarian, vegan, macrobiotic, and whole foods ingredients and products are available at conventional mainstream supermarkets across America.

The natural foods movement rose in response to an epidemic of degenerative diseases: Twentieth-century America saw an explosion of heart disease, diabetes, obesity, certain cancers, and more. Most of these diseases can be directly attributed to radical changes in our food supply, changes brought about by the industrial revolution. In response, authors and researchers began to identify and document the connection between industrialized food and the degenerative diseases suddenly plaguing America and began to tear down the myth that meat is a necessary part of a nutritious diet.

In 1971, Frances Moore Lappé published *Diet for a Small Planet*, a radical book for its time, telling people how they could thrive without meat. Lappé's book laid the foundation for a vegetarian movement to flourish among the Baby Boom generation. In 1987, John Robbins published *Diet for a New America*, waking up Gen Xers to the importance of plant-based foods. Robbins did more than just document the health consequences of a meat-based diet—he exposed the harm industrialized meat production does to the environment, and the horrific treatment animals endure in America's factory feedlots.

An industry of health, natural, organic, and macrobiotic foods was born, giving rise to companies like Eden Foods, Erewhon, Ohsawa, White Wave, and many others. People formed cooperatives in their communities to acquire these new ingredients. Some of the cooperatives evolved into full-fledged natural foods stores such as the Co-opportunity market in Santa Monica, California, where I shop today. Hand in hand with the natural foods movement, longevity centers opened where people could retreat, eat healthfully, and exercise. Today, the same principles are incorporated in health spas such as Canyon Ranch and California Health & Longevity Institute, where a balanced approach to wellness hinges on a clean, healthful diet.

The message has gone mainstream: We're hearing from medical doctors and public health advocates that we need to eat more plant-based foods. Contemporary best-selling authors Michael Pollan and Mark Bittman offer compelling arguments for eating far less meat, successfully catching the imaginations of a much wider audience than their predecessors. The United Nations has recommended one meatless day a week as a means of combating climate change; and Johns Hopkins Bloomberg School of Public Health sponsors Meatless Monday, a national nonprofit initiative that's working to reduce meat consumption by 15 percent to improve personal health and the health of our planet.

THE COOKBOOK YOU HOLD IN YOUR HANDS IS ENTIRELY VEGAN. People already know that looking after their family's long-term health means fitting more vegetables, fruits, and whole grains into every meal, and more plant-based meals and snacks into every week. You may be asking yourself, "How can I accomplish this?" The answer is contained within the book: home-cooked vegan meals.

If you're intimidated by the thought of preparing plant-based food, don't be. A standard peanut butter and jelly sandwich is vegan. Most of the easy vegan recipes that follow have fewer than a dozen ingredients—and they're much more delicious than a PB&J. How about Lasagna Rolls (page 166), Pinto Bean Enchiladas (page 142), or Burger in a Salad with Caramelized Onions, Avocado, Tomatoes, and Thousand Island Dressing (page 117)?

VEGAN FOOD IS HEALTHFUL AND BALANCED. Did you know that most Americans consume way too much protein? The USDA has shamelessly promoted the myth that we need more protein than we do, in order to bolster meat sales, which in turn increases sales of crops like corn and soybeans that are used to fatten up livestock. Excess protein has been linked to kidney stones and osteoporosis, among other health issues.

It's easy to get the protein you need from plant-based foods; protein-rich ingredients include beans, soy products, nuts, and seeds. Sprinkle a handful of toasted nuts onto your salad, or add tofu or tempeh to a vegetable stir-fry. With enough variety, you'll find that a plant-based diet will leave you feeling satisfied and energized.

I used to be concerned about getting enough vitamins and minerals. Of the fifty vitamins and minerals you need, forty-eight are plentiful in plants. Of the two that are not, vitamin D is produced in your body every time the sun shines on you, and the other, vitamin B12, is present in some fortified vegan foods like cereals, nondairy milks, nutritional yeast, and plant-based butter replacements and can also be taken as a supplement.

A plant-based diet, naturally high in fiber, low in fat, and rich in vitamins and minerals, will reduce your risk of heart disease, diabetes, obesity, and certain types of cancer. Dietary cholesterol is only present in animal products, so a vegan diet is inherently a cholesterol-free one.

The smartest plant-based diets go beyond avoiding animal products and focus on real food: In other words, whole foods as opposed to

processed, refined products. Consider rice, for instance: The complete milling and polishing that converts brown rice to white rice discards all dietary fiber and essential fatty acids; most of the iron and vitamins B3, B1, and B6; and half of the manganese and phosphorus. That's why I reach for brown rice even when I'm making dessert (check out my Coconut Rice Pudding on page 231)—it's that important.

VEGAN FOOD IS SUSTAINABLE. Eating lower on the food chain, or eating vegetables instead of animals that ate the vegetables, is health-smart, and environmentally smart, too. It takes only half an acre of land to feed a vegan, but seven acres to feed a meat-eater. Producing vegetables and grains uses a fraction of the water and fossil fuels that are required to produce the same calories from meat. Incredibly, the meat industry generates more man-made greenhouse gas emissions than all cars, trucks, and buses combined. Going meatless just a couple of days a week saves more energy and greenhouse gases than driving a hybrid car.

It's now clear that global climate change is directly related to agriculture: Every year we lose millions of acres of wilderness to cattle grazing lands. Factory feedlot operations release tons of methane, a gas that has twenty-five times more heat-trapping properties than other greenhouse gases. Energy-intensive fertilizers, polluting pesticides, food processing, and the transportation of animals all pollute the environment. By moving toward a more sensible and simple way of eating, we will be a healthier society while creating a better future.

It's no wonder that my organic vegan restaurants are filling up with people who aren't vegan or vegetarian full-time. People are thinking about their health and their impact on the

In 1975, my brother-in-law, organic farmer Larry Jacobs, was living on the property of back-to-the-land pioneers Scott and Helen Nearing, who followed a vegan lifestyle at their Maine homestead, working the land, growing their own foods, building, and writing (they published *Living the Good Life*, among many other books). In their heyday, it was nothing short of radical to be vegetarian.

Larry tells ironic stories of medical doctors traveling to Harborside, Maine, to see Scott Nearing, a strong ninety-year-old man who hadn't eaten an animal in more than forty years. In disbelief, these doctors performed tests on the Nearings, looking for maladies that must exist in someone who hadn't eaten meat for so long. Tests and observations proved the Nearings to be in superb health. In fact, the Nearings were far healthier than their meat-eating contemporaries and were entirely free of

Hale, Hearty, and vegan

the degenerative diseases plaguing Americans. The Nearings' vegan diet and vigorous lifestyle (they refused to exploit horses to pull their plows through their gardens, instead tilling the soil themselves at ninety years of age) left them in the physical condition of people one-quarter their age.

environment, with a growing interest in adding plant-based meals to their weekly repertoire.

VEGAN FOOD IS KIND. The ethical and environmental costs of factory farming have become impossible to ignore. Not eating meat is a more effective and immediate solution than campaigning for the rights of animals on their way to the slaughterhouse. Young people seem to know this inherently; they're quick to question why some animals are kept as pets and considered friends while others are eaten. My school-age kids don't always eat vegan meals outside our house, but they do stick to a vegetarian diet easily—and very much on their own.

For many people, becoming vegetarian is a great place to start. If you choose to eliminate dairy and eggs, too, you'll be doing that much more for your health and the environment. Both the commercial dairy and egg industries employ highly questionable practices to keep production up and costs down. Animal fats like those from eggs and dairy clog our arteries and leave us feeling sluggish. Fruits, vegetables, and whole grains—what I call "real food"—leave us feeling light and energized.

FAMILY AND FRIENDS MAY WONDER ABOUT SOME OF THE NEW FOODS YOU'RE EATING. Having grown up in the South, the new foods I started eating did not go unnoticed. My family of origin started calling the cuisine I ate "Ann's food," as if it were something really strange. On visits home to Memphis, I'd make meals in my mother's kitchen—meals that she enjoyed eating, but with some reserve. At some point during the meal, there would always be a reference to "Ann's food."

Many years later, after my first restaurant opened, my family started to embrace the food I ate. On trips to Los Angeles, my parents would eat at Real Food Daily and see how crowded the restaurant was. "There must be something to this food," they thought, "if all these people are eating here." I have won over many skeptics by entertaining with such dishes as my version of Bangers and Mash: Apple-Sage Field Roast Grain Sausage with Mashed Potatoes and Celeriac Root (page 162). My extended family and friends might not eat plant-based meals all the time, but they look forward to the ones we share—and I enjoy proving that plant-based meals are far more satisfying than they had imagined.

VEGAN FOOD IS DELICIOUS. A plant-based diet encourages creativity in the kitchen, with a seasonally rotating palette of fresh, colorful produce ripe for use. Prepare the best local and seasonal ingredients with a variety of cooking methods, and you'll have more interesting and diverse tastes, textures, and colors on your plate.

For inspiration, I often turn to recipes that come from traditions around the world. Recipes with a long culinary history are always heartfelt endeavors: There's a reason people pass them down from generation to generation. Consider India, with its many traditional vegetable dishes made sultry with exotic combinations of spices that lend layers of flavor and heat; the Far East, with its creative uses of tofu and tempeh, and its rich condiments like miso and tamari; and Mexico, with its earthy way of combining ingredients like chiles, beans, and corn for just the right balance. You'll find these traditions reflected in such recipes as Curried Red Lentil Soup (page 89), Sichuan Noodles with Hot Spicy

Peanut Sauce (page 147), and Southwestern Salad with Chipotle Ranch Dressing and Agave-Chili Tortilla Strips (page 112), among others.

Vibrant flavors help defy what people expect from vegan fare. Case in point: One time, a family friend from Tennessee who is a very successful soybean and cotton farmer came to Los Angeles and ate lunch at Real Food Daily. When he returned home, he told his friends, "I don't know what I ate, but it sure was good."

CHANGE IS POSSIBLE—AND IT STARTS AT HOME. While I hope you will visit me at Real Food Daily for a vegan meal and some culinary inspiration, I believe that real dietary changes happen at home—that's where you can support yourself with good cooking and eating habits. Cooking at home also has the advantage of being budget-friendly and family-friendly. Seasonal fresh vegetables cost less than meat, and you can adjust recipes to the tastes of those around your table. It's well worth the time: Showing your children and friends how to eat well is one of the most important life skills you can pass on.

As a busy working mother, I struggle with day-to-day challenges: Juggling work, kids, grocery shopping, exercise, and trying to squeeze in a little time for myself. So where do I find the time to prepare meals at home? First, I begin with simple meals. While it's nice to have four dishes at every meal, it's not necessary. Balance your nutrition intake across the week, and don't get hung up on making every meal complete. Instead, focus on one or two recipes, made with a variety of plant-based ingredients.

The dishes in this book are designed for family meals. They are simple vegan recipes with approachable ingredients lists and techniques, relatively short preparation times, and, of course, wide appeal. I consider your family to be whoever gathers around your table regularly; the recipes that follow can help you find ways to incorporate more plant-based meals and snacks more often, both for yourself and your loved ones.

GET STARTED TODAY. I've found it exciting and validating that so many people are enjoying the benefits of going meatless; that's what inspired this book. I've filled it with my favorite go-to recipes for home-cooking—more than 100 of them. For help with ingredients that might be new to you, simply turn to the Real Food Pantry listings throughout the book for extra information that will demystify the likes of spelt and umeboshi, and many more plant-based pantry staples. Keep in mind that many of my recipes are easily adapted to the ingredients you have on hand, so scan the recipe introduction for suggestions.

Quick and easy vegan recipes are what people in my restaurants have been asking for, and it's what we all need: Recipes that don't compromise our ethics or health, yet don't take all day to prepare. The reasons are plentiful and it's easy to make delicious food that's good for your family and good for the planet. Whether you're a committed vegan who's looking for new ways to prepare fresh, healthful meals at home or a life-long omnivore who wants to improve your health and do your part for the environment, you'll find that there's something very powerful in cooking plant-based meals for yourself, your family, and your friends.

breakfasts

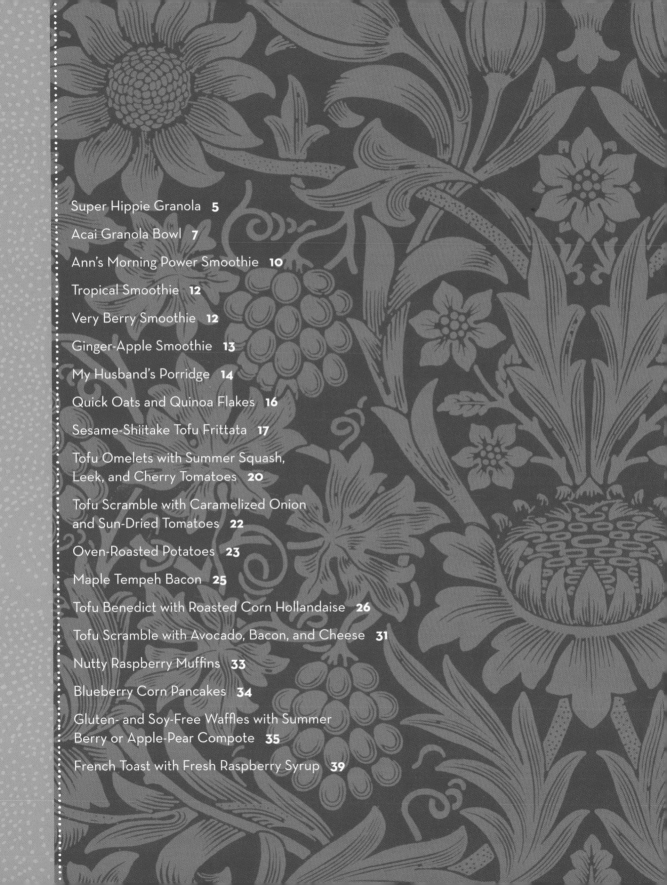

Believe me, I've heard all the reasons people don't eat breakfast: They don't have time, or they're not hungry in the morning, or all they need is a cup of coffee. In fact, I've been guilty of saying some of those things myself. I, too, was once a gal who never ate breakfast. These days, I eat breakfast daily—and I am a champion of good breakfasts because I've learned why they're so important.

In Chinese medicine, eating good-quality foods when you wake up is believed to kick-start your chi. Chi is energy—*your* energy. Think of eating breakfast as turning on the ignition to your body. Eating within the first hour of waking energizes your mind, too, helping you feel focused. Breakfast also makes a difference later on, when you might otherwise be tempted to reach for a quick (and less healthful) fix. In fact, eating breakfast is a widely recognized tool for maintaining a healthy weight—people who eat breakfast actually reduce their risk of obesity and improve their ability to make smart food choices the rest of the day.

While many breakfast foods can be taken along to work (it seems that modern life doesn't always allow room for more relaxed meals), I do try to allow myself time in the morning to eat a little something at my table. I enjoy the ritual of the morning news with my cup of tea and a wholesome breakfast. I've witnessed firsthand the difference a healthful breakfast makes to me and to my family, and I've come to think of it as a necessity rather than a luxury.

So what about those good-quality foods for optimizing chi? They're all in this chapter: from my Super Hippie Granola (page 5) and Nutty Raspberry Muffins (page 33) that can be prepared ahead of time for grab-and-go breakfasts all week long, to my Gluten- and Soy-Free Waffles (page 35) and Sesame-Shiitake Tofu Frittata (page 17) that you can whip up when you have a few extra minutes. I have included recipes for healthful smoothies to enjoy at home or on the run, and pancake breakfasts worthy of serving to weekend guests, whether they're vegan or not. My recipes are all free of animal products, naturally, and they're packed with the good stuff that will help you feel your brightest and most energetic as the day begins.

super Hippie granola

Granola has long been thought of as hippie food. I call my granola "Super Hippie" because it contains superfoods like goji berries and Hunza mulberries, which make it even more nutrition-packed than the original (for more on superfoods, see page 8). The best granola has just the right amount of sweetness and crunchiness and has been baked to a golden brown. For perfectly balanced sweetness, cut the maple syrup with rice syrup. Rice syrup is also essential to the texture, as it helps create clusters, which granola-lovers know are key to exceptional results (ideally, granolas are equal parts loose ingredients and small clusters). If you don't have coconut oil on hand, using an unflavored neutral cooking oil is fine. Granola makes a great snack on its own and is delicious served with any nondairy milk, including homemade nut milk (page 30). **Makes 6 cups**

1½ cups old-fashioned rolled oats

½ cup raw Brazil nuts, coarsely chopped

½ cup raw shelled sunflower seeds

½ cup raw whole almonds, coarsely chopped

1 teaspoon ground cinnamon

½ teaspoon fine sea salt

2 tablespoons melted unrefined coconut oil (see Cooking Tip)

½ cup pure maple syrup

¼ cup brown rice syrup

2 tablespoons water

1 tablespoon vanilla extract

¼ cup dried apricots, diced

¼ cup dried goji berries

¼ cup dried Hunza mulberries

¼ cup golden raisins

Position a rack in the middle of the oven and preheat the oven to 300°F. Line a large, heavy baking sheet with parchment paper.

Mix the oats, Brazil nuts, sunflower seeds, almonds, cinnamon, and salt in a large bowl.

Heat the coconut oil in a small, heavy saucepan over low heat. Add the maple syrup, rice syrup, water, and vanilla, and whisk just until blended and heated through. Drizzle the syrup mixture over the oat mixture, and stir with a whisk to coat. Spoon the granola mixture evenly over the prepared baking sheet.

Bake the granola for about 40 minutes, or until it is golden brown and clusters form. As the granola bakes, gently stir it about every 15 minutes with a fork to ensure it cooks evenly but being careful not to break up the clusters. Add the dried apricots, goji berries, mulberries, and raisins and continue baking for 10 minutes longer. Set the granola aside to cool (it will become crunchy when cool).

The granola can be stored in an airtight container for up to 2 weeks.

Cooking Tip: You'll need to melt the coconut oil before measuring it. In a small saucepan, place 2 generous tablespoons of solid coconut oil over the lowest heat and melt. Once it's liquid, measure to 2 tablespoons of oil.

Variations: It's fun to experiment with some of the superfoods, but don't let these unusual ingredients or their unavailability turn you away from making granola: While they are easily found in many areas in natural foods stores, you may choose to substitute dried coconut, cranberries, cherries, dates, or figs. Golden raisins add a beautiful color, but any black raisin or currant will do. Feel free to use your favorite nuts and seeds; I often use walnuts, pecans, or hazelnuts.

The evolution of granola

Even though hippies helped to ignite the popularity of granola in the 1960s right along with the natural foods movement, the first boxes of mainstream, commercially prepared granola didn't hit the shelves until 1972. I went to college in the 1970s and missed the height of the hippie movement, but I can remember eating granola out of a box for many a meal. It was inexpensive, it gave me energy, and I loved the ease of it: At that time, I had no clue how to cook anything, so sweet, crunchy granola and a carton of milk made for a perfect meal in my dorm room. Little did I know then that this exact time period marked a veritable granola revival all over the country, as the natural foods movement took hold and what had once been limited to health enthusiasts went mainstream.

"Granula," as it was first called, was made from graham flour and resembled oversized Grape-Nuts. Dr. James Caleb Jackson, who ran a health spa in Dansville, New York, won bragging rights for being the first to make and sell it in the late 1800s. Around the same time, Dr. John Harvey Kellogg developed a similar cereal—and only renamed it "Granola" when he got into legal issues with Jackson. When the colorful 1960s kicked off granola's enduring popularity, rolled oats were the recipe's main ingredient. By the 1970s, there were several people who claimed to have revived or re-invented granola. One was Layton Gentry—no kin of mine—who developed a successful recipe and sold it to two companies: The first was Sovex Natural Foods in Tennessee, whose granola sales were over $1 million in 1971.

After buying back the western U.S. rights from Sovex, Gentry then sold the recipe to Lassen Foods in California. *Time* magazine profiled Gentry in 1972, calling him "Johnny Granola-Seed."

These days, I'm happy to continue the ever-evolving tradition of refining granola's recipe to create a breakfast cereal that's packed with nutrition. Using my Super Hippie Granola (page 5) as inspiration, feel free to adapt it with your own mix of favorite fruits, nuts, and seeds.

acai granola bowl

This recipe presents a whole new way to enjoy the Super Hippie Granola (page 5)—blending acai berry bars (from the frozen foods section of many natural foods stores) with a small amount of nondairy milk. I prefer the unsweetened frozen acai berry bars, to which you can add a bit of agave nectar; if that's too tart for your taste buds, then use the bars that are sweetened with organic cane sugar. I use a rice, hemp, or coconut milk beverage, as I like the flavor of these nondairy milks. As an alternative, you can skip the nondairy milk entirely for a thicker, more yogurt-like consistency. Either way, the results are delicious. I also like to top the granola with seasonal fresh fruits, such as peaches, berries, pears, or bananas. **Serves 4**

2 (3½-ounce) frozen unsweetened acai berry bars, thawed until soft

1 ripe banana, peeled

6 fresh strawberries, hulled

¼ to ½ cup nondairy milk

1 tablespoon agave nectar

⅛ teaspoon ground cinnamon

2 cups Super Hippie Granola (page 5)

Assorted seasonal fresh fruits (optional)

Blend the acai berry bars, banana, whole strawberries, ¼ cup milk, agave nectar, and cinnamon in a blender on high speed until smooth. If necessary, add enough milk to achieve the desired consistency. You should have a little bit more than 2 cups of the acai mixture.

Divide the acai mixture among 4 bowls. Spoon ½ cup of the granola over the acai mixture in each bowl. Top with seasonal fresh fruits, and serve immediately.

exotic
superfoods

In the last few years, exotic superfoods have made it into our marketplace, gaining a great deal of attention from nutritionists and the media alike. *Superfood* is a term for a food with a high phytonutrient content—exceptionally high, considering its calories per serving—with possible health benefits as a result. Not all superfoods are exotic: Even common foods like spinach and blueberries qualify. Spinach, for example, is especially dense in iron; when you eat even easily found superfoods, you're getting the most out of every calorie you consume.

While it's encouraging to know that some of our everyday favorites are such smart choices, more exotic superfoods like acai berries are fun to experiment with, too: They bring new flavors, textures, and health benefits to the table. Exotic superfoods are popular with people following a raw diet; advocates claim that such foods are capable of virtual nutritional miracles, such as increasing longevity and healing disease. Whether or not that's the case, these nutritional powerhouses are well worth trying. They're excellent for snacking or for using in recipes: The three fruits listed here make my Super Hippie Granola (page 5) really outstanding. Remember that there's no one magic ingredient; you get different health benefits from different foods, which is why variety and moderation are so important.

ACAI is a small, round berry native to Central and South America; it looks very similar to a small grape or a blueberry. It's considered to be one of nature's most complete and healthy foods, as it's loaded with antioxidants, amino acids, essential fatty acids, fiber, and protein. With a flavor that's been described as between a berry and dark chocolate, acai berries aren't naturally sweet, so they're often blended with other ingredients. Mostly, you'll find acai in juice blends, smoothies, yogurts, instant drink mixes, and frozen acai berry bars..

FLAXSEEDS are highly recommended for whole-body nutrition; research is ongoing, but some people believe that they can reduce your risk of heart disease, stroke, some cancers, and diabetes. Flaxseed oil is a rich source of essential fatty acids: I often use flaxseed oil as an ingredient, as it's an easy way to boost the nutritional content of my salad dressings (page 106). I also add it to the mix I use to coat my French toast (page 39), where it lends a golden color and deep flavor to the dish. Whole flaxseeds are rich in fiber and lignans (compounds in plants that act as antioxidants) as well as essential fatty acids.

GOJI BERRIES (also called wolfberries) are shriveled bright red berries native to China; when dried, they have a shape and chewy texture similar to raisins. The taste is slightly sweet and sour with a mild tanginess—a cross between a cranberry and a cherry. They are rich in antioxidants, particularly carotenoids such as beta-carotene. I love to snack on these little gems; they're chewy and satisfying.

DRIED MULBERRIES are known for their distinctively tangy, rich flavors; they are plump and chewy and offer vitamin C, iron, calcium, protein, and dietary fiber. Look for Hunza mulberries, which are indigenous to one region of Pakistan, at your natural foods store. Harvested wild and dried, Hunza mulberries are a raw food that never undergoes treatment or processing.

ann's morning power smoothie

This is my favorite smoothie. Sometimes I make slight fruit variations depending upon what I have on hand, but I pretty much stick to these ingredients. Look for coconut water at your local natural foods store, or in the beverage section of some supermarkets. Coconut water is an excellent source of potassium, and it naturally rehydrates the body with electrolytes. Apple juice, berry juice, or orange juice will also work well in its place. I like to add a green vitamin powder to give my smoothies an extra boost of nutrition: There are many kinds available, so read the labels carefully, and choose a green vitamin powder that's made mostly from fruits and vegetables. **Makes about 3½ cups**

1 (11.2-ounce) container coconut water

3 tablespoons soaked almonds (recipe follows), drained

1 tablespoon soaked flaxseeds (recipe follows), drained

1 tablespoon green vitamin powder

1 ripe banana, peeled

1 cup assorted fresh or frozen berries

½ cup fresh or frozen peach or mango chunks

Blend all the ingredients in a blender until smooth. Pour the smoothie into glasses and serve immediately.

During the warm-weather months, a smoothie is the perfect way to start your day: It's cool and delicious, and it's also a smart tool for incorporating into your diet the extra antioxidants, fiber, and other nutritional powers that various fruits offer. I like a smoothie with just the right amount of texture—not thin like a juice, but not so thick that you'll have to eat it with a spoon. The ideal smoothie is also balanced in flavor; it allows a hint of each fruit, but no one ingredient overpowers the others. When nuts and seeds are blended in, they give the blended fruit more body and a subtle crunch, not to mention a boost in the health benefits.

smoothies

soaked almonds

In addition to their appealing fragrance and flavor, almonds are nutritionally dense: With more dietary fiber and calcium than any other nut, it's no wonder they're on the superfoods list (for more on superfoods, see page 8). Soaking almonds makes them much easier to digest—and their nutrients easier to absorb. If you want to, you can remove the skins, which will fall off easily after soaking; otherwise, just leave the almonds intact (I use them that way all the time). For smoothie recipes that call for soaked almonds, just scoop the soaked almonds out of the water, drain, and toss them into the blender. **Makes 2 cups**

2 cups organic raw whole almonds

Place the almonds in a medium bowl and rinse them under cold running water until the water runs clear. I rinse the almonds 3 or 4 times, using my hand or a colander to drain the water each time.

Place the rinsed almonds in a 4-cup glass mason jar (I like to use a mason jar because it has a tight-fitting lid). Add enough fresh cold water to cover the almonds by at least 1 inch. Cover with the lid and set the jar on the kitchen counter away from direct sun for at least 8 hours or up to 24 hours. The almonds will swell and the water will turn amber.

Once the almonds are soaked, they're ready to use. For storage, pour the soaking water out and add fresh cold water to the jar, swishing the almonds around to ensure they aren't stuck to the bottom of the jar, then drain the water and repeat this a few times.

Fill the jar with fresh cold water, then cover and refrigerate. Every 2 or 3 days, drain the water, rinse the almonds, and refill the jar with fresh cold water. The almonds will keep for up to 2 weeks in the refrigerator with this method.

soaked flaxseeds

Besides the subtle nutty, earthy flavor of flaxseeds, they have an abundance of antioxidants and omega-3 fatty acids. They are low in carbohydrates and high in fiber, making flaxseeds an ideal food to start your day, helping you to feel full and satisfied. When you're ready to use the soaked flaxseeds, you probably won't have to drain them—usually there isn't any excess liquid, as the flaxseeds absorb the soaking water. **Makes 1 cup**

1 cup organic whole flaxseeds

Place the flaxseeds in a fine-meshed strainer and rinse them under cold running water, stirring them with your fingers.

Place the flaxseeds in a 4-cup glass mason jar and add enough fresh cold water to cover the flaxseeds by 2 inches. Cover with the lid and set the jar on the kitchen counter away from direct sun for at least 8 hours or up to

24 hours. Once the flaxseeds are soaked, they're ready to use. (The flaxseeds will completely swell with the water, making draining unnecessary.) For storage, using a spoon, stir them and add more water to cover them as needed. Refrigerate the soaked flaxseed mixture. Every few days, drain any soaking liquid, rinse the flaxseeds, and cover them with fresh cold water. The flaxseeds will keep for up to 1 week in the refrigerator with this method.

Tropical smoothie

This is another favorite smoothie of mine, especially on a hot summer day. The coconut water complements the juiciness of the pineapple (although pineapple juice may be substituted for the coconut water in a pinch). The fruits in this smoothie are rich sources of antioxidants; the pineapple and papaya contain strong digestive enzymes as well. **Makes about 3½ cups**

1 (11.2-ounce) container coconut water

1 ripe banana, peeled

1 cup fresh or frozen pineapple chunks

1 cup fresh or frozen papaya chunks

½ cup fresh or frozen mango chunks

3 tablespoons soaked almonds (page 11), drained

Blend all the ingredients in a blender until smooth. Pour the smoothie into glasses and serve immediately.

Very Berry smoothie

This smoothie is my kids' favorite: They love the vibrant color and flavor of the berries. Any one berry or any combination of berries may be substituted, so use what is in season and on hand. This smoothie is the perfect place to use the frozen acai bars you'll find in the frozen foods section of many natural foods stores, as the acai blends right into the berries, without affecting their color. I also like knowing that my children are getting the extra benefits of this superfood, including antioxidants, fiber, and so much more. **Makes about 3½ cups**

2 cups berry juice or grape juice

1 cup fresh or frozen blueberries

1 cup hulled fresh or frozen strawberries

½ cup fresh or frozen raspberries

1 (1-inch) chunk frozen unsweetened acai berry bar

2 dates, pitted

Blend all the ingredients in a blender until smooth. Pour the smoothie into glasses and serve immediately.

ginger-apple smoothie

This smoothie is a refreshing tonic, and one I enjoy making in the afternoon as a pick-me-up. Ginger is known for its many healing properties, and combining it with fruit mellows its pungency and spiciness. The green tea powder adds a smooth, rich texture and turns the smoothie a beautiful pale green color. I usually find green tea powder in the baking section or the tea area of the grocery store; look for matcha green tea powder, as it's the purest. **Makes about 1¼ cups**

1 (6-inch) piece fresh ginger, peeled

1 ripe banana, peeled

½ cup unsweetened apple juice

¼ cup soaked almonds (page 11), drained

2½ tablespoons fresh lemon juice

1 teaspoon green tea powder

Grate the ginger using a Microplane or ginger grater over a bowl lined with cheesecloth or a paper towel. Gather the edges of the cloth and squeeze the ginger pulp to extract the juice. Discard the pulp.

Add the ginger juice and all the remaining ingredients to the blender, and blend until smooth. Pour the smoothie into glasses and serve immediately.

choosing the best blender

For making smoothies (not to mention nut milks, puréed soups, and sauces), a good high-powered countertop blender is indispensable. While blenders are useful for all cooks, they seem to be especially important for those following a plant-based diet. If you are preparing food at home on a consistent basis, you could run through several blenders in a lifetime of cooking, so it's worth investing in a good one that will give you a few extra years (and far fewer frustrations). At the very least, look for a high-powered countertop blender with a few speeds. If you can spring for the admittedly steeper price tag, consider purchasing a Vitamix, which is the premier blender on the market. It produces smoother results: If you add nuts to your smoothies, they'll disappear into the mix more than they would with a less powerful blender, which would leave a bit of crunch in the texture. I use my Vitamix for blending smoothies, of course, but also for dozens of other kitchen tasks, including making nuts into nut butters and puréeing hot liquids.

My Husband's porridge

My husband, Robert, and I have an ongoing morning debate: Who makes the best hot cereal? He thinks he does, while I prefer my Quick Oats and Quinoa (page 16). This recipe is Robert's, and I will admit it is very tasty. Soaking the oats brings out their natural sweetness, and a very ripe banana sweetens the porridge even more. Adding granola gives it crunchiness, which leads us to another debate: My husband actually prefers this recipe made with Post Grape-Nuts, rather than my granola, because he likes the malt flavor of the Grape-Nuts. And that's okay by me—it means my crunchy homemade granola will last longer. **Makes 4 cups**

1¼ cups old-fashioned rolled oats

1¼ cups plain unsweetened soy milk or oat milk

1 cup rice milk

1 very ripe banana (must be covered with brown speckles), peeled

About ½ cup boiling water

½ cup Super Hippie Granola (page 5)

Combine the oats, soy milk, and rice milk in a medium saucepan, then cover and refrigerate overnight.

Cook the oat mixture over medium heat, stirring occasionally, until the mixture comes to a near boil. Reduce the heat to low, partially cover the oatmeal, and simmer until the oats are tender and the mixture is thick and creamy, about 5 minutes. Watch closely to be sure the oatmeal doesn't boil over.

Coarsely mash the banana with a fork, then stir the banana into the oatmeal.

Meanwhile, pour enough boiling hot water over the granola in a small bowl to just cover. Set aside until the granola softens and soaks up some of the water, about 5 minutes. Drain the soaking liquid and stir the soaked granola into the oatmeal. Cook for 1 minute longer.

Spoon the oatmeal into bowls and serve.

A box of brown rice cream is the perfect quick breakfast for those with sensitive stomachs or for those who want their first meal of the day to be light but nutritious and satisfying. My kids love this creamy porridge. It's also an excellent choice if you aren't feeling so grand but still want to eat something.

There are two brands, Erewhon and Lundberg, that are easily found at natural foods stores. Simply follow the measurements on the back of the box—and my tips for making the rice cream even better.

Quick and Easy Hot Rice Cereal

1. Instead of water, use a watery nondairy milk like rice milk, almond milk, or hemp milk. First, bring the nondairy milk to a simmer, then slowly add the rice cream, whisking to make sure no clumps form. Cook over low heat, whisking frequently, for 2 to 3 minutes.

2. If you wish to embellish the hot cereal, add a maple syrup or agave nectar swirl upon serving, or top with chopped toasted nuts. And don't forget to pour extra nondairy milk on top of it: Serving it this way always reminds me of the oatmeal my mother made for me when I was growing up.

quick oats
and quinoa flakes

This is one of my favorite hot cereals: It's lighter than traditional oatmeal and it's just as fast to make. Both the quick oats and the quinoa flakes cook to a smooth, soft consistency. Quinoa is considered a supergrain because it contains a balanced set of essential amino acids, making it an unusually complete protein source among plant foods. This is a perfect recipe to use oat milk because of its creamy oat flavor. While I love this dish unembellished, those who crave a bit more sweetness might like to add a swirl of maple syrup or agave nectar. For extra protein, add chopped toasted nuts. **Makes about 4 cups**

4 cups oat milk or nondairy milk, plus more as needed

2 cups quick-cooking oats

⅔ cup quinoa flakes

¼ teaspoon fine sea salt

2 teaspoons vanilla extract

¼ teaspoon ground cinnamon

Pure maple syrup or agave nectar

Chopped toasted walnuts

Raisins or currants

Stir the 4 cups milk, the oats, quinoa flakes, and salt in a medium, heavy saucepan over high heat until the mixture comes to a boil. Decrease the heat to medium-low and cook, stirring occasionally, until the oats and quinoa are creamy, about 5 minutes. Stir in the vanilla and cinnamon and continue cooking for 1 minute longer. Add more milk, as needed, to form a soft, creamy consistency that pours easily from the pot.

Pour the cereal into bowls and drizzle with the maple syrup. Sprinkle the walnuts and raisins over the cereal and serve immediately.

sesame-shiitake tofu frittata

This breakfast dish reminds me of *okonomiyaki*, a savory Japanese pancake. Its long name means something along the lines of "cook what you like." You can take that to mean that variations on the vegetables in the dish are welcome and encouraged. The first time I ate this savory pancake, it was made with noodles and vegetables in the batter, and I doused it with soy sauce, not maple syrup. When I started making this pancake at home, I found my version to be thick, so I treated it like a frittata—starting it on the stovetop and finishing it in the oven. You can use dried shiitake mushrooms in place of the fresh ones: Pour enough boiling water over 8 dried mushrooms to cover them, and let them steep for 30 minutes, or until they soften. Drain and then proceed the same way you would if using fresh mushrooms. **Serves 6**

FRITTATA
1 tablespoon toasted sesame oil

6 fresh shiitake mushrooms (about 5 ounces), stemmed and thinly sliced

2 carrots, peeled and cut into matchstick-size strips

6 scallions, thinly sliced diagonally

4 cloves garlic, minced

2 tablespoons sesame seeds

2 tablespoons tamari

1 (14-ounce) container water-packed firm tofu, drained

½ cup garbanzo-fava flour or whole-wheat flour

2 tablespoons nutritional yeast

1 tablespoon arrowroot

1 teaspoon fine sea salt

½ teaspoon ground turmeric

¼ teaspoon freshly ground black pepper

1¼ cups plain unsweetened soy milk

2 tablespoons olive oil

Nonstick olive oil cooking spray

ASPARAGUS
13 ounces fresh asparagus, tough ends trimmed

1 tablespoon olive oil

Fine sea salt and freshly ground black pepper

Frittata: Preheat the oven to 400°F. Heat the sesame oil in a large, heavy sauté pan over medium-high heat. Add the mushrooms, carrots, scallions, one-half of the minced garlic, and the sesame seeds and sauté until the mushrooms are tender and the carrots are crisp-tender, about 4 minutes. Stir in the tamari. Set aside.

Blend the tofu, flour, nutritional yeast, arrowroot, salt, turmeric, pepper, and the remaining minced garlic in a food processor until the mixture is smooth. With the machine running, slowly add the soy milk and the 2 tablespoons oil. Process until the mixture is smooth and thick like yogurt.

Heat a heavy 9½- to 10½-inch nonstick sauté pan over medium heat. Spray the pan with nonstick olive oil spray, then spoon half of the mushroom mixture into the pan. Pour the tofu mixture over the mushroom mixture, then sprinkle with the remaining mushroom mixture. Cover and cook until the tofu mixture begins to simmer in the center. Decrease the heat to low and continue cooking until the tofu mixture is set around the outer ½-inch edge of the pan, about 8 minutes. Transfer the pan to the oven and bake, uncovered, until a toothpick inserted into the center comes out with some tofu mixture attached, about 45 minutes. Set the frittata aside to cool for 10 minutes. (Keep the oven hot for roasting the asparagus.) Alternatively, you can use a 12-inch nonstick sauté pan and bake the frittata until a toothpick comes out clean, about 30 minutes.

Asparagus: Place the asparagus on a baking sheet and drizzle with the olive oil. Sprinkle with salt and pepper and toss to coat. Roast the asparagus until it is crisp-tender, turning once, about 10 minutes.

Top the frittata with the roasted asparagus and serve.

nutritional yeast

Nutritional yeast is an inactive yeast similar to brewer's yeast, but with more flavor. It's yellow in color; it has a distinct, pleasant aroma; and it has a delicious nutty, cheesy taste. Nutritional yeast is also a valuable nutritional supplement, as it contains high levels of protein, folic acid, and vitamins. Most important, it provides vegans and vegetarians with a non-animal source of vitamin B12. I use nutritional yeast in tofu-based breakfast dishes, but it can also be added to salads, salad dressings, casseroles (like Baked Penne and Cauliflower with Cheesy Sauce on page 152), soups, sauces, and gravies; some people even like it sprinkled on freshly popped popcorn. Look for nutritional yeast at your natural foods store, either in the bulk section or in the baking section.

tofu omelets with summer squash, leek, and cherry tomatoes

This recipe is for all those vegans who used to love egg omelets—like me. If your store doesn't have garbanzo-fava flour, garbanzo flour by itself works just fine; a sturdy whole-wheat flour will also do. I like bean flours because they are gluten-free, and I also like that they add a certain savory flavor to the omelet. The consistency of the omelet is crispy on the outside with a soft, almost runny egg-like inside. This omelet recipe makes for a fun nighttime meal, too: Dream up any favorite combination of vegetables and nondairy cheeses to fill it with. **Makes 5 omelets**

SUMMER SQUASH TOPPING

1 tablespoon olive oil

1 leek (white and pale green parts only), finely diced

2 cloves garlic, minced

1 large yellow squash, such as pattypan or crookneck, cut into half-moon slices

1 zucchini, cut into half-moon slices

½ cup cherry tomatoes, halved

2 teaspoons chopped fresh dill

Fine sea salt and freshly ground black pepper

OMELET

½ (14-ounce) container water-packed firm tofu, drained

¼ cup garbanzo-fava flour or whole-wheat flour

1 tablespoon nutritional yeast

1½ teaspoons arrowroot

1 clove garlic, minced

½ teaspoon fine sea salt

¼ teaspoon ground turmeric

⅛ teaspoon freshly ground black pepper

⅔ cup plain unsweetened soy milk

1 tablespoon olive oil, plus more for coating the pan

3 ounces nondairy mozzarella-style cheese, grated (about ⅔ cup)

Summer Squash Topping: Heat the oil in a large, heavy sauté pan over medium heat. Add the leek and garlic and sauté until the leek begins to soften, about 2 minutes. Add the squash and zucchini and cook over medium-high heat until they are almost tender but do not lose their shape, about 6 minutes. Remove the pan from the heat and stir in the cherry tomatoes and dill. Season to taste with salt and pepper. Set aside.

Omelet: Blend the tofu, flour, nutritional yeast, arrowroot, garlic, salt, turmeric, and pepper in a food processor until the tofu breaks down and the mixture is smooth. With the machine running, slowly add the soy milk and the 1 tablespoon oil. Process until the mixture is smooth and thick like yogurt.

Heat 1 teaspoon of olive oil in an 8-inch nonstick sauté pan over medium-low heat. Using about ⅓ cup of the batter, pour the batter into the center of the hot oiled pan and tilt the pan to form a 5- to 6-inch-diameter round with an even thickness. Don't worry if the batter does not form a perfect round shape. Cook the omelet until the edges start to brown and begin to pull away from the bottom of the pan and the top looks dry, about 3 minutes. Using a silicone spatula, loosen the omelet from the pan, then flip the omelet. Sprinkle with one-fifth of the cheese and one-fifth of the squash mixture and cook for another 2 minutes. Slide the omelet onto a plate, serving it open-faced or folded. Repeat with the remaining omelet mixture, cheese, and topping, adding more oil to the pan as needed.

1.   2.

CUTTING TECHNIQUES

HALF-MOON and QUARTER-MOON CUTS are used for elongated vegetables such as carrots, parsnips, yellow squash, and zucchini. First, cut off the stem or root end. Next, cut the vegetable in half lengthwise. (For quarter moons, cut each half lengthwise in half again, forming four long pieces.) Next, with the cut side down, slice each piece crosswise into ⅛- to ¼-inch-thick slices, forming half-moon-shaped (or quarter-moon-shaped) pieces.

tofu scramble with caramelized onion and sun-dried tomatoes

The key to this dish is using a water-packed tofu (I prefer the firm), which results in the most scrambled-egg-like texture. The nutritional yeast (page 19) adds a subtle cheesy, nutty flavor and a nutritional boost. For this recipe, be sure to choose a nondairy cheese that melts well; if you don't already have a favorite, turn to page 36 for some recommendations. **Serves 4**

1 (14-ounce) container water-packed firm tofu, drained

2 tablespoons olive oil

1 tablespoon water

1 tablespoon nutritional yeast

4 cloves garlic, minced

1 teaspoon fine sea salt

½ teaspoon chopped fresh thyme

½ teaspoon ground turmeric

⅛ teaspoon ground white pepper

½ medium yellow onion, thinly sliced

8 dry-packed sun-dried tomatoes, soaked in warm water for 30 minutes, drained, and thinly sliced

1½ ounces nondairy mozzarella-style cheese, grated (about ⅓ cup)

1 tablespoon thinly sliced fresh basil

Wrap the drained tofu block in paper towels and set aside on a plate for 10 minutes. Rewrap the tofu with dry paper towels and squeeze gently to remove any excess water. Coarsely break the tofu into 1-inch pieces, allowing some of the pieces to crumble more than others.

While the tofu is sitting, whisk 1 tablespoon of the oil with the 1 tablespoon water, the nutritional yeast, one-half of the minced garlic, the salt, thyme, turmeric, and white pepper in a large bowl to blend. Add the tofu and toss just enough for the pieces to absorb the seasonings (do not overmix).

Heat a medium to large cast-iron skillet over medium heat. Add the remaining 1 tablespoon oil, then the onion, and sauté for about 8 minutes, or until the onion is almost caramelized. Add the sun-dried tomatoes and the remaining minced garlic and cook for 1 minute. Add the seasoned tofu. Using a stainless steel spoon, stir the tofu to keep it from sticking to the bottom of the skillet and to break up the larger tofu chunks into desired pieces until it is heated through, about 5 minutes. If the mixture seems too dry, add 3 tablespoons of water (it will cook off). Remove the pan from the heat. Add the grated cheese and the basil and toss gently just until the cheese melts, about 1 minute. Transfer the scramble to plates and serve.

oven-roasted potatoes

This hearty side dish goes perfectly with scrambled tofu for breakfast, but it's also satisfying any other time of the day—a great addition to lunch or dinner. While I like the dramatic visual impact of using red-, tan-, and purple-skinned potatoes, feel free to use just one kind of potato, or any combination that you like. **Serves 4 to 6**

2½ pounds assorted potatoes (such as red-skinned, Yukon Gold, and purple; about 3 medium of each variety), cut into 1½-inch-long wedges

2 tablespoons olive oil

2 teaspoons minced fresh rosemary

1 teaspoon minced fresh dill

1 clove garlic, minced

1 teaspoon fine sea salt

½ teaspoon freshly ground black pepper

Preheat the oven to 375°F. Line a large, heavy baking sheet with parchment paper.

Toss the potatoes with the oil, rosemary, dill, garlic, salt, and pepper in a large bowl to coat. Arrange the herbed potatoes in a single layer on the prepared baking sheet and roast for 35 to 40 minutes, until the potatoes are tender and browned. Serve immediately.

I ventured into the world of silicone kitchen tools even when it sounded futuristic and unnatural, with pop-up measuring cups and spatulas in a rainbow of colors. Silicone spatulas were the first to win me over: With their heat resistance and durability, they quickly took the place of my rubber spatulas, which needed to be replaced every few months after getting caught in a flame and melting, or showing worn edges that could no longer be trimmed.

silicone spatulas and pans

Once silicone spatulas passed the test, it was on to bigger silicone baking equipment such as soft, colorful muffin pans, and eventually Bundt pans and loaf pans made from the same FDA food-grade silicone. The biggest benefit of silicone bakeware is that you do not have to oil the pans. Although I didn't really believe that at first, I finally took the risk and found that the pans work perfectly without oil. They heat quickly and bake evenly, leaving no burned or dark edges or bottoms. Plus, it's super easy to remove muffins from the pans: Just gently pull on the sides to release the muffins.

Silicone bakeware is safe to put in the freezer, refrigerator, microwave, dishwasher, and oven. It doesn't rust; cleanup is quick and easy; and it doesn't take up much storage space. And I have to admit that part of its appeal is that it can be found in many cheerful colors.

maple tempeh bacon

This recipe is adapted from my first book, *The Real Food Daily Cookbook*. I couldn't help but revisit it: There is something very seductive about this vegan bacon. Besides eating it with breakfast, you can use it as an ingredient in many other dishes. Here, I have simplified the steps to make the prep time shorter and the process easier. You'll still need a stovetop smoker (available at most specialty cookware stores)—it's the key to great-tasting vegan bacon. You'll also need a very sharp large knife. **Makes about 48 strips**

½ cup warm water

2 tablespoons fine sea salt

1½ (8-ounce) packages soy tempeh

2 tablespoons high-heat sunflower or safflower oil

¼ cup pure maple syrup

Whisk the warm water and salt in a small baking dish until the salt dissolves. Soak the tempeh in the salted water for 10 minutes, turning after the first 5 minutes. Drain well.

Prepare a stovetop smoker according to the manufacturer's instructions. Smoke the tempeh over medium heat for 40 minutes, or until it is golden brown. Let the tempeh cool.

Preheat the oven to 300°F. Line 2 large, heavy baking sheets with parchment paper. Lightly coat the paper with 2 teaspoons of the oil. Using a very sharp large knife, cut the tempeh lengthwise into ⅛-inch-thick strips. Arrange the tempeh strips in a single layer on the prepared baking sheets. Brush 2 teaspoons of the oil over the tempeh strips, then brush the tempeh with 2 tablespoons of the maple syrup. Bake the tempeh strips for 20 minutes, turning the strips after 10 minutes and brushing them with the remaining 2 teaspoons oil and 2 tablespoons maple syrup, or until they are crisp and golden brown.

The tempeh bacon will keep for 1 week. Let it cool to room temperature, then store it in an airtight container at room temperature.

tofu benedict with roasted corn hollandaise

A corn-based vegan version of hollandaise sauce brings its creamy, rich texture to this delicious special-occasion breakfast dish. In the hollandaise, the sweetness of the corn is balanced with just a hint of heat from the cayenne. The sauce is ladled over savory tofu set atop a thick slice of sourdough bread and then topped with tomatoes and spinach, making this a perfect start to the day. Heirloom tomatoes are especially tender and flavorful and come in a variety of appealing colors, but any ripe, juicy tomato will do. **Serves 6**

SAUCE

1 (10-ounce) package frozen corn kernels, thawed, or 1 ¾ cups fresh corn kernels

¾ teaspoon fine sea salt

1¼ cups plain unsweetened soy milk

2 tablespoons fresh lemon juice

1 tablespoon olive oil

⅛ teaspoon cayenne pepper

TOFU

1 (14-ounce) container water-packed extra-firm tofu

¼ cup fresh lemon juice

2 tablespoons olive oil

2 tablespoons water

1 tablespoon red wine vinegar

1 teaspoon Dijon mustard

1 teaspoon ground turmeric

½ teaspoon ground cumin

½ teaspoon fine sea salt

1 tablespoon minced fresh dill

1½ teaspoons minced fresh tarragon, or ½ teaspoon crumbled dried tarragon

Nonaerosol nonstick cooking spray

ASSEMBLY

3 medium heirloom tomatoes (preferably yellow and green tomatoes), thickly sliced

Fine sea salt

2 teaspoons plus 2 tablespoons olive oil

2 cloves garlic, minced

1 (6-ounce) bunch fresh baby spinach, stems trimmed

Freshly ground black pepper

6 (½-inch-thick) slices sourdough or country white rosemary bread

2 large scallions, thinly sliced

Sauce: Preheat the oven to 375°F. Line a large, heavy baking sheet with parchment paper. Scatter the corn kernels over the baking sheet and sprinkle with the salt. Roast until the corn is crisp and begins to brown, about 30 minutes.

Transfer the roasted corn kernels to a blender. With the machine running, slowly blend in the soy milk, lemon juice, oil, and cayenne. Allow the mixture to continue blending until it thickens to the consistency of a runny pudding, about 3 minutes. Strain the corn mixture through a fine-meshed strainer and into a bowl, pressing on the solids to extract as much liquid as possible. You should have about 1½ cups of sauce. Discard the solids.

Just before serving, warm the sauce in a small saucepan over medium heat.

Tofu: Drain the liquid from the tofu, then place the tofu on a plate lined with paper towels. Cover the tofu with a folded paper towel and place another plate on top of the tofu to weigh it down. Set aside while you make the marinade.

Whisk the lemon juice, olive oil, water, vinegar, mustard, turmeric, cumin, and salt in a medium bowl to blend. Whisk in the dill and tarragon.

Cut the block of tofu horizontally twice, then cut it in half to get six 3½ by 2 by ½-inch slices. Place the tofu slices in an 8 by 8-inch baking dish. Pour the marinade over the tofu and marinate for at least 1 hour at room temperature or cover and refrigerate for up to 1 day.

Do-Ahead Tip: At this point, the sauce and the tofu can be prepared up to 1 day ahead. Transfer the sauce to a covered container and refrigerate separately. Rewarm the sauce before serving.

Heat a ridged grill pan over medium-high heat. Spray the pan with nonaerosol cooking spray. Grill the tofu, brushing with the remaining marinade, until char marks form and the tofu is heated through, about 2 minutes per side.

Assembly: Meanwhile, place the tomatoes in a medium bowl and sprinkle lightly with salt. Set aside until the tomatoes begin to exude their water, about 10 minutes. Drain the accumulated water.

Heat 2 teaspoons of the oil in a large, heavy sauté pan over medium heat. Add the garlic and sauté until fragrant and softened, about 30 seconds. Add the spinach and toss just until it is heated through and begins to wilt, about 1½ minutes. Season to taste with salt and pepper.

Lightly brush both sides of the bread slices with the remaining 2 tablespoons olive oil and grill on the grill pan until toasted, about 2 minutes per side.

Place 1 slice of toast on each of 6 plates. Top with the tofu, then spoon the sauce over the tofu and around the toast. Top with the tomato slices and spinach. Garnish with the scallions and serve immediately.

nondairy milk and ice cream

NONDAIRY MILK

Finding an appealing nondairy milk is one key to making a plant-based diet easier. While vegans avoid dairy as part of a strict vegetarian diet, growing numbers of people are looking for alternatives for other reasons, too: Dairy is among the leading causes of food allergies, and many people are also finding that they are lactose-intolerant.

There are several delicious options, both store-bought and homemade. Be aware that many store-bought nondairy milks are sweetened with organic cane sugar, so read the labels; you'll also find options that are unsweetened or sweetened with rice syrup. While there is nothing wrong with a little sugar here and there, I don't want extra sugar in nondairy milk that I'm giving to my kids to drink, or that I'm using in a savory dish. (Even dessert recipes benefit from reducing the sweetener when you are using a nondairy milk that already has sugar in it.)

Experiment with any of the following; they're indispensable for pouring over cold or hot cereals, stirring into your tea or coffee, and using in recipes.

ALMOND MILK is great in every aspect of cooking and baking as well as over cereal and in your morning tea or coffee. It is high in fiber, protein, vitamin E, and monounsaturated fats. Those allergic to soy should be aware that almond milk is not soy-free, as it almost always contains soy lecithin. For a soy-free almond milk that you can make at home, see my recipe for Homemade Nut Milk (page 30).

coconut milk beverage, made by So Delicious, can be found in the refrigerated section of natural foods stores, right next to the dairy milk. It's free of cholesterol, trans-fats, soy, and gluten. It's a good source of vitamin B12, and it's also fortified with calcium, vitamin A, and vitamin D. Coconut milk beverage is delicious on cereal. I love it on my Super Hippie Granola (page 5), in tea or coffee, and just for drinking. (Note that this is a different product from canned coconut milk, which is thicker.)

HemP MILK is a creamy, nutty beverage that's perfect at breakfast. It is high in protein and it's a good source of balanced omega-3 and omega-6 fatty acids. Although hemp milk can be overpowering in some dishes (I wouldn't use it to make mashed potatoes), it is interchangeable with soy milk in many recipes; I especially like to use it when making my Acai Granola Bowl (page 7).

Oat MILK is quite light and has a mild, slightly sweet taste. It's a good alternative to soy or rice milk, breaking the monotony of always using the same product. Try oat milk on breakfast cereal, such as my Quick Oats and Quinoa Flakes (page 16), as it adds a rich milky oat flavor.

RICe MILK is not as thick as soy milk and has a somewhat translucent appearance. Because it is slightly sweet and a bit watery, rice milk works well in dessert recipes but is not suited for savory or salty dishes. Compared to soy and nut milks, rice milk has less protein; some versions are fortified, so read the labels.

SOY MILK has almost as much protein as dairy milk, but less fat and no cholesterol. Most soy milks are fortified, making them an excellent source of calcium as well. Each brand of soy milk is slightly different, so read the labels, try a few, and see which one suits your taste buds and needs the best. I use soy milk when I want a thicker, richer consistency in my cooking.

HOMEMADE NUT MILK
Milk made from almonds, cashews, or hazelnuts will have a creamy consistency similar to soy milk and a nutty taste perfect for making fruit smoothies or other creamy drinks and desserts.

3 cups raw nuts such as almonds, cashews, hazelnuts, or macadamia nuts

6 cups cold water, plus more water to soak the nuts

A few teaspoons agave nectar or vanilla extract (optional)

Cover the raw nuts with (additional) water, and allow them to soak for at least 8 hours or up to 24 hours. Drain and rinse.

Place the soaked nuts and the filtered water in a high-speed blender or a food processor and process until creamy and smooth, at least 1 full minute.

Line a large fine-meshed strainer with a double thickness of cheesecloth, and place the strainer over a large bowl. Pour the nut mixture into the strainer and let drain. Grab the corners of the cheesecloth, hold tightly, and squeeze the cheesecloth to extract all of the nut milk. (This will take some time, but it's worth the end result.)

Discard the pulp. To store the nut milk, transfer it to a covered container and refrigerate for up to 3 days.

When ready to use the nut milk, reblend with a hint of agave nectar or vanilla.

NONDAIRY ICE CREAM

You don't have to give up all creamy frozen desserts to stick to a plant-based diet: There are some great-tasting nondairy ice creams available, and it seems like new ones are coming out all the time. These frozen desserts are made with nondairy milk—various brands use soy milk, rice milk, coconut milk, and even hemp milk. In my experience, it's best to try a few and find your own favorite: There are plenty of flavors to choose from, ranging from classic vanilla to mint chip to chocolate—peanut butter swirl. Enjoy these frozen desserts the same way you would ice cream: I love putting a scoop atop a serving of my Summer Blueberry Crumble (page 219). Nondairy ice creams are also fantastic bases for my milkshake recipes (beginning on page 242).

Tofu scramble with avocado, bacon, and cheese

This breakfast recipe really showcases the strong flavors of the tempeh bacon on page 25. Its chewy texture contrasts nicely with the soft textures of scrambled tofu and fresh avocado. The vegan bacon is well worth the effort, but in a pinch, you may substitute purchased vegan sausage. This dish will impress anyone who is a bit wary of giving up eggs at breakfast time. **Serves 4**

1 (14-ounce) container water-packed firm tofu, drained

1 tablespoon water

2 tablespoons olive oil

1 tablespoon nutritional yeast

2 cloves garlic, minced

¾ teaspoon fine sea salt

½ teaspoon chopped fresh thyme

½ teaspoon ground cumin

½ teaspoon ground turmeric

¼ teaspoon ground white pepper

⅓ cup coarsely crumbled Maple Tempeh Bacon (about 8 strips; page 25)

½ firm but ripe avocado, peeled, pitted, and diced

1½ ounces nondairy cheddar-style cheese, grated (about ⅓ cup)

Freshly ground black pepper

1 large scallion, thinly sliced

Wrap the drained tofu block in paper towels and set aside on a plate for 10 minutes. Rewrap the tofu with dry paper towels and squeeze gently to remove any excess water. Coarsely break the tofu into 1-inch pieces, allowing some of the pieces to crumble more than others. While the tofu is sitting, whisk the 1 tablespoon water, 1 tablespoon of the oil, the nutritional yeast, garlic, salt, thyme, cumin, turmeric, and white pepper in a large bowl to blend. Add the tofu and toss just enough for the pieces to absorb the seasonings (do not overmix).

Heat a medium to large cast-iron skillet over medium heat. Add the remaining 1 tablespoon oil, then add the seasoned tofu. Using a stainless steel spoon, stir the tofu to keep it from sticking to the bottom of the skillet and to break up the larger tofu chunks into desired pieces until it is heated through, about 5 minutes. If the mixture seems too dry, add 3 tablespoons of water (it will cook off). Remove the pan from the heat. Add the bacon, avocado, and cheese and toss gently just until the cheese melts, about 2 minutes. Season to taste with black pepper. Sprinkle with the scallion and serve.

Nutty Raspberry Muffins

This muffin recipe lends itself to many variations: Fresh fruit practically melts into the mix, spreading the fruit color and flavor throughout the muffins, while frozen fruit holds its shape better. (Thaw frozen fruit for just a few minutes to allow it to loosen up.) At my house, we especially love the combination of fresh raspberries and chopped pecans; another delicious duo is bananas and walnuts (use very ripe bananas, and blend them into the tofu mixture until smooth). Although the recipe calls for a standard muffin tin and paper liners, I also like to use silicone muffin pans, which allow me to skip spraying the pan or lining it with paper cups. A muffin recipe is a great place to try out different flours: Spelt flour has a nuttier and slightly sweeter taste than whole-wheat flour. **Makes 12 muffins**

2 cups spelt flour or whole-wheat pastry flour

2 teaspoons baking powder

¾ teaspoon baking soda

¾ teaspoon ground cinnamon

½ teaspoon fine sea salt

1 cup pecans, coarsely chopped

8 ounces vacuum-packed soft silken tofu (such as Mori-Nu)

⅔ cup plain unsweetened soy milk

⅔ cup pure maple syrup

⅓ cup neutral cooking oil

2 teaspoons apple cider vinegar

2 teaspoons vanilla extract

1 (6-ounce) container fresh raspberries

Preheat the oven to 350°F. Line 12 standard (⅓ cup) metal muffin cups with paper liners.

Whisk the flour, baking powder, baking soda, cinnamon, salt, and ¾ cup of the pecans in a large bowl to blend.

Blend the tofu, soy milk, maple syrup, oil, vinegar, and vanilla in a food processor until completely smooth and creamy.

Stir the tofu mixture into the flour mixture just until blended. Fold the raspberries into the batter, but do not overmix the batter. Divide the batter equally among the prepared muffin cups. Sprinkle the remaining ¼ cup pecans over the muffins and bake for 25 to 30 minutes, until a toothpick inserted into the center of a muffin comes out dry.

Transfer the muffin pan to a cooling rack and let the muffins cool for 10 minutes. Invert the pan to remove the muffins. Turn the muffins upright and serve them warm or let them cool completely on the cooling rack.

Do-Ahead Tip: The muffins can be made up to 2 days ahead. Store them in an airtight container at room temperature.

Fruit Variations: All fresh summer berries, such as raspberries, strawberries, blackberries, and blueberries, work well in this recipe. During other seasons, use frozen berries, bananas, or chopped apples or pears.

blueberry corn pancakes

The sweetness of the blueberries, cornmeal, maple syrup, and cinnamon complements the slight bitterness of the buckwheat flour in these pancakes—as does the extra maple syrup you'll serve with them. The batter should be pourable: As you are cooking the pancakes, you may need to add a tablespoon of water to thin out the mixture, which tends to thicken as it sits. **Makes about 10 (4-inch) pancakes**

½ cup old-fashioned rolled oats

½ cup cornmeal, sifted to remove any coarse grains

½ cup buckwheat flour

½ teaspoon ground cinnamon

1 teaspoon baking powder

½ teaspoon fine sea salt

¼ teaspoon baking soda

1 ¼ cups plain unsweetened soy milk

1 tablespoon apple cider vinegar

2 tablespoons high-heat sunflower or safflower oil, plus more as needed

2 tablespoons pure maple syrup, plus more for serving

1 tablespoon vanilla extract

1 cup fresh or frozen blueberries

Nonaerosol nonstick cooking spray

Blend the oats in a food processor until they are ground into flour. Mix the oat flour, cornmeal, buckwheat flour, cinnamon, baking powder, salt, and baking soda in a medium bowl to blend. Mix the soy milk and vinegar in a large bowl and set aside until the soy milk begins to curdle, about 5 minutes. Mix in the 2 tablespoons oil, the 2 tablespoons maple syrup, and the vanilla. Stir in the dry ingredients. Fold the blueberries into the batter.

Preheat a large, heavy cast-iron skillet or flat nonstick griddle pan over medium heat. Spray the cast-iron pan with cooking spray or brush the nonstick pan with oil. Working in batches and using about ¼ cup of the batter for each pancake, spoon the batter into the hot pan, forming 4-inch pancakes. Cook for 3 minutes, or until the pancakes are dry around the edges, the bubbles burst on top, and the blueberry juices start to ooze. Turn the pancakes over and continue cooking for about 3 minutes. As the pancakes cook, adjust the heat as needed to ensure the pancakes cook evenly.

Transfer the pancakes to plates and serve immediately with maple syrup.

Gluten- and soy-free waffles with summer berry or apple-pear compote

When you bite into this crisp waffle with its soft fruit compote, whipped cream, and maple syrup, it is amazingly delicious. The waffles' almond flavor also pairs nicely with apricots, so another way to enjoy these crispy cakes is to simply spread apricot jam on top. Both the powdered egg replacer and the xanthan gum can be found at regular grocery stores as well as natural foods stores: These two ingredients take the place of eggs, helping the flours bind. **Makes about 5 waffles**

3 tablespoons water

1 tablespoon powdered egg replacer

2 cups almond milk

3 tablespoons agave nectar

1 tablespoon sunflower or safflower oil

2 teaspoons almond extract

1½ cups brown rice flour

¼ cup almond meal

¼ cup tapioca flour

2 teaspoons baking powder

1 teaspoon baking soda

1 teaspoon fine sea salt

¼ teaspoon xanthan gum

Nonaerosol nonstick cooking spray

Apple-Pear Compote (recipe follows) or Summer Berry Compote (recipe follows)

Soy whipped topping or Tofu Whipped Cream (page 233), for serving

Pure maple syrup

Toasted sliced almonds

Preheat a standard waffle iron over high heat. Whisk the 3 tablespoons water with the egg replacer in a medium bowl until well blended. Whisk in the 2 cups almond milk, the agave nectar, oil, and almond extract.

Whisk the brown rice flour, almond meal, tapioca flour, baking powder, baking soda, salt, and xanthan gum in a large bowl to blend. Stir the wet ingredients into the dry ingredients just until moistened, being careful not to overmix. Let the batter sit for 10 minutes to thicken.

Spray the hot waffle iron generously with cooking spray. Pour about ⅔ cup of the batter onto the waffle iron. Close the lid and cook until the waffle is golden brown and crisp, about 5 minutes. Using tongs, gently loosen the waffle from the iron and transfer it to a plate.

Immediately top the hot waffle with the compote and soy whipped topping, or with maple syrup. Garnish with toasted almonds and serve immediately. Repeat to make more waffles.

SUMMER BERRY COMPOTE

The key to this recipe is to allow the heat to soften the berries to the point where they're just about to begin losing their shape: When you bite into them, they'll be even sweeter than when picked. These berries go perfectly on top of waffles, and they also make a delicious ice cream or sorbet topping. Leftovers can even be added to your granola in the morning. **Makes about 3 cups**

½ cup fresh orange juice

⅓ cup pure maple syrup

1 teaspoon grated orange zest

1 teaspoon ground mace

½ teaspoon ground cinnamon

1 (10-ounce) container fresh strawberries, hulled and quartered

1 (6-ounce) container fresh blueberries

2 tablespoons water

1 tablespoon arrowroot

1 (6-ounce) container fresh raspberries

Stir the orange juice, maple syrup, orange zest, mace, and cinnamon in a large saucepan to blend, and bring to a boil over medium-high heat. Decrease the heat to medium-low and add the strawberries and blueberries to the syrup mixture. Simmer gently until the berries begin to release their juices and soften, about 8 minutes.

Stir the 2 tablespoons water and the arrowroot in a small bowl to blend. Stir the arrowroot mixture into the berry mixture and increase the heat to medium. Allow the compote to simmer for about 2 minutes, or until the compote thickens. Remove the compote from the heat and stir in the raspberries. Set aside to cool slightly (the compote will thicken further as it cools).

Refrigerate the compote in an airtight container for up to 5 days.

APPLE-PEAR COMPOTE
When apples and pears are in season, this is an excellent topping for waffles and French toast. This simple cooked fruit is also a winner if you need to whip up a quick last-minute dessert: I've served it many times with a cookie or two, and it always hits the spot. You might sprinkle some chopped toasted nuts on top to give it a little crunch. **Makes about 3 cups**

¼ cup pure maple syrup

3 tablespoons fresh lemon juice

½ teaspoon ground cinnamon

¼ teaspoon fine sea salt

⅛ teaspoon ground cloves

⅛ teaspoon ground nutmeg

½ vanilla bean, split lengthwise

3 apples, such as Gala, Pink Lady, or Rome Beauty (about 1¼ pounds), peeled, cored, and cut into 1-inch chunks

3 ripe pears, such as Anjou (about 1¼ pounds), peeled, cored, and cut into 1-inch chunks

2 teaspoons water

1 teaspoon arrowroot

Stir the maple syrup, lemon juice, cinnamon, salt, cloves, and nutmeg in a large saucepan to blend. Scrape the seeds from the vanilla bean into the syrup, then add the bean. Stir in the apples and bring the syrup mixture to a simmer over medium-high heat. Decrease the heat to medium-low and cook, stirring occasionally, for 3 minutes. Add the pears and continue cooking until the apples and pears are tender, about 15 minutes.

Stir the 2 teaspoons water and the arrowroot in a small bowl to blend. Quickly stir the arrowroot mixture into the apple-pear mixture and simmer until the liquid thickens, about 3 minutes.

Remove from the heat and discard the vanilla bean. Let cool slightly before serving.

Refrigerate the compote in an airtight container for up to 5 days.

french toast with fresh raspberry syrup

This is one recipe where white bread—a key to exceptional French toast—is preferable to whole-grain bread. The bread must be sturdy enough to maintain its texture (standard French bread will get too soggy), yet remain tender when cooked. If you have a local bakery, try using one of their signature white breads; at the grocery store, look for a country loaf that has not been sliced. The raspberry syrup makes a nice addition; if you don't have the time to prepare it, simply serve this French toast with maple syrup or a favorite jam. **Serves 6**

1 cup drained water-packed soft tofu (about 8 ounces), crumbled

4 teaspoons arrowroot

2 teaspoons baking powder

2 teaspoons ground flaxseeds

½ teaspoon ground cinnamon

¼ teaspoon freshly grated nutmeg

⅛ teaspoon fine sea salt

⅛ teaspoon ground turmeric

1 cup plain unsweetened soy milk

⅓ cup high-heat sunflower or safflower oil, plus more for coating the pan

⅓ cup pure maple syrup

¼ teaspoon vanilla extract

12 (½-inch-thick) slices crusty country-style white sourdough bread

Fresh Raspberry Syrup (recipe follows)

Blend the tofu, arrowroot, baking powder, ground flaxseeds, cinnamon, nutmeg, salt, and turmeric in a food processor until smooth, stopping the machine occasionally to scrape the bottom and sides of the bowl. Combine the soy milk, the ⅓ cup oil, maple syrup, and vanilla in a liquid measuring cup. With the food processor running, gradually pour the soy milk mixture through the feed tube and into the tofu mixture, blending until the mixture is smooth, and stopping the machine to scrape the sides and bottom of the bowl. Pour the batter onto a large rimmed baking sheet. Arrange the bread slices in a single layer in the batter and turn to coat. Set aside, turning the bread occasionally, for 30 minutes, or until the bread absorbs most of the batter.

Heat a large, heavy flat griddle pan over medium heat. Working in batches, brush a little oil over the griddle and grill the soaked bread until it is heated through and golden brown, about 3 minutes per side. Transfer the French toast to plates, spoon the raspberry syrup over, and serve.

Fresh Raspberry Syrup
I always prefer fresh berries when they're in season, but frozen raspberries, strawberries, or blueberries will also work well in this recipe. **Makes 2 cups**

3 (6-ounce) containers fresh raspberries

½ cup pure maple syrup

1 teaspoon arrowroot

1 tablespoon cold water

Combine 2 containers of the raspberries and the maple syrup in a heavy medium saucepan over medium heat, and cook until the syrup comes to a near simmer, about 2 minutes. Meanwhile, stir the arrowroot and the 1 tablespoon cold water in a small bowl to blend. Stir the arrowroot mixture into the raspberry mixture. Continue cooking, stirring often, until the raspberries are very soft and mushy and the syrup boils and thickens, about 3 minutes. Strain the mixture through a fine-meshed strainer and into a bowl. Discard the raspberry seeds. Fold the remaining container of raspberries into the hot syrup to coat, and let the syrup stand until the raspberries are heated through.

snacks
and
sandwiches

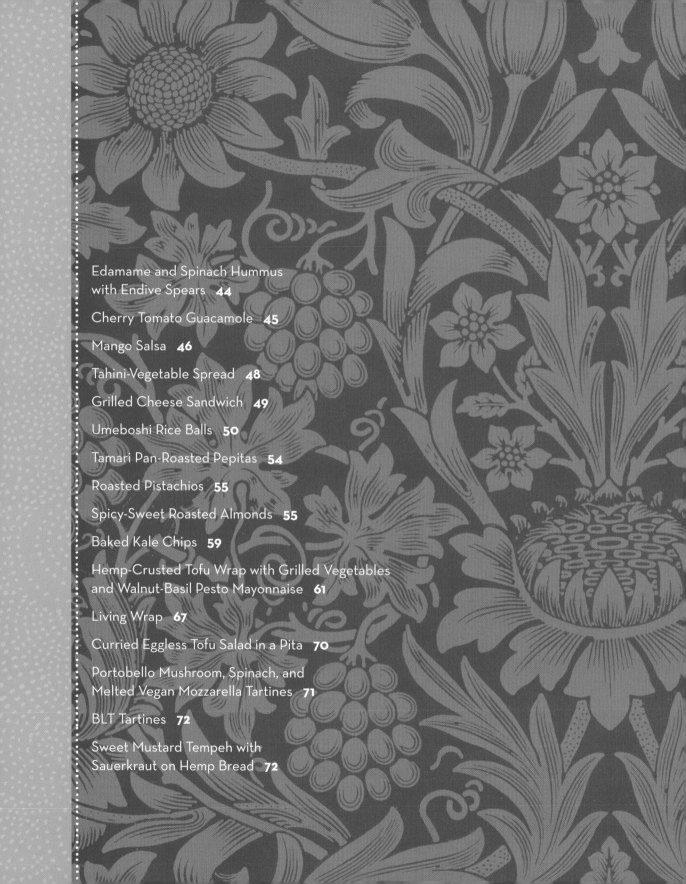

When we think of snacks, we often think of something sweet—at least I know I used to. I grew up drinking Dr Pepper after school, and snacking on something made with sugar and white flour. As I began experimenting with a more healthful diet, I limited sweets but found myself indulging in salty snacks all the time. Many of us are tempted to swing between sweet and salty snacks to dampen our cravings, until we're not sure where the salt ends and the sweet begins. It's not a healthful cycle, nor one that ever seems to leave us feeling full or recharged.

This chapter shows you how filling and energizing wholesome, savory snacks can be. My Tahini-Vegetable Spread (page 48), incorporates spices and herbs to tempt your tastes, and it has a satisfyingly creamy texture, too. The Cherry Tomato Guacamole (page 45) is big on flavor— and big on fresh, raw vegetables. What's truly different about these snacks is that instead of just satisfying a passing craving, they're actually giving you something your body needs: more vegetables, fruit, and whole grains. In fact, some of these recipes might seem more like small meals rather than snacks—and that's exactly the point. Eating frequent small meals is thought to be more healthful than the old model of three larger meals a day. Every

recipe in this chapter is flexible enough to suit changing needs—whether it's a mid-morning snack, an appetizer, or a small meal. For instance, prepare any of the spreads from this book, such as the Edamame and Spinach Hummus (page 44), the Red Pepper–Sunflower Seed Spread (page 67), or the Walnut-Basil Pesto (page 88), pair it with your favorite bread, and you've got an appealing and wholesome snack. Add a bowl of soup or a salad, and you've got a meal. Dips and spreads are also fantastic served with crudités—a colorful assortment of raw or blanched vegetables that might include carrots, celery, green and red peppers, and jicama.

In addition to the nuts, sandwiches, and dips, I've included some more unusual snacks in this chapter; these are snacks that make a regular appearance in my home kitchen. Baked Kale Chips (page 59) and Umeboshi Rice Balls (page 50) have wide appeal and bring more vegetables and grains to the table. Either one can be enjoyed as a snack on its own or paired with another recipe to make a delicious small meal.

The recipes in this chapter help redefine what we think of as snacks, creating a healthful pattern of reaching for nourishing foods to help us stay energized and satisfied throughout the day.

edamame and spinach hummus with endive spears

This is an easy spin on a traditional hummus; it has a little spinach for color and flavor, and edamame (fresh soybeans) to add a jolt of plant protein as well as texture. Instead of serving it with bread or crackers, I like to use endive leaves; their size and shape are perfect for scooping the creamy hummus. This hummus also makes an excellent addition to the Grecian Goddess Salad with Quinoa Tabbouleh (page 130). **Makes about 4 cups**

8 cloves garlic, peeled

4 cups loosely packed spinach, stems trimmed

2 (15-ounce) cans garbanzo beans, drained and rinsed

1 cup thawed frozen shelled edamame

½ cup fresh lemon juice

⅓ cup roasted tahini

½ cup olive oil

1½ teaspoons fine sea salt

¼ teaspoon freshly ground black pepper

⅛ teaspoon cayenne pepper

2 Belgian endives (red and green), spears separated

Mince the garlic cloves in a food processor. Add the spinach, beans, edamame, lemon juice, and tahini. Pulse until the mixture is smooth. With the machine running, slowly drizzle in the oil until the mixture is smooth and creamy. Blend in the salt, black pepper, and cayenne pepper.

Transfer the hummus to a bowl and serve with the endive spears.

44

cherry tomato guacamole

There is nothing better than farm-fresh tomatoes to enhance a bowl of guacamole. Fortunately for me, my brother-in-law and sister-in-law grow gourmet organic cherry tomatoes: Their Del Cabo co-operative of small family farmers in Baja California produces some of the most flavorful varieties of cherry tomatoes you'll ever taste. And that certainly sweetens the deal for me when they drop in unannounced—they always come with armloads of fresh organic produce. Their cherry tomatoes inspired this guacamole, which has become an extended-family favorite. Any color or shape of bite-size tomatoes will work; using a variety of colors makes this dish even more festive. Of course, ripe, juicy plum tomatoes will work, too—just chop them coarsely. **Makes about 3 cups**

1 (4-ounce) basket cherry tomatoes, halved if small, quartered if large

½ small white onion, finely diced

⅓ cup finely chopped fresh cilantro

2 tablespoons fresh lime or lemon juice

¾ teaspoon fine sea salt, plus more as needed

¼ teaspoon ground cumin

2 cloves garlic, minced

4 firm but ripe avocados (about 1¾ pounds total), peeled, pitted, and coarsely diced

Toss the tomatoes, onion, cilantro, lime juice, the ¾ teaspoon salt, cumin, and garlic in a medium bowl. Let stand for 20 minutes to allow the flavors to blend.

Mash one-half of the diced avocados in a large bowl. Gently stir the mashed avocados and the remaining diced avocados into the tomato mixture, keeping the diced avocados intact. Season the guacamole to taste with more salt, if desired.

mango salsa

This snack satisfies that afternoon craving for a sweet treat, but because the sugars come from the mango's natural fruit juices, it's much healthier than a sugar-sweetened snack. I like using minced jalapeño chile to provide the heat, but for those of you who like a little more spice, you can use cayenne pepper for an extra kick. This salsa is great served with tortilla chips, and it's a nice addition to a leafy green salad. **Makes about 2 cups**

1 large ripe mango (about 13 ounces), peeled, pitted, and cut into ½-inch dice

1 ripe tomato, finely diced (about ½ cup)

1 Persian cucumber, peeled and finely diced (about ¼ cup)

½ red bell pepper, finely diced

2 tablespoons finely diced red onion

2 tablespoons chopped fresh cilantro

1 small jalapeño chile, minced, or 1 teaspoon cayenne pepper

1 tablespoon fresh lime juice

2 tablespoons fresh orange juice

½ teaspoon fine sea salt

Gently toss all the ingredients in a small bowl. Serve immediately, or cover and refrigerate until cold, at least 1 hour or up to 6 hours.

Pictured from left to right: Walnut-Basil Pesto (page 88),
Mango Salsa (opposite), and Tahini-Vegetable Spread (page 48).

tahini-vegetable spread

This is a versatile recipe that can be used as a dip or a spread. As the mixture sits, it will thicken up, so allow some time for it to rest between when you make it and when you intend to serve it. Serve it as a spread on rice crackers (or any other favorite crackers), or serve it as a dip with carrots and celery. It's also great for using in a wrap, as the flavors go well with roasted vegetables: You can use the ones from the Hemp-Crusted Tofu Wrap with Grilled Vegetables (page 61). **Makes about 1⅔ cups**

½ cup roasted tahini

⅓ cup water

¼ cup white or yellow miso

¼ cup fresh lemon juice

1 small clove garlic, minced

¾ teaspoon ground cumin

Pinch of cayenne pepper

1 medium carrot, peeled and finely chopped

1 celery stalk, finely chopped

2 tablespoons finely chopped scallions

2 tablespoons chopped fresh cilantro

Combine the tahini, the ⅓ cup water, the miso, lemon juice, garlic, cumin, and cayenne in a food processor and blend until smooth, about 3 minutes. Transfer the mixture to a small bowl.

Stir in the carrot, celery, scallions, and cilantro. The spread can be prepared up to 3 days ahead. Cover and refrigerate.

grilled cheese sandwich

Making a great grilled cheese sandwich using vegan cheeses is a two-step process, both to ensure melting of the vegan cheese and to give the outside of the bread its golden, crusty texture. Follow the steps below, and you will make a very satisfying sandwich. I prefer using a vegan cheese that comes in a block so I can use a cheese-cutter and slice the cheese to any thickness. I also like to use two different types of cheese per sandwich. See the variations at the end of the recipe for some ways to make the sandwich more gourmet. **Makes 4 sandwiches**

8 slices whole-wheat sandwich bread

½ cup vegan mayonnaise

8 (¼-inch-thick) slices Cheddar or American vegan cheese

8 (¼-inch-thick) slices Swiss or Monterey Jack vegan cheese

6 tablespoons vegan butter

Preheat the broiler. Heat a heavy flat grill pan or a cast-iron skillet over medium-low heat. (You want it hot when you lay your first sandwich down.)

Lay the 8 bread slices on a heavy baking sheet. Spread the vegan mayonnaise on the bread slices, then top each of 4 bread slices with 2 slices of the Cheddar cheese and each of the remaining 4 bread slices with 2 slices of the Swiss cheese. Broil until the cheese melts, watching closely, about 1½ minutes. Sandwich the bread slices together, forming 4 sandwiches that include both types of cheese.

Melt 3 tablespoons of the vegan butter on the hot grill pan. Place the sandwiches on the grill pan and cook, gently pressing down on the sandwiches with a spatula once or twice, until golden brown, about 3 minutes. Add the remaining 3 tablespoons of butter to the pan and turn the sandwiches over. Cook the second side of the sandwiches until they are golden brown and the cheeses are fully melted, about 3 minutes. Transfer the sandwiches to plates and serve immediately.

Variations:

- Mince a small clove of garlic and add to the vegan butter melting on the grill pan.

- Add a slice of tomato between the melted cheeses before sandwiching the bread.

- Add strips of Maple Tempeh Bacon (page 25) between the melted cheeses before sandwiching the bread.

- For a little zing, spread stone-ground mustard instead of the vegan mayonnaise on the bread slices. Or spread one side with the vegan mayonnaise and the other side with mustard.

umeboshi Rice Balls

My kids and I enjoy preparing these together. Even though it can get a little messy and sticky, it's all part of the fun. The idea is to hide a little treasure inside and surprise your diners—at least that's what I tell my children. These are great as an appetizer or a snack; they are very portable, which makes them perfect for a lunch box. **Makes about 20 rice balls**

3¾ cups Sushi Rice (recipe follows)

About 10 teaspoons umeboshi paste, or 5 whole umeboshi plums, pitted and quartered

2 tablespoons sesame seeds, toasted

4 sheets nori, cut into 1-inch-wide strips

Using wet hands and about 3 tablespoons of rice, form the rice into Ping-Pong-size balls. Press a hole in the center of 1 ball with your thumb. Using a small spoon or chopsticks, place about ½ teaspoon of umeboshi paste or a piece of plum in the hole. With your wet fingers, close the hole and smooth the opening completely. Repeat with the remaining balls.

Sprinkle the sesame seeds over the rice. Wrap a piece of nori around each rice ball, trimming the nori as needed and moistening the ends to seal. Serve immediately.

Variations: Incorporate any of the following ingredients by spooning 1 to 2 teaspoons inside the rice ball before closing and wrapping with the nori: minced scallions, chopped nuts, Kale Dust (page 60), or nut butter, such as almond, cashew, or peanut butter.

Nori, the thin sheets of dried seaweed best known for wrapping sushi, is widely available at natural foods stores and Asian grocery stores. I use it in these Umeboshi Rice Balls, among other recipes. It comes in flat packages of 10 to 50 sheets. Most companies today are selling nori that has been pre-toasted. When I was first introduced to nori, that was not true—you always had to toast the sheets prior to using. Recently, I've noticed that you can purchase smaller nori sheets that have been oiled and salted, sometimes with sesame seeds included. But why pay a premium price for these when you can easily do it yourself for a lot less—and control the amount of salt, too?

To prepare nori, preheat your oven to 300°F. On 1 cookie sheet, lay as many nori sheets as you can side by side. Using a small culinary brush, lightly brush each side of the nori with sesame

toasted nori

or olive oil. (Sesame oil will produce a definite flavor, while olive oil will be more subtle.) Lightly sprinkle both sides of the nori with fine sea salt. Bake on one side for 5 minutes. Remove from the oven, let cool. Keep whole or cut into smaller squares.

SUSHI RICE

Makes 6 cups

3½ cups water

1 cup short-grain brown rice, rinsed well

1 cup sweet brown rice, rinsed well

¼ teaspoon sea salt

2 tablespoons brown rice vinegar

1 tablespoon mirin

Combine the 3½ cups water and both types of rice in a 4¼-quart pressure cooker. Lock the lid into place. Bring the pressure to high over high heat. Decrease the heat to medium-low and simmer for 30 minutes. Remove from the heat and let stand for 10 minutes to allow the pressure to reduce. Carefully unlock the lid and remove it from the pot.

Transfer the rice to a large bowl. Drizzle the vinegar and mirin over the rice. Using chopsticks, gently toss the rice to coat it with the vinegar and mirin. Let the rice cool completely to room temperature.

Variation: If you don't have a pressure cooker, cook the rice in a large, heavy saucepan. Bring to a boil and then decrease the heat to low. Cover and simmer gently, without stirring, for 35 minutes, or until the rice is tender and the liquid is absorbed. Remove from the heat. Let stand, covered, for 5 minutes. Proceed with drizzling and tossing the rice with the vinegar and mirin, as explained above.

There are so many different types of eaters these days that feeding your family and friends can be a big challenge, whether you're cooking at home or heading out on the town. Here is a short guide to who is eating what these days, with its often overlapping—and frequently misunderstood—categories. (For more on gluten-free diets, see page 161; for more on macrobiotics, see page 202.)

LIVING Or raw FOODISTS eat foods that have been heated up to but not above 118°F (this number varies; I've heard as low as 102°F). These diets are usually vegan, but not always—I have seen raw milk offered at my local farmers' market, for instance. The theory behind raw foods is that cooking destroys the enzymes and life force of food. Macrobiotic teachings discuss the energy of food, and I find credence in this idea. I've included a few recipes in this book that come from my exploration of living food. These recipes are wonderfully light and cooling in the summertime, but I still find nothing more energizing than a hot bowl of soup on a cold winter day.

who is at the table?

LOCavores choose foods grown within a geographic region they've defined as local. In addition to supporting local agriculture, locavores are interested in more nutritious and better-tasting produce. I embrace these tenets of the locavore movement: The less time fruits and vegetables have spent on the road, the better they taste and the more nutrients they deliver. Being a locavore does not necessarily mean eating vegan or vegetarian. Today's locavores are connoisseurs of meat, poultry, fish, and dairy, seeking out local ranchers and producers of animal-based foods. Those more committed to the movement slaughter the animal in their own backyard. No exaggeration. Frankly, I find the slaughter of animals, whether done at home or in a factory, to be unappetizing and repulsive. Labeling an animal "local" does not justify the wasteful and inhumane practice of enslaving and slaughtering animals.

organic eaters aim to avoid the pesticides, herbicides, and petrochemical fertilizers that have transformed agriculture in the years following World War II—they consume organic foods both for health and for environmental concerns. As the organic foods movement blossomed in the late 1980s and the 1990s, people found the produce to be much better tasting, and some studies are showing these foods to be more nutritious than their conventionally grown counterparts. Many gourmet chefs have started seeking out locally grown organic produce to enhance the flavors of their dishes. While vegans and vegetarians often appreciate organic foods, organic eaters are not necessarily vegan or vegetarian.

vegans are the strictest of vegetarians; they don't eat meat, poultry, fish, dairy, eggs, or anything derived from animals, including honey. Some people stop there, with food as their only commitment. But other vegans are more politically involved as animal activists: They extend their animal-products ban to cosmetics and materials like leather, fur, and silk, to make sure that their purchases don't support animal testing or cruelty.

vegetarians rely primarily upon a plant-based diet, but vegetarians do come in many stripes: Some eat milk products (lacto-vegetarians), while others eat eggs (ovo-vegetarians), and many eat both (lacto-ovo vegetarians). Some people who identify themselves as vegetarians eat fish (pescatarians). In short, if someone tells you that they are vegetarian or vegan, and you will be preparing food for them, it's helpful to politely ask for clarification.

roasted nuts

Roasting nuts either in the oven or on the stovetop enhances their flavor and makes them easier to digest. These three roasted nut recipes are delicious eaten out of hand or used as a garnish for any green salad. They are also suggested for use in particular salads: Try the pepitas in the Buckwheat Salad with Oil-Free Sesame Sauce (page 184), the pistachios in the Watercress and Butter Lettuce Salad (page 128), and the almonds in the Harvest Kale Salad (page 115).

Tamari Pan-Roasted Pepitas

Makes 3 cups

3 cups unsalted shelled (green)
pumpkin seeds (pepitas)

3 tablespoons tamari

Wash the pumpkin seeds in a fine-meshed strainer under cold running water. Shake out any excess water.

Heat a large (9½- to 10½-inch) cast-iron skillet over medium-low heat to allow the skillet to get hot, about 2 minutes. (It shouldn't smoke.)

Add the wet pumpkin seeds to the hot skillet. Using a long-handled rice paddle or a square-tipped wooden spoon, move the pumpkin seeds around in the skillet. Continue to do this as they cook. After a few minutes, the seeds will start to swell and turn brown, and some will pop (all good). Keep stirring gently to make sure no seeds burn by sitting too long on the bottom of the skillet. This takes about 8 minutes.

At this point, add the tamari and continue to move the seeds around in the skillet. The tamari will coat the bottom of the skillet, so use the paddle or spoon to push the tamari to keep it from sticking. You want the tamari on the seeds, not on the bottom of the pan. Cook for another 10 minutes, or until all the seeds have turned a beautiful green-brown color and most are puffed.

Serve hot, or let cool completely and store in a glass jar. The pepitas will stay fresh in a tightly sealed glass jar for up to 1 week. Store the jar of seeds away from bright sunlight and in a cool area of your kitchen.

ROASTED PISTACHIOS

Makes about 1 cup

1 cup raw shelled unsalted natural pistachios

2 tablespoons agave nectar

1 tablespoon neutral cooking oil

⅛ teaspoon fine sea salt

⅛ teaspoon cayenne pepper

Preheat the oven to 350°F. Line a heavy rimmed baking sheet with parchment paper.

Toss the pistachios, agave nectar, oil, salt, and cayenne pepper in a large bowl to coat. Spread the pistachio mixture in a single layer on the prepared baking sheet. Bake, stirring frequently, until the pistachios turn golden, 8 to 10 minutes. Let cool.

SPICY-SWEET ROASTED ALMONDS

Makes about 1 cup

1 cup raw whole almonds

2 tablespoons pure maple syrup

1 tablespoon neutral cooking oil

¼ teaspoon chili powder

⅛ teaspoon cayenne pepper

⅛ teaspoon fine sea salt

Preheat the oven to 350°F. Line a heavy rimmed baking sheet with parchment paper.

Toss the almonds, maple syrup, oil, chili powder, cayenne pepper, and salt in a large bowl to coat. Spread the almond mixture in a single layer on the prepared baking sheet. Bake, stirring every 5 minutes, until the almonds turn golden and the syrup begins to thicken and coat the almonds, about 15 minutes. Let cool. (The almonds and coating will become crunchy when cool.)

real food pantry

nondairy cheeses

Nondairy cheese alternatives can satisfy cheese cravings without compromising a plant-based diet; use them to top nachos, make sandwiches, and sprinkle on salads or pastas. For homemade nondairy cheese, try my Vegan Cashew Cheese (recipe follows); it's easy to prepare and very versatile, but it requires planning ahead to allow the cheese time to set if you'll be slicing or grating it. There is also Tofu Ricotta Cheese (page 169), which I use in my Lasagna Rolls (page 166), and Cashew Cream (page 83), which I love using in soups and in my Baked Penne (page 152).

There are several good nondairy cheeses on the market these days, too. Up until a few years ago, it was difficult to find a nondairy cheese that could melt well. Fortunately, some companies have mastered this key attribute. I suggest you try them all to see which one you like the most; I keep a few brands on hand and choose the one that works the best for each recipe. As with all products, it's important to read the labels carefully when choosing nondairy cheeses: Some use casein, the protein found in milk.

ALMOND-BASED cheese alternatives produced by Lisanatti are soy-free, gluten-free, and cholesterol-free, but these products do contain casein. Lisanatti almond cheeses come in cheddar, mozzarella, jalapeño Jack, and garlic-herb flavors; they can be shredded and melted.

RICE-BASED cheese alternatives are perfect for those with soy allergies. Rice cheese is also one of the best for melting among nondairy cheeses, although its flavor tends to be less assertive than that of soy-based cheese. Galaxy Nutritional Foods' rice vegan slices, which come in cheddar, pepper Jack, and American cheese flavors, are a good source of calcium, and they are free of gluten, soy, preservatives, and all animal ingredients (including casein).

SOY-BASED cheese alternatives are the most common (and therefore the most widely available) of the nondairy cheeses. Popular brands of soy-based cheeses include Follow Your Heart, Teese, and Tofutti. Soy cheeses are available both in shredded and sliced forms and often melt much like traditional dairy cheeses. Dairy-free cheeses are not as commonly found in mainstream supermarkets as nondairy milks are, but they are available in most natural foods stores. These cheeses are great on sandwiches; I've used them to make my Grilled Cheese Sandwich (page 49).

TAPIOCA-BASED cheese alternatives are the newest innovation in the alternative cheese market: Look for a vegan product called Daiya, which is free of dairy, nuts, soy, and gluten. I've found that Daiya, which comes shredded in cheddar and mozzarella flavors, is the closest to tasting like a dairy-based cheese, and it melts the best, too. I use it in my Baked Penne (page 152), in my tofu scrambles in the Breakfasts chapter, and, of course, on my Grilled Cheese Sandwich (page 49).

vegan cashew cheese

I've used this cheese recipe for over a decade at my restaurants, Real Food Daily, and I published it in my first cookbook, *The Real Food Daily Cookbook*. It is an excellent nondairy cheese that slices, shreds, and melts. **Makes 4 cups**

1¼ cups raw cashews

½ cup nutritional yeast

2 teaspoons onion powder

2 teaspoons sea salt

1 teaspoon garlic powder

⅛ teaspoon ground white pepper

3½ cups plain unsweetened soy milk

1 cup (about 1½ ounces) agar agar flakes

½ cup canola oil

¼ cup white or yellow miso

2 tablespoons fresh lemon juice

Using the pulse button, finely grind the cashews in a food processor (do not allow the cashews to turn into a paste). Add the nutritional yeast, onion powder, salt, garlic powder, and white pepper. Pulse 3 more times to blend in the spices.

Combine the soy milk, agar, and oil in a medium, heavy saucepan. Bring to a simmer over high heat. Decrease the heat to medium-low. Cover and simmer, stirring occasionally, for 10 minutes, or until the agar is dissolved. With the food processor running, gradually pour the hot soy milk mixture through the feed tube and into the cashew mixture. Blend for 2 minutes, or until the mixture is very smooth and creamy. Blend in the miso and lemon juice.

For grated or sliced cheese, transfer the cheese to a container, and cover and refrigerate until it is very firm, about 4 hours. Once it is firm, grate or slice the cheese as desired.

For melted cheese, use the cheese immediately. To make the cheese in advance, cover and refrigerate it. When ready to use, melt it in a saucepan over medium heat until it is smooth and creamy, stirring frequently and adding more soy milk to the melted cheese to thin it, if necessary.

The cheese will keep for 4 days, covered and refrigerated.

Baked Kale Chips

Sure, kale is versatile, but who knew that you could make it into crunchy chips? Kale chips have become quite popular, but the price is prohibitive. When I saw them going for ten dollars a bag, that's when I set out to make my own. The store-bought ones are dehydrated, which is a method used often in living and raw foods cuisine. I've found that baking the kale on low heat can produce an excellent result. The main thing is to spread it out on the baking sheet, keeping space between each piece; otherwise, it tends to get soggy. When coming out of the oven, the kale might still look a little limp, but give it time to cool, and you've got yourself a batch of kale chips—all for a few bucks. **Serves 2 to 4**

1 (8-ounce) bunch large curly kale

1 tablespoon olive oil

⅛ teaspoon fine sea salt

Preheat the oven to 300°F. Line 2 large, heavy baking sheets with parchment paper.

Spin the kale pieces in a salad spinner, or pat them with paper towels, until they're dry. It is important that the leaves are very dry, as oil doesn't mix with water.

Cut away the center spine from each kale leaf and discard the spine. When removing the spine, go ahead and cut through to the top of the leaf so you have 2 pieces. Keep the leaves as halves, or cut each piece in half again. (I cut or tear these pieces so I get 4 pieces from each leaf, or I just leave them as whole as possible, since the kale shrinks to less than half its size while baking.)

Place the kale, oil, and salt in a large bowl and, using your hands, rub the oil to coat the kale pieces thoroughly. (Be prepared to get your hands oily and salty.)

Arrange the kale pieces in a single layer on the prepared baking sheets and then bake until they are crisp, about 25 minutes. Check the kale every 10 minutes or so and turn some pieces over if they look too toasty.

The kale chips will stay crisp and fresh for up to 1 week, stored in a sealed container or bag.

Variations: Wash, cut, coat, and bake the kale according to the directions above. Instead of seasoning the kale with just olive oil and salt, try any of these variations. Because some of these variations include maple syrup, which makes the kale brown faster, cooking times will range from 15 to 25 minutes, so check the kale often to determine doneness.

Vinegar and Sea Salt: Combine 1 tablespoon vinegar (balsamic, apple cider, or brown rice), 1 tablespoon olive oil or a neutral cooking oil, and ⅛ teaspoon fine sea salt.

Maple-Coconut: Combine 2 tablespoons finely shredded unsweetened dried coconut, 2 tablespoons pure maple syrup, 1 tablespoon sunflower oil or a neutral cooking oil, and ⅛ teaspoon fine sea salt.

Garlic-Sesame: Combine 2 tablespoons sesame seeds or hemp seeds, 1 tablespoon olive oil or a neutral cooking oil, 1 tablespoon tamari, and 1 clove garlic, minced.

Hot and Spicy: Combine 1 tablespoon olive oil or a neutral cooking oil, 1 tablespoon pure maple syrup, ⅛ teaspoon cayenne pepper, ⅛ teaspoon chili powder, and ⅛ teaspoon fine sea salt.

Kale Dust for Popcorn: Crush the baked kale chips with your fingers or with a mortar and pestle into a fine powder. Sprinkle the crushed kale over popcorn. It's colorful and nutritious; my kids love this one.

Parchment paper is a heavy-duty paper product that you can find in any grocery store, where the plastic wrap and aluminum foil is found. It is a relative of wax paper, but it is much more versatile and environmentally friendly. The lack of a petroleum-

parchment paper

based wax coating means that, unlike wax paper, you can cook with parchment paper.

Parchment paper is a relatively recent addition to my tool kit, and I honestly don't know how I lived without it. Now a staple in my kitchen, I use it for lining baking pans, thereby eliminating the need to use baking sprays or oils; it also makes cleanup a breeze.

Hemp-Crusted Tofu Wrap with Grilled Vegetables and Walnut-Basil Pesto Mayonnaise

A little vegan mayo in this walnut-basil pesto and the benefits from the omega fatty acids in hemp seeds make this one fantastic wrap. Feel free to substitute your favorite seasonable vegetables. **Makes 6 wraps**

PESTO MAYONNAISE
1 cup Walnut-Basil Pesto (page 88)

¼ cup vegan mayonnaise

WRAPS
2 red onions, cut crosswise into ¼-inch-thick rings

2 yellow crookneck squash, cut on a sharp diagonal into ¼-inch-thick slices

2 zucchini, cut on a sharp diagonal into ¼-inch-thick slices

1 red bell pepper, cut lengthwise into ¼-inch-thick slices

2 tablespoons olive oil

Fine sea salt and freshly ground black pepper

6 (8- to 9-inch) flour tortillas (preferably made with spinach or sun-dried tomatoes)

12 pieces Hemp-Crusted Tofu (recipe follows)

3 cups chopped mixed baby lettuces

Pesto Mayonnaise: Stir the pesto and vegan mayonnaise in a small bowl to blend. Set aside.

Wraps: Heat a large, heavy grill pan over medium heat, or prepare a barbecue for medium-high heat. Brush the vegetables with the oil and season them with salt and pepper. Place the onions on the hot pan and cook, turning them over once, until they are tender and beginning to brown, about 10 minutes. Add the squash, zucchini, and bell pepper and cook until they are tender and just cooked through but not mushy, about 8 minutes for the squash and zucchini and 12 minutes for the bell pepper. Keep the vegetables separate and set aside.

To warm the tortilla, place one tortilla at a time in a nonoiled griddle or pan over low to medium heat for 15 seconds per side, or until warmed through. Keep the tortilla warm in a clean kitchen towel while you heat up the remaining 5 tortillas.

Lay the tortillas flat on the work surface. Spread 2 tablespoons of the pesto mayonnaise on each tortilla, leaving about ½ inch of the outer edges uncovered. Be generous with the pesto—it's what makes the wrap moist and delicious. Layer the vegetables and tofu in the following order from top to bottom, dividing equally: zucchini, red bell pepper, tofu pieces, lettuce, yellow squash, red onions.

Roll up the tortillas tightly, enclosing the filling, and tuck in the ends. Using a large sharp knife, cut each wrap diagonally into 2 pieces.

HEMP-CRUSTED TOFU

While this recipe was designed to use in the wrap above, it's a great example of how flexible the components of so many of my recipes are. Hemp-crusted tofu is the perfect protein to serve with a bowl of rice and a vegetable dish to make a simple and satisfying meal. Just know, some of the hemp seeds will fall off during the cooking process, and that's okay. **Serves 4**

2 (14-ounce) containers water-packed extra-firm tofu, drained

2 tablespoons olive oil

¾ cup hemp seeds

1½ teaspoons fine sea salt

Nonstick olive oil spray

Pat the tofu dry with paper towels. Cover a large baking sheet with more dry paper towels. Arrange the tofu over the towels on the baking sheet and let drain for 2 hours, changing the paper towels after 1 hour.

Cut each block of tofu horizontally twice to equal 6 pieces total. Now, cut these in half vertically and you'll end up with a total of 12 pieces.

Brush the tofu with the oil. Gently press the hemp seeds and salt onto each side of the tofu pieces to cover generously.

Preheat a flat griddle pan or a large cast-iron skillet over medium-low heat. Spray the pan with oil and lay the hemp-coated tofu pieces on the pan. Cook until the tofu is heated through and the hemp crust is golden, about 3 minutes on each side.

Alternatively, the prepared tofu can be baked. To do so, preheat the oven to 400°F. Arrange the tofu on a baking sheet and bake for 10 minutes on each side, or until it is golden brown and heated through.

If you're wondering how to be greener in the kitchen, then congratulations: You already made a big step forward when you bought this book. Eating a plant-based diet is one of the most powerful ways to have a positive impact on the planet. However, there are lots of other simple, low-cost ways that you can make a difference in your kitchen.

BE CONSCIENTIOUS. Challenge yourself to be more thoughtful in your everyday tasks: Turn off the tap when it's not needed, only run the dishwasher when it's full, and turn off lights and unplug appliances when not in use. Another simple way to be more thoughtful every day

Greening your kitchen

is to think about your consumption, and try to limit waste as much as possible. One of the best ways to do this is through recycling, and not just the bottles-and-cans variety: See if you can reuse jelly jars as small-wares containers, for example. If you're really ambitious, start a backyard compost for kitchen scraps.

VOTE WITH YOUR DOLLAR. Every purchase you make is an opportunity to let businesses know that consumers want greener products. Start by making an effort to purchase organic and natural versions of the products you already buy—most manufacturers are getting hip to the fact that there is a growing demand for these items. Another way you can shop smart is to purchase items that are reusable, rather than disposable, such as reusable lunch bags, shopping totes, and water bottles. I've gotten my kids involved in packing their zero-waste school lunches. Finally, one of the best ways to vote with your dollar is to support local businesses—from buying produce from local farmers to buying your screwdriver at the mom-and-pop hardware store. These small businesses make up the fabric of a community and are often invested in making your neighborhood a better place to live.

KEEP IT CLEAN AND GREEN. If you are enjoying the recipes in this book, then you are probably spending a fair amount of time in your kitchen. By making an effort to keep your kitchen as bright and clean as possible, you will be helping to make the time spent cooking that much more enjoyable. Fortunately, there are many brands of green cleaning products available today—look for those with the EcoLogo or Green Seal certification, as you can be sure those products have been tested and reviewed to meet high standards for a green clean. In addition to purchasing green cleaning products, simple steps like opening windows and allowing sunshine into your kitchen can make a big difference by introducing positive energy into the space. And although it's not practical for everyone, container gardens can help to both beautify and purify the kitchen, not to mention that they're very handy when the recipe calls for fresh herbs.

Pictured with Very Berry Smoothie, page 12.

Living wrap

The ingredients in this recipe are absolutely raw. If eating raw is not your thing, you can still enjoy this delicious wrap: Try regular tamari as opposed to the nama shoyu, which is a raw organic unpasteurized soy sauce. You can also use regular agave nectar rather than its raw version. The salad greens need to be tossed with the dressing before you make the wrap; otherwise, the wrap will be too dry. This salad dressing can easily be doubled and used on another salad. To learn more about raw cuisine, see page 52.

Makes 16 wraps

RED PEPPER–SUNFLOWER SEED SPREAD

1 cup diced red bell pepper

1 cup raw shelled sunflower seeds

½ cup firmly packed fresh basil leaves

1 tablespoon fresh lemon juice

1 tablespoon nama shoyu

1 teaspoon fine sea salt

2 cloves garlic, minced

CITRUS DRESSING

1 tablespoon apple cider vinegar

1 tablespoon fresh orange juice

1 teaspoon raw agave nectar

1 teaspoon chopped fresh dill

1 small clove garlic, minced

1½ tablespoons extra-virgin olive oil

Fine sea salt and freshly ground black pepper

WRAPS

4 large collard green leaves (each at least 11 by 11 inches)

2 Persian cucumbers, peeled, seeded, and cut into long strips about ¼ inch thick

2 large ripe avocados, peeled, pitted, and thinly sliced

2 ripe tomatoes, halved and thinly sliced

6 cups mixed salad greens

Red Pepper–Sunflower Seed Spread: Combine all the ingredients in a food processor and blend until the mixture is spreadable but still a bit chunky.

Citrus Dressing: Whisk the vinegar, orange juice, agave nectar, dill, and garlic in a medium bowl to blend. Gradually whisk in the oil. Season to taste with salt and pepper.

Wraps: Using a sharp knife, cut out the center vein from each of the collard green leaves. This will pretty much cut the leaves in half, which is what you want. Now, cut each half in half again to make 16 equal pieces.

Lay the pieces of collard greens on the work surface. Spread 1½ tablespoons of the red pepper mixture in the center of each piece of collard green. Lay 2 cucumber strips, 2 avocado slices, and 1 tomato slice over the spread on each piece. Toss the mixed salad greens with just enough of the dressing to coat lightly. Place a few leaves of the mixed salad greens on top of the tomatoes. Roll up the collard green pieces around the fillings, tucking under one side to hold the filling in.

Stick toothpicks through the wraps to keep them together. Serve the remaining mixed salad greens alongside.

favorite Asian condiments

What I've done best as a chef is to create American vegan cuisine that's influenced by global flavors. The secret to my style of cooking can be found in this list of Asian condiments and seasonings. They add rich, earthy, pure flavors to my dishes—and a depth that I find is often missing from vegan cooking. An easy way to elevate your own home cooking is to stock your pantry with the following ingredients:

MIRIN is a mildly sweet cooking wine made from whole-grain rice. Its flavor rounds out acidic ingredients, and it goes well with tamari and sesame oil. I love to use mirin in sautéing; you'll find it enhances my South American Stew (page 148), and brings an unusual flavor to my Peaches and Nectarines with Sweet Almond-Cashew Cream (page 241).

MISO is a rich fermented paste made from ingredients such as soybeans, barley, and brown rice. You might want to think of it as a clean, animal-free version of chicken stock or bouillon. When eaten on a regular basis, miso aids circulation and digestion. Besides using it as the star ingredient in miso soup, I love to add miso to other soups—as I did with my Fennel and Roasted Garlic Soup with Walnut-Basil Pesto (page 87). Miso is also great in sauces, gravies, dressings, and spreads: My Tahini-Vegetable Spread (page 48) is one delicious example.

RICE VINEGAR has been called the eastern version of apple cider vinegar. Its flavor has about half the sharpness, with a subtle sweetness. I prefer brown rice vinegar, but will settle for rice vinegar that has not been tampered with by the addition of sugar.

SHIITAKE MUSHROOMS are available either dried or fresh and may be used to flavor soup stocks or vegetable dishes. Dried shiitake mushrooms are often used in medicinal preparations, too. And they are a must in any good miso soup: You'll find dried shiitake mushrooms in my Ginger Miso Soup (page 98), and fresh shiitakes in my One-Pot Vegetables and Tofu (page 145).

TAMARI is a traditional, naturally made soy sauce. The big difference between tamari and soy sauce is that tamari is brewed and aged for a longer time than soy sauce, producing a rich, smooth, and complex flavor that distinguishes it from chemically processed soy sauce. Tamari has a small amount of wheat added to it, while soy sauce can contain 40 to 60 percent wheat. In today's marketplace, you can also find gluten-free tamari. I use tamari often in my savory dishes, from vegetables to sauces.

UMEBOSHI are beautiful dark-red-skinned plums; technically, they are a Japanese variety of pickled Asian plums. I can't live without umeboshi, as they help with digestion and increase my energy when I am feeling sluggish. They are a potent food, so you only need a very small amount. Umeboshi are quite medicinal and may be eaten whole—but no more than one at a time. The plums are often made into a paste or vinegar, which is best used for cooking. You'll see how I use the paste in my Boiled Vegetable Salad with Umeboshi-Scallion Dressing (page 204).

curried eggless tofu salad in a pita

When I was living in New York, I worked for a time at a popular bistro in SoHo, where I used to indulge in the curried tuna salad. What made it so different from the classic tuna fish salad that I was brought up on was the curry—and the currants. I couldn't get enough of those two flavors together. Years later and no longer eating tuna fish, I created this recipe to enjoy those same flavors. This might be my daughter Halle's favorite recipe in the book—it's a special treat when I can pack her lunch with this exotic sandwich. **Serves 4**

1 (14-ounce) container firm tofu, drained

4 pita pockets, tops trimmed 1½ inches

6 tablespoons vegan mayonnaise

3 tablespoons finely chopped fresh cilantro

2 tablespoons fresh lemon juice

5 teaspoons curry powder

1 tablespoon umeboshi paste

½ teaspoon fine sea salt

¼ teaspoon freshly ground black pepper

¼ red onion, minced (about ⅓ cup)

1 celery stalk, finely chopped

¼ cup currants, plumped in warm water for 10 minutes and drained

4 romaine lettuce leaves

1 tomato, thinly sliced

Pat the tofu dry with paper towels. Cover a large baking sheet with more dry paper towels. Arrange the tofu over the towels on the baking sheet and let drain for 2 hours, changing the paper towels after 1 hour.

Preheat the oven to 350°F. Wrap the pita breads in foil and bake them in the oven until they're hot, about 10 minutes.

Using a fork, break up the tofu in a medium bowl, making sure no big chunks remain, but being careful not to turn it into mush. Remember, it will smooth out even more when you add the mayonnaise. Whisk the vegan mayonnaise, cilantro, lemon juice, curry powder, umeboshi paste, salt, and pepper in a large bowl to blend. Mix in the tofu, onion, celery, and currants.

Stuff the tofu salad, lettuce leaves, and tomato slices into the pita breads and serve immediately.

open-faced sandwiches

The French call them *tartines;* in Italy, they are beloved as crostini; and in the States, we call them open-faced sandwiches. These can be great appetizers to serve at a party, enjoyed as a savory snack, or paired with a bowl of soup or a simple salad to make a whole meal. You can be as creative as possible. It's really all about your favorite bread, a spread, a plant-based protein, and your choice of vegetables to top it all off. The following are my favorite *tartine* recipes:

PORTOBELLO MUSHROOM, SPINACH, AND MELTED VEGAN MOZZARELLA TARTINES

As the executive chef of *Vegetarian Times* magazine, I prepared this *tartine* on the *Today* show. Here, I've put my vegan mark on the recipe; among the changes, I use vegan mozzarella cheese instead of the Parmesan. **Serves 4**

6 ounces vaccum-packed soft silken tofu (such as Mori-Nu)

6 cloves garlic, roasted

Fine sea salt and freshly ground black pepper

1 tablespoon olive oil

2 large portobello mushrooms, cut into ½-inch-thick slices

2 large shallots, thinly sliced

1 (8-ounce) bag fresh spinach

6 tablespoons grated vegan mozzarella cheese (such as Daiya)

½ French baguette, halved lengthwise, then cut crosswise in half

Preheat the broiler for low heat. Blend the tofu and roasted garlic in a food processor until smooth. Season with salt and pepper.

Heat the oil in a large, heavy skillet over medium heat. Add the mushrooms and shallots and sauté until softened, about 5 minutes. Stir in the spinach and cook until wilted, about 2 minutes. Add 2 tablespoons of the cheese, then remove the pan from the heat. Season to taste with salt and pepper.

Spread 1 tablespoon of the tofu-garlic mixture on each baguette piece. Top with the mushroom-spinach mixture, then sprinkle with the remaining ¼ cup cheese. Broil until the cheese begins to brown, about 3 minutes.

BLT Tartines Watch out; this vegan take on the classic BLT will become addictive.
Makes 4 tartines

4 (½-inch-thick) diagonal slices sourdough baguette

¼ cup vegan mayonnaise

4 lettuce leaves

12 slices Maple Tempeh Bacon (page 25)

8 slices tomatoes (from 1 large ripe tomato), or 8 small cherry tomatoes, halved

1 ripe avocado, peeled, pitted, and cut lengthwise into slices

Preheat the oven to 400°F. Place the bread slices on a baking sheet, and toast for about 2 minutes on each side, or until the bread is golden brown. Alternatively, toast the bread in a toaster oven.

Spread the vegan mayonnaise generously on the toasted bread. Top with the lettuce, bacon, tomato, and avocado.

Sweet Mustard Tempeh with Sauerkraut on Hemp Bread This is another use for the Sweet Mustard Tempeh from my Harvest Kale Salad (page 115). Instead of cutting it into bite-size pieces, for this recipe, I just cut the tempeh horizontally in half, then use a vertical cut to make 4 large pieces, perfect to fit on this sandwich. I like to use French Meadow's hemp bread, as the slices are smaller than usual sandwich bread. If you don't care for the hemp, this national bakery has lots of other delicious choices. **Makes 4 tartines**

4 (¼-inch-thick) slices hearty whole-grain bread

2 tablespoons stone-ground mustard

4 slices Sweet Mustard Tempeh (page 116; prepared in slices rather than cubes)

1 cup sauerkraut, drained

Toast the bread slices in a toaster oven or set under the broiler 2 to 3 minutes per side, until brown. Spread 1½ teaspoons of the mustard on each slice of toasted bread. Top with 1 slice of Sweet Mustard Tempeh. Finish the tartines by topping each with ¼ cup of the sauerkraut.

Variation: To make the recipe into a warm tempeh melt, spread each bread slice with 1 tablespoon Thousand Island dressing instead of the mustard, place a slice of Sweet Mustard Tempeh on top of each, and then place a slice of nondairy Swiss cheese atop the tempeh on each. Bake in a 400°F oven for 4 minutes, or until the cheese melts. Top the tartines with the sauerkraut and serve.

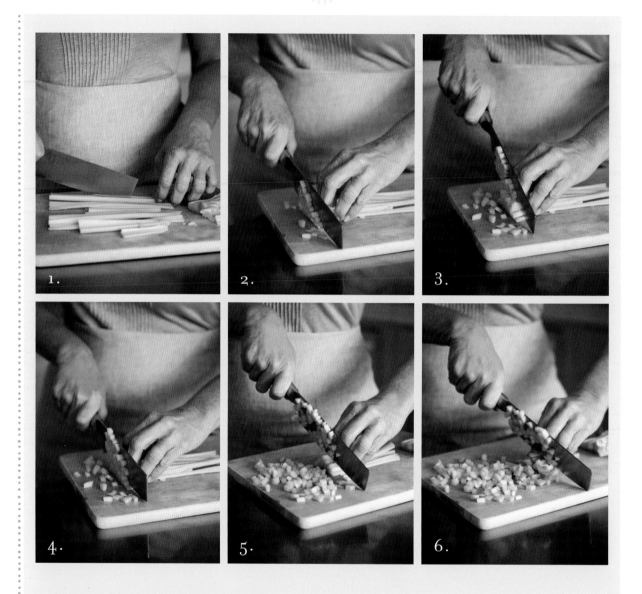

CUTTING TECHNIQUES

DICING is cutting vegetables into uniformly small pieces, ranging from ¼-inch pieces up to ½-inch pieces. To dice celery into ½-inch pieces, cut off the root end and then slice each celery stalk lengthwise into ½-inch-wide strips. Finally, slice it crosswise into ½-inch pieces.

soups

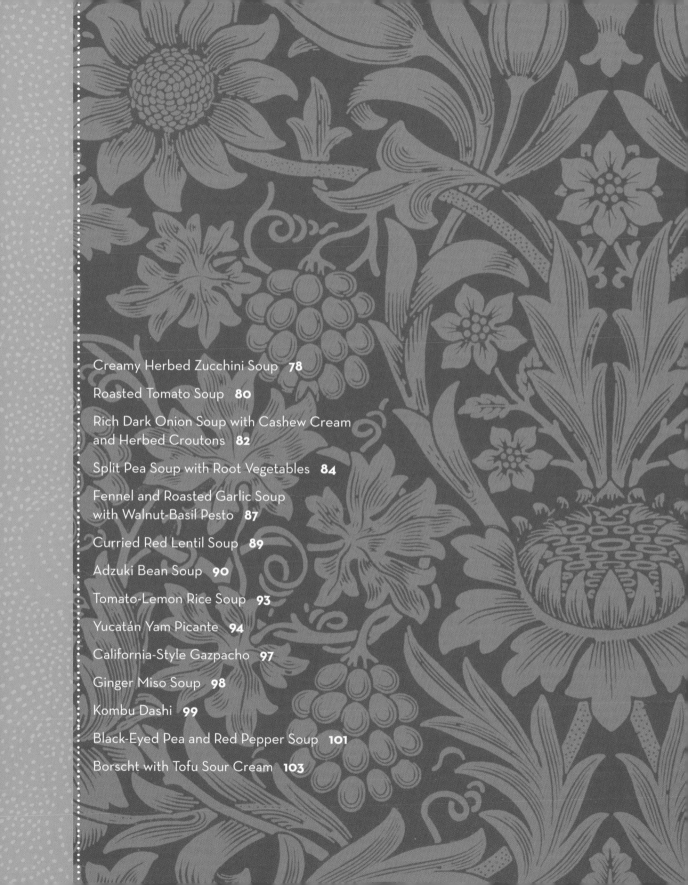

soups

Homemade soup is one of the most satisfying meals I know; bubbling on the stove, its scent will entice your family to come into the kitchen or gather around the table, eager for dinner and the conversation that comes with it. A hot, comforting bowl of homemade soup is what your kids will miss when they're away from home, and what they'll crave when they're sick. When you're making it from scratch, you decide which vegetables, grains, and seasonings to include in your soup, and the results are always superior to supermarket offerings—and far less salty, too. One-pot cooking means soups are unfussy to prepare, and most happen to be low in fat and high in fiber, making them a healthful menu staple for busy families. Soups hold well for anyone working or playing late, and many soups freeze well, too.

The little effort and expense you put into making soup will produce results that stretch beyond one meal. Served alone, soup makes a nourishing lunch or dinner—just add a thick slice of crusty bread or serve with a favorite salad. I always look forward to the next day when I can pack a lunch that includes a thermos of soup. In addition, soups have a calming and soothing effect, and from a practical perspective, starting a meal with a cup of soup can help prepare your digestion for the courses to follow.

You don't need much equipment to get started: A stockpot, a blender, a cutting board, a good knife, and a ladle will do. Add to that a variety of basic ingredients like vegetables, beans, some grains, a little tofu, herbs, and a well-stocked spice rack, and you've got everything you need. In fact, soups make good use of the main ingredients in my Real Food Pantry: I like to draw on global inspiration, using herbs and spices liberally, in ways that always seem to work. I can also use my imagination and throw leftover grains or beans into a pot with vegetables and reliably come up with a filling and delicious soup.

The recipes that follow are my go-to soups, the ones I regularly prepare for my family and friends. While certain ingredients are seasonal—zucchini shows up in the late spring (for Creamy Herbed Zucchini Soup, page 78) and yams show up in the fall (for Yucatán Yam Picante, page 94)—there are enough soups in this chapter to keep you and your family satisfied year-round. Consider the Adzuki Bean Soup (page 90), which is best in the winter, and my California-Style Gazpacho (page 97), which is refreshing in the summer months. There is truly something for every taste and time.

creamy herbed zucchini soup

This is a fantastic soup for late spring, when zucchini starts to make an appearance at the farmers' market. I use both rolled oats and a potato to thicken this soup; don't overblend it, as the potato can become gummy. If you don't have fresh herbs available, use half the amount in dried herbs—it will still be a pleasing soup. While a handheld blender will also work, I prefer puréeing this soup in a full-size blender, to create a smooth, silky consistency that turns the soup into a sophisticated bowl of pure green goodness.

Serves 6 to 8 (makes about 8 cups)

1½ teaspoons olive oil

1 large onion, chopped

2 cloves garlic, chopped

1½ teaspoons fine sea salt, plus more to taste

1 pound green zucchini, coarsely chopped

2 celery stalks, chopped

1 small Yukon Gold potato, peeled and cut into ¾-inch pieces

¼ head cabbage, coarsely chopped

⅛ teaspoon ground white pepper

4 cups water

3 tablespoons old-fashioned rolled oats

1 tablespoon fresh basil leaves

1 tablespoon fresh tarragon leaves

¼ teaspoon fresh oregano leaves

2 tablespoons thinly sliced fresh chives or scallions, for garnish

Heat the oil in a heavy pot over medium-high heat. Add the onion, garlic, and the 1½ teaspoons salt. Sauté until the onion is translucent, about 5 minutes. Add the zucchini, celery, potato, cabbage, and white pepper. Cook, stirring often, until the vegetables soften, about 10 minutes.

Add the water and oats, then cover and bring to a simmer over high heat. Decrease the heat to medium-low and, with the lid on, continue to simmer, stirring occasionally, until the vegetables are tender, about 30 minutes. Stir in the basil, tarragon, and oregano. Taste and adjust salt if necessary.

Working in batches, purée the soup in a blender until it is smooth.

Ladle the soup into bowls. Sprinkle with the chives and serve.

The soup will keep for 2 days, covered and refrigerated, or for 1 month frozen. To rewarm, bring the soup to a simmer over medium heat, stirring occasionally and adding water to thin the soup to the desired consistency.

great soup thickeners

Thickening soup gives it more body, enhancing its texture, character, and appeal. But there are many ways to thicken a soup, and not all of them are equal. Conventional cookbooks recommend everything from flour to bread crumbs to making a full-fledged roux, and from milk to cream to eggs to lard (really). Others simply use arrowroot or cornstarch. And still others use whole foods like beans, nuts, puréed vegetables, potatoes, and grains. When you use whole foods as a thickening agent, you'll add more nutrition to the recipe. This is especially important when serving soup as a main course.

For creamy puréed soups, I find that white potatoes or rolled oats do a nice job of blending well with vegetables and disappearing into the flavor profile. Cashew Cream (page 83) is a thickener that adds not only body, but a mellow, nutty flavor and extra protein, too; it works equally well in soups with a brothy texture or a creamy texture. I also like using grains or beans to thicken brothy soups; when blended, they contribute a creamy texture and sound nutrition.

ROasted TOmato soup

From Roma to cherry to beefsteak, any kind of tomatoes can be used to make this soup. You can play around with the colors of the tomatoes, too. Look for heirloom varieties at your local farmers' market: They might be red, orange, yellow, purple, or even green. For a shortcut—or when it's not tomato season— you can use canned fire-roasted tomatoes; Muir Glen makes a great one that's organic, too. Besides basil and flat-leaf parsley, sage is added to lend an even deeper flavor. This soup is hearty and satisfying, and it makes a fantastic meal served with any of my open-faced sandwiches or tartines, starting on page 71.

Serves 6 to 8 (makes about 9 cups)

4 pounds ripe tomatoes, quartered

¼ cup plus 2 tablespoons extra-virgin olive oil

¼ cup balsamic vinegar

12 large cloves garlic, chopped

3 teaspoons fine sea salt

1 teaspoon freshly ground black pepper

2 medium red onions, coarsely chopped

¼ cup lightly packed chopped fresh basil

2 tablespoons finely chopped fresh flat-leaf parsley

1½ tablespoons finely chopped fresh sage

5 cups water

About 2 cups Herbed Croutons (page 83)

Preheat the oven to 500°F. Toss the tomatoes with ¼ cup of the olive oil, the vinegar, garlic, 2 teaspoons of the salt, and the 1 teaspoon black pepper in a large bowl. Transfer the tomato mixture (including all of the liquid) to a large, heavy rimmed baking sheet, arranging the tomatoes in a single layer, skin side down. Roast until the tomatoes are charred on the edges, about 40 minutes. Allow the mixture to cool slightly. Slip the skins off the tomatoes.

Heat the remaining 2 tablespoons olive oil in a heavy pot over medium heat. Add the onions and the remaining 1 teaspoon salt, and cook, stirring often, until the onions are very soft, about 10 minutes. Add the basil, parsley, and sage and sauté for about 1 minute. Stir in the roasted tomatoes and all the accumulated juices from the baking sheet and bring to a simmer. Add the water and simmer gently to allow the flavors to blend, about 8 minutes.

Ladle the soup into bowls, garnish with the croutons, and serve.

This soup is best eaten the day it is made, but it can be covered and refrigerated for up to 1 day. To rewarm, bring the soup to a simmer over medium heat, stirring occasionally and adding water to thin the soup to the desired consistency.

Pictured with Portobello Mushroom, Spinach, and Melted Vegan Mozzarella Tartine, page 71.

Rich Dark Onion Soup with Cashew Cream and Herbed Croutons

The slowly caramelized onions in this soup create a beautifully fragrant broth, which is appealing in its own right. But what we all really want is a bready, cheesy topping. I've tried adding grated nondairy cheeses, but it never seems to be the right consistency, as these cheeses tend to separate and go gummy in hot soup. Fortunately, my Cashew Cream (recipe follows) makes just the right rich, creamy addition. While this recipe can be prepared with a dry white wine, I prefer red wine, as it gives the soup a bolder, richer flavor and aroma. **Serves 8 to 10 (makes about 12 cups)**

2 tablespoons olive oil

4½ pounds red onions, thinly sliced

3 pounds yellow onions, thinly sliced

3 cloves garlic, minced

¼ cup minced fresh flat-leaf parsley

1 tablespoon fresh thyme leaves

1 teaspoon fine sea salt

2 teaspoons freshly ground black pepper, plus more to taste

2 small bay leaves

1¼ cups dry red wine

2 tablespoons tamari, plus more to taste

8 cups low-sodium vegetable stock (two 32-ounce boxes)

2 cups water

About 3 cups Herbed Croutons (recipe follows)

1 cup Cashew Cream (recipe follows)

Heat the olive oil in a large, heavy pot over medium heat. Add the red onions and cook, stirring often, until they reduce by a third, about 30 minutes. Stir in the yellow onions and continue cooking, stirring occasionally, until the onions release their liquid, then become a dark golden brown color, about 1 hour 45 minutes. After the first 1½ hours, stir the onions more frequently and scrape the bottom of the pot to prevent the mixture from burning. The onions will reduce to less than one-fourth of their original volume.

Stir the garlic, 3 tablespoons of the parsley, the thyme, the salt, the 2 teaspoons black pepper, and the bay leaves into the onions and cook for 5 minutes. Add the wine and the 2 tablespoons tamari. Decrease the heat to medium-low and simmer gently until the mixture thickens slightly, about 15 minutes.

Add the stock and water, and bring the soup to a boil over high heat. Decrease the heat again to medium-low. Cover and simmer gently until the flavors blend, about 20 minutes. Season the soup to taste with more tamari and pepper, and remove the bay leaves.

Ladle the soup into bowls and top with the croutons. Spoon a dollop of the cashew cream atop each bowl of soup. Garnish with the remaining 1 tablespoon parsley and serve.

The soup will keep for 2 days, covered and refrigerated, or for 1 month frozen. To rewarm, bring the soup to a simmer over medium heat, stirring occasionally and adding water to thin the soup to the desired consistency.

Herbed Croutons

These crisp croutons would also be delicious tossed into your favorite green salad. **Makes about 3½ cups**

½ loaf crusty French bread (about 8 ounces), crust removed, cut into ½-inch cubes

½ teaspoon dried basil

½ teaspoon dried dill

½ teaspoon dried rosemary

¼ teaspoon freshly ground black pepper

⅛ teaspoon fine sea salt

2 tablespoons extra-virgin olive oil

Preheat the oven to 375°F. Toss the bread cubes, basil, dill, rosemary, black pepper, and salt in a medium bowl. Drizzle the oil over the herbed bread cubes and toss to coat.

Arrange the bread cubes in a single layer on a rimmed baking sheet.

Bake until the croutons are golden brown, stirring occasionally to ensure even browning, about 15 minutes. Let cool completely.

Cashew Cream

This recipe is quite versatile: Once I prepare it, I use it to thicken soups and sauces. If allowed to set overnight, it will thicken to a soft cheese-like consistency perfect for spreading on sandwiches and crackers. **Makes about 1¼ cups**

1½ cups raw cashews

⅓ cup water

2 teaspoons fresh lemon juice

2 cloves garlic

½ teaspoon sea salt

Place the cashews in a medium bowl. Add enough cold water to cover the nuts by 2 inches. Let soak for 2 hours. Drain.

Combine the cashews, water, lemon juice, garlic, and salt in a food processor or heavy-duty blender and blend, scraping down the sides of the bowl or container occasionally, for 5 minutes, or until very smooth. To store, transfer to a small bowl, cover, and let stand at room temperature for up to 24 hours to allow the cashew cream to thicken. Refrigerate for up to 5 days.

split pea soup with root vegetables

I've added lots of hearty root vegetables like carrots, parsnips, and sweet potatoes to this traditional soup. I like to use butternut or acorn squash, but some of the other winter squashes like kabocha or hubbard will work, too. There is no need to blend this soup; the split peas cook until they fall apart and dissolve, resulting in an appealingly creamy texture. **Serves 8 to 10 (makes about 12 cups)**

8 cups water

2 cups green split peas, picked through and rinsed

2 bay leaves

3 cloves garlic, minced

1 large onion, finely chopped

2 celery stalks, finely chopped

1 large carrot, peeled and finely chopped

1 large parsnip, peeled and finely chopped

1 large sweet potato, peeled and finely chopped

1 cup diced peeled winter squash

2 teaspoons fine sea salt, plus more to taste

1 teaspoon paprika

2 tablespoons thinly sliced fresh thyme

Combine the water, split peas, and bay leaves in a heavy pot. Bring to a simmer over high heat, skimming off the foam that rises to the top. Decrease the heat to medium-low. Cover and simmer, stirring occasionally, for 45 minutes, or until the split peas are just tender and falling apart.

Add the garlic, onion, celery, carrot, parsnip, sweet potato, squash, the 2 teaspoons salt, and the paprika. Return the soup to a simmer over high heat. Decrease the heat to medium-low and simmer uncovered, stirring occasionally, for 40 minutes, or until the vegetables are tender and the soup is thick. Remove the bay leaves and add the fresh thyme. Season the soup to taste with more salt, if desired.

Ladle the soup into bowls and serve.

The soup will keep for 2 days, covered and refrigerated, or for 1 month frozen. To rewarm, bring the soup to a simmer over medium heat, stirring occasionally and adding water to thin the soup to the desired consistency.

cutting techniques

MINCING is chopping ingredients into very fine pieces. Garlic and fresh herbs are most often minced before they're used. To mince a clove of garlic, first cut off the root end and remove the papery peel. Next, use the flat side of a chef's knife to crush the garlic clove on a cutting board, releasing the garlic's aroma and making it easier to mince. Finally, slice it vertically and then crosswise, producing a fine mince.

fennel and Roasted garlic soup with walnut-Basil pesto

Take one look at this luxuriously creamy soup, and you might wonder how it could possibly be dairy-free. Yogurt is often added to this type of soup to lend a creamy texture, but my plant-based recipe relies on the deliciously versatile Cashew Cream (page 83) instead. Topping the soup with a swirl of pesto adds vibrant, fresh flavors to this otherwise mellow recipe—and it looks pretty, too. I recommend making my Walnut-Basil Pesto on page 88 to use here, but prepared pesto from the market makes for a convenient shortcut; feel free to use the one you like the best. **Serves 6 to 8 (makes about 8 cups)**

2 heads of garlic, unpeeled

1 teaspoon plus 2 tablespoons olive oil

2 large leeks (white and pale green parts only), chopped

½ teaspoon fine sea salt, plus more to taste

2 large fennel bulbs, trimmed and coarsely chopped

4 celery stalks, coarsely chopped

7 cups water

1 medium Yukon Gold potato, peeled and coarsely chopped

2 bay leaves

½ cup Cashew Cream (page 83)

3 tablespoons white miso paste

1 tablespoon minced fresh thyme

½ cup Walnut-Basil Pesto (recipe follows)

Preheat the oven to 375°F. Cut ¼ inch off the tops of the garlic heads. Drizzle 1 teaspoon of the olive oil over the garlic heads and wrap the heads together in foil. Roast until the garlic is tender, about 50 minutes. Let cool. Press the garlic to release the cloves from the skin. Transfer the garlic cloves to a small bowl and set aside.

Heat the remaining 2 tablespoons olive oil in a heavy pot over medium-high heat. Add the leeks and the ½ teaspoon salt and sauté until the leeks are translucent, about 2 minutes. Add the fennel and celery and cook, stirring often, until the vegetables begin to soften, about 4 minutes.

Stir in the roasted garlic, water, potato, and bay leaves. Simmer until the potato is very tender, about 20 minutes. Whisk in the cashew cream and miso paste. Remove the bay leaves.

Working in batches, purée the soup in a blender until it is smooth. Wipe the pot clean and return the soup to the pot. Add the thyme and bring the soup to a simmer. Season to taste with salt.

Ladle the soup into bowls. Swirl a large dollop of the pesto into each bowl of soup and serve.

The soup will keep for 2 days, covered and refrigerated, or for 1 month frozen. To rewarm, bring the soup to a simmer over medium heat, stirring occasionally and adding water to thin the soup to the desired consistency.

walnut-basil pesto

Makes 1 cup

2 cups firmly packed fresh basil leaves

½ cup walnuts, toasted

¼ cup extra-virgin olive oil

8 garlic cloves

3 tablespoons yellow or white miso

1 teaspoon freshly ground black pepper

Blend all the ingredients in a food processor until smooth and creamy.

The pesto will keep for 2 days, covered and refrigerated.

While there is nothing that beats a good counter-top blender for turning chunky soups into silky purées (in recipes like Creamy Herbed Zucchini Soup [page 78] and Fennel and Roasted Garlic Soup with Walnut-Basil Pesto [page 87], among others), a handheld immersion blender is a great tool to have in your kitchen, too. I don't know what took me so long: After decades of cooking, I finally bought one just a few years ago. They are inexpensive; I paid all of about twenty bucks for mine. I love it and wonder how I managed in the kitchen before.

Handheld immersion blenders do a nice job of puréeing soup with the bonus of doing so right in the cooking pot, leaving less to clean up.

handheld immersion blenders

Although they won't blend soup to quite as silky smooth a texture as countertop blenders, the end result will still be nice and creamy. Hand-held blenders are great for blending gravies and sauces, too—anything hot in a pot.

curried red lentil soup

Red lentils are high in protein and rich in iron. Allow them to cook all the way through; they will fall apart and melt into a thick, hearty consistency. Curry and ginger give the sweet vegetables just the right amount of heat, and a sprightly splash of fresh lemon juice at serving time makes for the perfect bowl of soup. Like many soups, this one is even more delicious the day after it's made, when the spices have had more time to mingle. If the soup seems too thick the following day, add a little water to achieve the original consistency. **Serves 8 to 10 (makes about 10 cups)**

8 cups water

2 cups red lentils, picked through and rinsed

1 large onion, finely chopped

4 celery stalks, finely chopped

2 large carrots, peeled and finely chopped

3 cloves garlic, minced

1 tablespoon minced peeled fresh ginger

1 tablespoon olive oil

2 teaspoons fine sea salt

¼ cup chopped fresh cilantro

1 tablespoon curry powder

1 teaspoon ground cumin

1 lemon, halved

Combine the water and lentils in a heavy pot. Bring to a simmer over high heat, skimming off the foam that rises to the top. Decrease the heat to medium-low. Cover and simmer, stirring occasionally, until the lentils begin to soften, about 5 minutes.

Add the onion, celery, carrots, garlic, ginger, olive oil, and the 2 teaspoons salt and cook, stirring occasionally, until most of the lentils are falling apart, about 20 minutes. Stir in the cilantro, curry powder, and cumin. Cover and cook, stirring occasionally, until the vegetables are very tender and the soup thickens slightly, about 20 minutes.

Ladle the soup into bowls. Squeeze a few generous drops of lemon juice into each bowl of soup and serve.

The soup will keep for 2 days, covered and refrigerated, or for 1 month frozen. To rewarm, bring the soup to a simmer over medium heat, stirring occasionally and adding water to thin the soup to the desired consistency.

adzuki bean soup

This soup brings together the nourishing earthiness of adzuki beans with the warming spiciness of ginger. Adzuki beans are small and pearly red in color; they're loaded with protein and fiber. Kombu is a sea vegetable popular in Japanese cooking and in macrobiotics; when cooked with beans, it renders the beans more digestible. If you don't want to take the time to cook dried adzuki beans, use canned ones instead. **Serves 8 to 10 (makes about 10 cups)**

7 cups water

2 cups dried adzuki beans, rinsed

1 (6 by 1½-inch) piece dried kombu

2 teaspoons fine sea salt

2 large onions, finely chopped

3 large carrots, peeled and finely diced

4 celery stalks, finely diced

2 medium turnips (about 8 ounces), peeled and finely diced

2 tablespoons tamari

1 (2-inch) piece fresh ginger, peeled and finely chopped

2 teaspoons minced garlic

1 teaspoon dried thyme

1 teaspoon freshly ground black pepper

Combine the water, adzuki beans, and kombu in a heavy pot and bring to a boil over high heat. Decrease the heat to medium-low, then cover and simmer until the beans are semisoft, about 25 minutes. As the beans boil, skim off any foam that rises to the top. Uncover the beans and stir in the salt. Cook uncovered for 5 minutes (simmering the beans uncovered releases the gases). Since they will finish cooking with the vegetables, be sure they are not too tender at this point.

Increase the heat to medium-high. Add the onions to the beans and bring to a simmer. Decrease the heat again to medium-low. Cover and simmer, stirring occasionally, until the onions are translucent, about 15 minutes. Stir in the carrots, celery, turnips, tamari, ginger, garlic, thyme, and black pepper. Cover and cook until the soup thickens slightly but is still loose and pourable and the beans are tender, about 25 minutes.

Ladle the soup into bowls and serve.

The soup will keep for 2 days, covered and refrigerated, or for 1 month frozen. To rewarm, bring the soup to a simmer over medium heat, stirring occasionally and adding water to thin the soup to the desired consistency.

to prepare stock or not to prepare stock

If your challenges are anything like mine (and I bet they are), managing to cook for yourself and your family is rewarding, but not always convenient. Given all the time constraints in our modern lives, the thought of adding the preparation and storage of homemade stock to your to-do list might seem a little much. I used to always make stock for my soups: I had a chef's bias and said it wasn't a good soup unless it was made with homemade stock. But once better-quality stocks came on the marketplace—ones that were lower in sodium and some with no salt added at all—I started to replace my homemade stock with these. After a while, I noticed many of them did the opposite of enhancing my soups, and instead interfered with the soups' flavors. Some of these stocks even added an off-putting too-orange color.

That's when I stopped relying on stocks and instead began using plain water—that's right, the free stuff from the tap. I found that since my soups were filled with so many vegetables, grains, herbs, and spices, they were still delicious and satisfying without stock. And because my soups were rich in texture and loaded with flavor, no one ever noticed I wasn't using a stock—not even me.

With the exception of two soups (Rich Dark Onion Soup and Ginger Miso Soup), I've made the soups in this chapter with water instead of stock. If you prefer to make a stock from scratch or to use a store-bought one, feel free to do so. For me, omitting stock means one less step I have to worry about.

Tomato-Lemon Rice Soup

This is a great way to get your grains for the day. I like the fragrance and flavor of basmati rice, but you can also try using any variety of brown rice or a wild rice, which will bring even more earthiness to the soup. In the summertime, I use juicy fresh tomatoes instead of canned. When shopping for canned tomatoes, choose a product without added salt. If you use canned tomatoes with salt, be sure to decrease the amount of salt in this recipe by half. **Serves 6 to 8 (makes about 8 cups)**

2 tablespoons olive oil

2 medium onions, chopped

2 cloves garlic, minced

1 (14.5-ounce) can low-sodium diced tomatoes, with juices

3 celery stalks, diced

¼ cup minced fresh flat-leaf parsley

2 tablespoons chopped fresh oregano

1 tablespoon fine sea salt, plus more to taste

1 teaspoon freshly ground black pepper, plus more to taste

⅓ cup tomato paste

8 cups water

2 cups cooked Plain Basmati Rice (page 182)

2 cups loosely packed fresh spinach

¼ cup fresh lemon juice

Heat the oil in a heavy pot over medium heat. Add the onions and garlic and sauté until the onions are translucent, about 5 minutes. Add the tomatoes with their juices, celery, parsley, oregano, the 1 tablespoon salt, and the 1 teaspoon pepper. Cook, stirring often, until the celery softens, about 10 minutes.

Stir in the tomato paste, then the water. Bring the soup to a boil, then decrease the heat to medium-low and simmer until the flavors blend, about 30 minutes.

Stir in the cooked rice, the spinach, and lemon juice, and simmer until the spinach wilts, about 5 minutes. Season the soup to taste with salt and pepper.

Ladle the soup into bowls and serve immediately.

The soup will keep for 2 days, covered and refrigerated, or for 1 month frozen. To rewarm, bring the soup to a simmer over medium heat, stirring occasionally and adding water to thin the soup to the desired consistency.

yucatán yam picante

I like making this soup with garnet yams; besides their bright orange color, yams are sweeter and less mealy than sweet potatoes. (You can use sweet potatoes, though the soup will be lighter in color.) The creamy sweetness of the coconut milk counters the intense spices. Crushed red pepper lends this soup a nice amount of heat: You'll taste it and feel it—it has to live up to its name, after all—but it's not overpowering. This soup is the perfect beginning to a festive gathering: Serve it in small cups or shooters.
Serves 10 to 12 (makes about 12 cups)

2 tablespoons olive oil

1 large onion, coarsely chopped

3 cloves garlic, chopped

2 teaspoons ground coriander

1 teaspoon ground cumin

1 teaspoon crushed red pepper

3 celery stalks, chopped

2 red bell peppers, coarsely chopped

2 teaspoons fine sea salt

2 pounds garnet yams or red-skinned sweet potatoes, peeled

8 cups water

1 (13.5-ounce) can unsweetened light coconut milk

2 teaspoons dried basil

¼ cup chopped fresh cilantro

Heat the oil in a large, heavy pot over medium heat. Add the onion and sauté until translucent, about 7 minutes. Add the garlic, coriander, cumin, and crushed red pepper and sauté until fragrant, about 2 minutes. Add the celery, bell peppers, and the 2 teaspoons salt and sauté until the vegetables begin to soften, about 12 minutes. Cut three-fourths of the yams into about 1-inch chunks and add them to the soup.

Stir in the water, coconut milk, and basil. Bring to a boil over high heat, then decrease the heat to medium and simmer until the yams are very soft, about 30 minutes.

Working in batches, purée the soup in a blender until it is smooth. Return the soup to the pot and bring to a simmer.

Meanwhile, cut the remaining one-fourth of the yams into ½-inch cubes and add them to the puréed soup. Simmer until the yams are tender, about 15 minutes. Stir in the cilantro.

Ladle the soup into bowls and serve.

The soup will keep for 2 days, covered and refrigerated, or for 1 month frozen. To rewarm, bring the soup to a simmer over medium heat, stirring occasionally and adding water to thin the soup to the desired consistency.

california-style gazpacho

I loved V8 juice as a kid: I found the tartness of the vegetables and the burst of citrus to be delicious. Of course, once I grew up and learned more about healthy living, I snubbed my nose at such a beverage, judging it to be way too salty for my new palate. But I still think V8 has its heart in the right place—and now it comes in a low-sodium version. I am thrilled to have found a way to use V8 in my repertoire: It makes a terrific base for the chunky vegetables in this fresh, summery soup. **Serves 6 to 8 (makes about 9 cups)**

2 pounds ripe tomatoes (about 6)

2 cucumbers, peeled, seeded, and coarsely chopped

1 red onion, coarsely chopped

1 large red bell pepper, coarsely chopped

½ cup fresh corn kernels

3 tablespoons minced garlic

2 teaspoons fine sea salt, plus more to taste

¾ teaspoon freshly ground black pepper, plus more to taste

3 cups low-sodium tomato-vegetable juice (such as low-sodium V8 or R.W. Knudsen Family Very Veggie juice), plus more to taste

3 tablespoons extra-virgin olive oil

3 tablespoons fresh lemon juice

3 tablespoons red wine vinegar

¼ cup finely chopped fresh basil

¼ cup finely chopped fresh cilantro

¼ cup finely chopped fresh parsley

1 large ripe avocado, peeled, pitted, and diced

¼ cup pine nuts, toasted

Bring a large saucepan of water to a boil. Cut an "X" in the bottom of each tomato. Cook the tomatoes in the boiling water just until the skin around the "X" begins to pull away, about 1 minute. Using a slotted spoon, remove the tomatoes from the boiling water and submerge them in a large bowl of ice water to stop them from cooking. Remove from the ice bath and using a small paring knife, peel away the skins. Cut the tomatoes in half crosswise, scoop out the seeds, and coarsely chop the tomatoes.

Combine the tomatoes with the cucumbers, onion, bell pepper, corn, garlic, the 2 teaspoons salt, and the ¾ teaspoon black pepper in a large bowl. Stir in 3 cups of the tomato-vegetable juice, oil, lemon juice, and vinegar. Working in batches, pulse the mixture in a food processor until the mixture is soupy but the vegetables are still chunky.

Pour the gazpacho into a glass or stainless steel container or bowl. Stir in the basil, cilantro, and parsley. Add more tomato-vegetable juice, salt, and pepper to season the soup to taste.

Cover and refrigerate for 2 hours to allow all the flavors to blend and the soup to become very cold.

Ladle the soup into bowls and garnish with the avocado and toasted pine nuts. Serve well chilled.

This soup is best eaten the day it is made.

ginger miso soup

Miso soup is one of the first dishes I learned to cook, and I still love it. A staple in the macrobiotic diet, miso soup is often eaten for its healing properties, and you can enhance even more by adding dried shiitake mushrooms, which are also known for their health benefits. I make a quick kombu dashi (recipe follows), which is a Japanese kelp stock, and I like to add some of the kombu pieces back to the soup for extra texture. Even though the dashi is prepared with fresh ginger, the addition of extra fresh ginger juice to the soup adds a bit of welcome heat. **Serves 4 to 6 (makes about 5 cups)**

1 cup hot water

3 dried shiitake mushrooms

4 cups Kombu Dashi (including half of the reserved kombu, sliced into thin strips; recipe follows)

1 (3-inch) piece daikon radish, peeled, quartered lengthwise, then cut crosswise into ¼-inch-thick slices

1 large carrot, peeled and cut into matchstick-size strips

½ small onion, thinly sliced

3 ounces firm tofu, drained and cut into ½-inch cubes

1 (2-inch) piece fresh ginger, peeled

⅓ cup mellow barley miso

2 scallions, thinly sliced diagonally

Combine the 1 cup hot water and the mushrooms in a medium bowl and let stand until the mushrooms soften, about 30 minutes.

Using a slotted spoon, transfer the mushrooms to a work surface. Make sure any grit from the mushrooms has been rinsed away in the soaking. If some grit still remains, run the mushrooms under cold water and rub off any grit from under the rim of the caps. Cut the mushrooms into thin matchstick-size slices. Strain the mushroom-soaking liquid into a large, heavy saucepan, leaving any sediment behind.

Add the mushrooms, kombu dashi, the reserved kombu strips, the daikon radish, carrot, and onion to the mushroom-soaking liquid. Bring to a simmer over high heat, then decrease the heat to medium-low. Cover and simmer, stirring occasionally, until the vegetables are very tender, about 20 minutes. Remove the pan from the heat and stir the tofu into the soup.

Grate the ginger using a Microplane or ginger grater over a bowl lined with cheesecloth or a paper towel. Gather the edges of the cloth and squeeze the ginger pulp over the pan to extract the ginger juice into the soup. Discard the pulp.

Just before serving, rest a fine-meshed strainer atop the pan of hot soup, submerging the bottom of the strainer in the soup. Place the miso in the strainer, and stir to dissolve it in the soup. Remove the strainer and stir the soup to fully blend in the miso.

Ladle the soup into bowls. Sprinkle with the scallions and serve.

The soup will keep for 1 day, covered and refrigerated. To rewarm, bring the soup to a simmer over medium heat, stirring occasionally and adding water to thin the soup to the desired consistency.

Cooking Tip: Never allow miso soup to come to a boil once the miso has been added, as this will deplete the nutritional benefits of the miso.

kombu dashi

This Japanese seaweed stock should be clean-tasting and not too salty; you will taste the tamari, the mirin, and, of course, the ginger. Typically, the kombu is discarded after the stock is prepared, but I like to cut half of the kombu into thin strips and add it to the miso soup I prepare with this stock.

Makes about 7 cups

2 (4 by 1-inch) pieces dried kombu

8 cups water

¼ cup reduced-sodium tamari

1 (4-inch) piece fresh ginger, peeled and sliced crosswise into coins

¼ cup mirin, sake, or dry sherry

Combine the kombu and the water in a large saucepan and set aside until the kombu becomes soft and pliable, about 1 hour.

Set the saucepan over medium-high heat and bring the water just to a simmer, about 12 minutes. Decrease the heat to medium-low. Add the tamari and ginger and simmer gently to allow the flavors to blend, about 10 minutes. Add the mirin. Strain the stock into another saucepan or container. Remove the kombu and discard half. Cut the remaining half in ⅛-inch strips and add to the Ginger Miso Soup. It's best to use the stock immediately.

black-eyed pea and red pepper soup

Popular in Southern cooking, black-eyed peas are small, tan beans that take their name from the black-eye-shaped mark on the inner curve of the bean. I have always loved eating them, though when I was growing up in Tennessee, I enjoyed them smothered with ketchup. Today, I prefer my black-eyed peas plain, as they have a unique flavor that I don't want to cover up. Their earthiness combines well with tomatoes and greens; add to that a dash of heat from cayenne, and this recipe makes a thick and hearty bowl of soup. **Serves 6 to 8 (makes about 8 cups)**

1 cup dried black-eyed peas

2 small bay leaves

2 cloves garlic, minced

About 6 cups water

1 teaspoon fine sea salt, plus more to taste

2 teaspoons olive oil

1 large onion, chopped

2 celery stalks, chopped

1 large red bell pepper, chopped

1 (15-ounce) can whole tomatoes, with juices

3 ounces collard greens, stemmed and cut into ½-inch squares (about 1 cup)

½ cup fresh or frozen corn kernels

2 teaspoons dried thyme

½ teaspoon freshly ground black pepper, plus more to taste

⅛ teaspoon cayenne pepper

2 tablespoons chopped fresh cilantro

Combine the black-eyed peas, bay leaves, and garlic in a heavy saucepan. Add enough water to cover the beans by about 2 inches (about 3 cups), then bring the water to a boil over high heat. Decrease the heat to medium-low and simmer uncovered for 25 minutes until the peas are par-cooked; they should be soft but still hold their shape. Add the 1 teaspoon salt and cook 5 minutes longer.

Heat the oil in a heavy pot over medium heat. Add the onion and sauté until translucent, about 7 minutes. Add the celery and bell pepper, then cover and cook until the pepper begins to soften, about 4 minutes. Break up the tomatoes by squeezing them in your hands over the pot, then add the tomatoes and their juices to the pot. Stir in the collard greens and corn. Cook for 2 minutes. Add the thyme, the ½ teaspoon black pepper, and the cayenne pepper and cook for 3 minutes, stirring frequently.

Add the black-eyed peas and their cooking liquid and 3 cups of water to the pot. Increase the heat to high and bring the soup to a simmer. Decrease the heat to medium-low and gently simmer until the peas and greens are tender, about 30 minutes. Remove the bay leaves.

Add more water, if needed, to thin the soup to the desired consistency. Stir in the cilantro, and season to taste with more salt and black pepper.

Ladle the soup into bowls and serve.

The soup will keep for 2 days, covered and refrigerated, or for 1 month frozen. To rewarm, bring the soup to a simmer over medium heat, stirring occasionally and adding water to thin the soup to the desired consistency.

Herbs
and spices

Herbs infuse dishes with flavor, adding a vibrant layer of taste, aroma, and color. Spices also bring unique aromas and flavors to a variety of dishes, both savory and sweet. Herbs and spices not only make food taste better, but promote health and aid digestion, too. They have been used medicinally for ages, and many appear on my list of superfoods.

I use herbs and spices anywhere I can. While both are commonly used dried, you'll find many recipes calling for fresh herbs. The rule of thumb is to use three parts fresh herbs to one part dried, so feel free to use dried herbs if fresh are not available.

My favorite herbs are basil, cilantro, dill, parsley, sage, and tarragon, and you'll find them sprinkled throughout my savory recipes. Among the spices in my pantry—cinnamon, nutmeg, cardamom, ginger, cloves— cinnamon is the one I reach for most. Its warm scent and flavor remind me of making sugar-and-cinnamon buttered toast as a teenager—not just for breakfast, but as a comforting snack, too.

When you're lucky enough to have fresh herbs on hand, make sure they last as long as possible by keeping them moist. Place the herbs in a glass of water, as you would cut flowers, and then refrigerate until you're ready to use them. Or wrap the stems in a damp paper towel before putting the herbs into a storage bag and refrigerating. Either way, handle fresh herbs gently.

Dried herbs and spices are best stored in glass jars with secure-fitting lids, away from moisture and extreme temperatures, and out of direct sunlight. Stored properly, dried herbs and spices can last for up to 6 months—some cooks say a whole year. You'll know by smelling them: If they still have a nice aroma and look bright and vibrant, they're going to give you the potency you expect.

borscht with tofu sour cream

There are two types of borscht: In one, the vegetables are kept chunky; in the other, they're puréed. I prefer the latter. The luscious purplish-red color of beets, a sign that they're naturally rich in nutrients, assures me I am getting the antioxidants, vitamins, and minerals that they offer. I love to use the beet greens, too: They can be boiled or sautéed, and they're highly nutritious. To play up the naturally sweet flavor of the beets, I use agave nectar in this soup; it adds just the right amount of mild sweetness to help counter the vinegar. This soup can be eaten hot or cold; if you plan to serve it cold, be sure to refrigerate it overnight to allow it to chill thoroughly. **Serves 6 to 8 (makes about 8 cups)**

2 teaspoons olive oil

1 large onion, chopped

1 pound red beets with green leaves attached (about 3 medium beets), beets peeled and cut into 1-inch pieces, center vein removed from leaves and leaves coarsely chopped

1 small russet potato (about 7 ounces), peeled and chopped

1 large carrot, peeled and chopped

2 celery stalks, chopped

2 cloves garlic, chopped

1 bay leaf

1½ teaspoons fine sea salt, plus more to taste

3 cups water

¼ head cabbage, chopped

½ (14.5-ounce) can chopped tomatoes, with juices

1½ tablespoons fresh lemon juice

1 tablespoon chopped fresh dill

1½ teaspoons agave nectar

1½ teaspoons red wine vinegar

¾ cup Tofu Sour Cream (recipe follows)

Dill sprigs, for garnish

Heat the oil in a heavy pot over medium-high heat. Add the onion and sauté until translucent, about 5 minutes. Add the beet pieces, chopped beet leaves, potato, carrot, celery, garlic, and bay leaf. Season with the 1½ teaspoons salt and sauté until the beets exude their juices, about 8 minutes.

Add the water and bring to a boil over high heat. Decrease the heat to medium-low and simmer until the vegetables are tender, about 30 minutes. Add the cabbage and the tomatoes with their juices and cook, stirring occasionally, over medium-high heat until the cabbage is tender, about 10 minutes. Remove the bay leaf.

Working in batches, purée the soup in a blender until it is smooth. Return the soup to the pot. Stir in the lemon juice, dill, agave nectar, and vinegar. Season the soup to taste with more salt.

Ladle the soup into bowls. Top each with a dollop of the tofu sour cream and a dill sprig, and serve warm. Alternatively, this soup can be chilled and served cold.

The soup will keep for 2 days, covered and refrigerated, or for 1 month frozen. To rewarm, bring the soup to a simmer over medium heat, stirring occasionally and adding water to thin the soup to the desired consistency.

Tofu Sour Cream

This is my go-to sour cream: It's quick to put together, and I've been using it ever since I started cooking. The umeboshi vinegar gives it a real kick. I often alternate my herbs, sometimes replacing the dill with basil or a combination of basil and oregano. **Makes about 1½ cups**

1 (12.3-ounce) container vacuum-packed firm silken tofu (such as Mori-Nu)

2 tablespoons umeboshi vinegar

1 tablespoon olive oil

1 teaspoon dry mustard

¼ teaspoon minced garlic

1 teaspoon dried dill

Blend the tofu, vinegar, oil, dry mustard, and garlic in a food processor until smooth. Transfer the tofu sour cream to a container. Stir in the dill. Cover and refrigerate for at least 2 hours or up to 2 days.

why use sea salt?

I recommend using fine sea salt in your cooking and baking, and fine or coarse sea salt (or even its fancier cousin, *fleur de sel*) for finishing dishes. Less processed than the more pedestrian table salt, sea salt is harvested through the evaporation of seawater, leaving any trace minerals intact. Table salt is mined from underground salt deposits, but it's then processed to remove minerals; iodine, a mineral we need in our diets, is then added back. It also has additives to prevent caking.

Besides the fact that I believe less processed foods are more healthful, sea salt is also superior to table salt from a purely culinary perspective: It just tastes better. Whereas table salt has a sharp, harsh bite to it, sea salt is more delicately flavored, perhaps because it's less dense. And when finishing dishes with coarser sea salts, I've found I need less to make an impact, as the larger flakes or crystals are more satisfying. My favorite salt is Celtic Sea Salt, a brand that offers a wide variety of unprocessed salts and salt mixes that are wonderful to cook with.

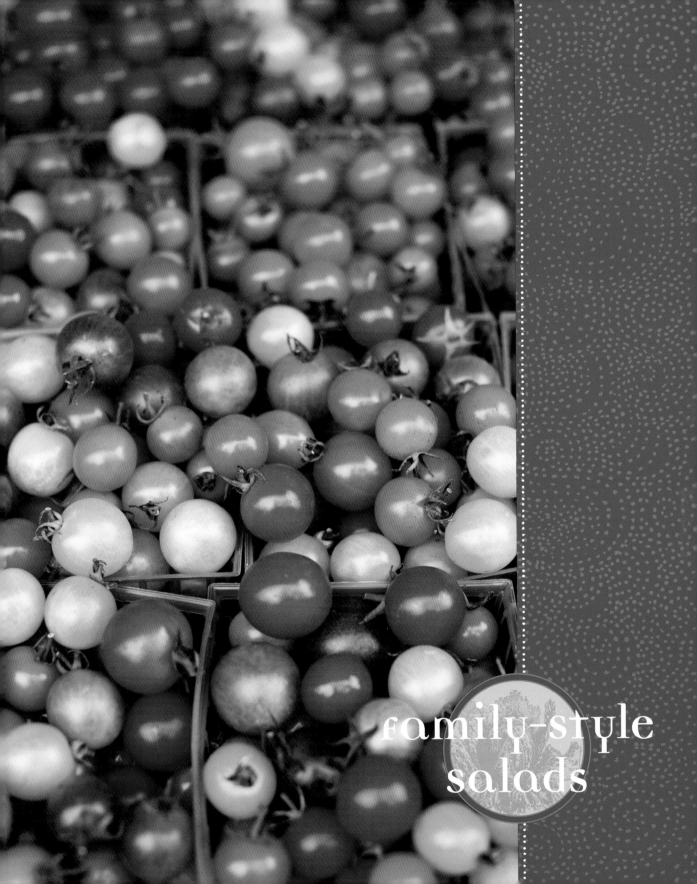

family-style
salads

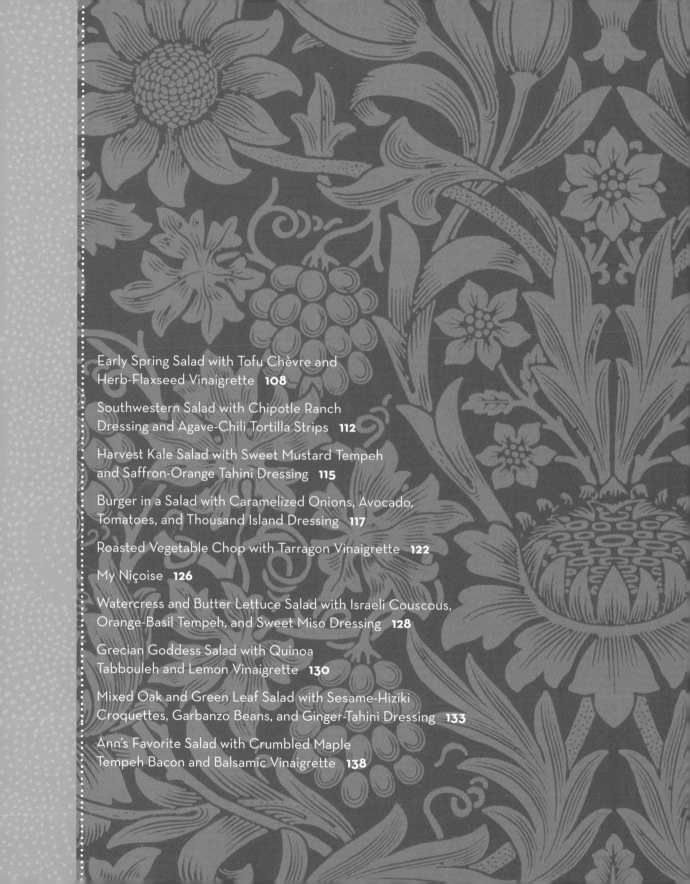

family-style salads

With the right ingredients, you can make a satisfying full meal out of a salad. I love the fact that salads as a whole meal can challenge the meat-and-three model of an animal protein, two starches, and a vegetable. Even vegans and vegetarians often feel that their main course needs to be a relatively large portion of plant protein, but with main-course salads, those plant proteins are moved from being the focus of the plate into a supporting role.

The best salads have a variety of colors, textures, and flavors. When I'm serving salad as a main course, I make sure to add plant proteins like tofu, tempeh, or beans; a colorful collection of vegetables like beets, carrots, and bell peppers; and healthy fats like olive oil, avocados, and nuts. It's everything you and your family need, in one cool, fresh dish.

While a main-course salad can truly stand alone as a great meal, for bigger appetites, it can also be paired with a soup (you'll see some specific suggestions throughout this chapter). And if you'd rather serve a salad as a starter or as an accompaniment, you can easily remove some of the heartier ingredients and adjust the serving size to suit your needs.

Main-course salads are budget-friendly and time-friendly, as they're a great way to use up leftovers. In my salad recipes, I often suggest substitutions, making it easier for you to use the items you might already have on hand: leftover cooked vegetables like potatoes and broccoli can be diced or sliced and added—and don't forget that you can incorporate leftover cooked grains like brown rice and quinoa, too. The ease of successfully substituting goes for lettuces as well: I love exploring new and exotic salad greens, but feel free to use the mixed greens that you can find at your local store or farmers' market.

Each main-course salad in this chapter serves four, and each is made for casual family-style serving; however, the recipes halve easily if you're preparing a meal for one or two. From the Roasted Vegetable Chop with Tarragon Vinaigrette (page 122) to the Southwestern Salad with Chipotle Ranch Dressing and Agave-Chili Tortilla Strips (page 112), you'll find some new favorites here that will inspire you to add main-course salads to your regular repertoire.

Early Spring Salad with Tofu Chèvre and Herb-Flaxseed Vinaigrette

This salad pairs well with the Creamy Herbed Zucchini Soup (page 78), as both recipes highlight the simple pleasures of spring produce. For the homemade Tofu Chèvre (recipe follows), choose the variation of that recipe that best suits your family's tastes. Look for a spring mix with fresh herbs, which add interesting colors, flavors, and textures to the salad. I've made the flaxseed oil optional because I realize that not everyone keeps it on hand, but I do highly recommend that you venture out to find this unique oil: Flaxseed oil is a great source for omega fatty acids in a vegan diet, and working flaxseed oil into your salads is a great way to incorporate this superfood into your day. Flaxseed oil is very delicate and must be refrigerated to keep it from going rancid; look for it in the refrigerated section of your local natural foods store. **Serves 4**

4 medium beets (about 1 pound total), trimmed

VINAIGRETTE
¼ cup brown rice vinegar

2 tablespoons apple cider vinegar

2 tablespoons chopped fresh flat-leaf parsley

1 tablespoon chopped fresh basil

2 teaspoons chopped fresh dill

2 teaspoons agave nectar

½ teaspoon fine sea salt, plus more to taste

½ teaspoon freshly ground black pepper, plus more to taste

½ cup extra-virgin olive oil

3 tablespoons flaxseed oil (optional)

Fine sea salt and freshly ground black pepper

SALAD
1 medium carrot, peeled

10 lightly packed cups mixed baby lettuces (about 6 ounces)

1 cucumber, peeled, seeded, and cut into half-moons (about 1½ cups)

6 radishes, thinly sliced (about 1 cup)

3 celery stalks, diced

Fine sea salt and freshly ground black pepper

½ log plain Tofu Chèvre (recipe follows)

Place the beets in a heavy saucepan and add enough cold water to generously cover them. Simmer until they are tender enough for a knife to easily glide through the center of one of the beets, about 30 minutes. Drain the beets in a colander and set them aside until you feel they are cool enough to handle. Slip off the beet skins and cut the beets into ½-inch-thick wedges.

Vinaigrette: While the beets are cooling, combine the brown rice vinegar, apple cider vinegar, parsley, basil, dill, agave nectar, the ½ teaspoon salt, and the ½ teaspoon pepper in a blender. With the blender on high speed, add the olive oil and flaxseed oil slowly in a steady stream, blending well. Season the dressing with salt and pepper.

Salad: Using a vegetable peeler and starting at the top end of the carrot, pull the peeler down the length of the carrot to shave off long ribbons. Toss the carrot ribbons, baby lettuces, cucumber, radishes, and celery in a large bowl with enough vinaigrette to coat. Season the salad to taste with more salt and pepper.

Assembly: Mound the salad on 4 plates. Toss the beets in a bowl with some of the remaining vinaigrette, then scatter the beets over the salad. Break the tofu chèvre into pieces, then place them on top of the salad and serve immediately.

TOFU CHÈVRE

I call this soft vegan cheese "chèvre" for its rich flavor, creamy texture, and log shape. It's easy to add texture and flavor to the basic tofu chèvre recipe simply by rolling the finished cheese log in a variety of ingredients, from ground peppercorns to fresh herbs to chopped nuts. The technique couldn't be simpler, or the results more sophisticated and satisfying. Be sure to plan ahead, as you'll need several hours for the tofu to completely drain and then another hour for the cheese log to chill.
Makes 1 (13-ounce) log

1 (12-ounce) container water-packed extra-firm tofu, drained and halved

1 large clove garlic

2 tablespoons yellow miso

3 teaspoons extra-virgin olive oil

¾ teaspoon fine sea salt

Pat the tofu dry with paper towels. Set the tofu in a colander and set the colander over a bowl to collect all the liquid that drains from the tofu. Cover the tofu with plastic wrap, then place 3 heavy cans, each at least 14 ounces, on the tofu to weigh it down. This weight will help extract all the excess liquid from the tofu. Refrigerate the tofu for at least 4 hours or overnight.

Mince the garlic in a food processor. Pat the tofu halves with paper towels to absorb any excess moisture, then add the tofu to the food processor. Add the miso, 2 teaspoons of the olive oil, and the salt, and blend until the mixture is very smooth, stopping the machine occasionally and scraping the bottom and sides of the bowl.

Lay a sheet of plastic wrap flat on the work surface. Scrape the tofu cheese onto the center of the plastic wrap, then wrap the cheese, forming a log. Refrigerate for 1 hour.

Preheat the oven to 375°F. Unwrap the cheese log and place it on a baking sheet. Brush the log lightly with the remaining 1 teaspoon oil. Bake just until the cheese is warmed through, but the center is still creamy, about 25 minutes.

Serve warm or cold.

Variations:

PEPPERCORN-CRUSTED: Coarsely grind whole black or multicolored peppercorns, then sprinkle them over the cheese, patting them gently to adhere.

HERB-CRUSTED: Chop fresh herbs, such as parsley, chives, dill, tarragon, basil, or thyme, then roll the cheese log over the herbs to coat.

NUT-CRUSTED: Finely chop toasted walnuts, then roll the cheese log over the nuts to coat completely. Other nuts, such as toasted pepitas, pine nuts, and Brazil nuts, work well too.

I've included a unique from-scratch salad dressing for each recipe in this chapter: Once you get started making your own salad dressings, you'll never see store-bought versions the same way. (I must confess, however, to always having one store-bought bottle in my fridge at any given time, to use in a pinch.) My grandmother always made her own salad dressings, but the base of her dressings was usually her homemade mayonnaise. Like her, I love to make my dressings from scratch, but I've lightened up from a mayonnaise base, relying more upon vinaigrettes and light oil-based dressings instead. (There are two exceptions: my Chipotle Ranch Dressing, page 112, and my rendition of Thousand Island Dressing, page 117, both of which make delicious use of vegan mayonnaise, a plant-based mayonnaise alternative.)

homemade salad dressings

Once you get the hang of making your own dressings, you'll love the opportunity it provides to get really creative with your salads, with fresher and more appealing results than dressings from a bottle can provide.

CUTTING TECHNIQUES

LONG STRIPS of ingredients are often called for in salads; this elegant cut shows off the beautiful color and texture of ingredients like bell peppers. (Long strips should not be mistaken with a julienne cut, which is a long cut as well, but more precise and smaller.) To create long strips with bell peppers, first cut each pepper into thirds or in half lengthwise, and remove the seeds, ribs, and stem. Place each bell pepper piece skin-side-down, and slice lengthwise into roughly ¼-inch-wide strips.

southwestern salad with chipotle Ranch Dressing and Agave-chili Tortilla strips

This salad is abundant in whole grains and plant protein, making it a meal in itself. The variety of fresh vegetables adds color and just the right amount of crunchy texture. When I have guacamole on hand, I use a dollop of it instead of the fresh avocado. The ranch-style dressing has a kick from the chipotle chiles, chives, and garlic, plus the tanginess of the lemon. Chipotle chiles not only add heat, they also lend a distinctive smoky flavor. While they're sold at many supermarkets these days, if they're not available in your area, simply substitute a chipotle-flavored hot sauce, starting with about ½ teaspoon and slowly adding more to achieve just the right amount of heat. **Serves 4 to 6**

DRESSING

¾ cup vegan mayonnaise

4 ounces vacuum-packed firm silken tofu (such as Mori-Nu)

¼ cup minced onion

¼ cup unsweetened soy milk

2 tablespoons fresh lemon juice

2 teaspoons Dijon mustard

2 teaspoons minced canned chipotle chiles in adobo sauce, plus 1 teaspoon adobo sauce

1 teaspoon minced garlic

1 teaspoon Worcestershire sauce

½ teaspoon celery seed

½ teaspoon fine sea salt, plus more to taste

¼ teaspoon freshly ground black pepper, plus more to taste

3 tablespoons finely chopped fresh chives

SALAD

1 head romaine lettuce, trimmed and cut into 1-inch pieces (about 10 cups)

2 cups cooked long-grain brown rice (see page 180), cooled

1 (15-ounce) can black beans, rinsed and drained well

½ small jicama, peeled and cut into ½-inch cubes (about ¾ cup)

Kernels from 1 ear of yellow corn (about ½ cup)

1 large red bell pepper, diced

1 cup cherry tomatoes, cut in half (quartered if large)

2 small firm but ripe avocados, peeled, pitted, and cubed

3 scallions, chopped

¼ cup grated cheddar-style vegan cheese (optional)

3 tablespoons minced fresh cilantro

Fine sea salt and freshly ground black pepper

¼ cup Agave-Chili Tortilla Strips (recipe follows; optional)

Dressing: Blend all the ingredients except the chives in a blender until smooth. Transfer the tofu mixture to a bowl. Whisk in the chives. Cover and refrigerate for at least 2 hours or up to 2 days to allow the flavors to blend. Season the dressing to taste with more salt and pepper.

Salad: Toss all the ingredients except the tortilla strips in a large bowl with enough of the dressing to coat. Season the salad to taste with salt and pepper. Mound the salad on 4 plates, dividing equally. Garnish with the tortilla strips and serve immediately.

AGave-CHILI TorTILLa STriPS

Makes 3 cups

1 tablespoon neutral cooking oil

2 teaspoons agave nectar

1½ teaspoons chili powder

½ teaspoon fine sea salt

6 (6-inch) corn tortillas

Preheat the oven to 350°F. Mix the oil, agave nectar, chili powder, and the ½ teaspoon salt in a bowl to blend. Brush the mixture over both sides of the tortillas and stack the tortillas as you coat them. Cut the tortillas in half, then cut the halves crosswise into ⅛-inch-thick strips.

Arrange the tortilla strips in an even layer on a heavy rimmed baking sheet. Bake, tossing occasionally, for 28 minutes, or until the tortilla strips are crisp. Set aside to cool. The strips will continue to crisp up as they cool.

The tortilla strips will keep for 2 days in an airtight container at room temperature.

Harvest Kale Salad with Sweet Mustard Tempeh and Saffron-Orange Tahini Dressing

Kale gets really sweet and delicious when it has been exposed to frost; therefore, winter kale such as lacinato (also known as "dinosaur kale") is ideal to use in a raw salad. Be sure to cut out the spine from the leafy part, as the spine can be too tough to chew. Beets and sweet potatoes are a fantastic combo that roast beautifully. However, this salad is a great opportunity for you to roast whatever vegetables you have on hand—regular potatoes, winter squash, or even carrots would also be lovely. The Sweet Mustard Tempeh has great flavor, in part from the marinade, which requires a bit of advance preparation. Incorporating a plant protein like tempeh makes this salad a satisfying and wholesome meal. **Serves 4**

ROASTED VEGETABLES

2 medium garnet yams (about 1 pound), peeled and cut into ½-inch cubes

4 medium red beets (about 14 ounces), peeled and cut into ½-inch cubes

1½ tablespoons olive oil

1 clove garlic, minced

¼ teaspoon fine sea salt

¼ teaspoon freshly ground black pepper

DRESSING

½ cup fresh orange juice

⅓ cup raw tahini

2 tablespoons brown rice vinegar

1 clove garlic, minced

½ teaspoon fine sea salt, plus more to taste

¼ teaspoon saffron strands (optional)

2 tablespoons extra-virgin olive oil

Freshly ground black pepper

ASSEMBLY

1 bunch lacinato kale (about 10 ounces), stems removed and leaves cut into ⅛-inch strips (about 4½ cups)

3 cups loosely packed baby spinach

1 cucumber, peeled, seeded, and cut into ½-inch pieces

1 red bell pepper, cut into ½-inch pieces

Sweet Mustard Tempeh (recipe follows), warm or at room temperature

Spicy-Sweet Roasted Almonds (page 55)

Roasted Vegetables: Preheat the oven to 400°F. Line a large, heavy baking sheet with parchment paper. Toss the yams and beets in a large bowl with the oil, garlic, salt, and pepper to coat. Transfer to the prepared baking sheet and roast, tossing after the first 20 minutes, until the yams are tender and browned, about 40 minutes. Let cool completely.

Dressing: Whisk the orange juice, tahini, vinegar, garlic, the ½ teaspoon salt, and the saffron in a medium bowl to blend. Gradually whisk in the oil to blend well. Season to taste with salt and pepper.

Assembly: Toss the kale, spinach, cucumber, and bell pepper in a large bowl with enough of the dressing to coat. Add the tempeh and the roasted yams and beets, and toss again, adding more dressing if necessary. Transfer the salad to a platter. Garnish with the almonds and serve.

SWEET MUSTARD TEMPEH
The tempeh needs at least an hour to marinate. This is a good do-ahead step, either the day before or make it your first order of business when you come into your kitchen to begin preparing the meal. **Serves 4**

3 tablespoons tamari	2 tablespoons water	1 (8-ounce) package grain-based tempeh, halved horizontally, then cut into ½-inch cubes
2 tablespoons Dijon mustard	1 tablespoon minced garlic	
2 tablespoons pure maple syrup	2 teaspoons neutral cooking oil	

Whisk the tamari, mustard, maple syrup, water, garlic, and oil in a 9- to 10-inch sauté pan to blend. Add the tempeh and turn to coat. Arrange the tempeh in the pan so it is in a single layer and submerged in the marinade. Set aside to marinate for at least 1 hour, or cover and refrigerate overnight.

Set the sauté pan over medium-low heat. Cover and cook until the tempeh is hot and the marinade has reduced, about 15 minutes. Serve the tempeh warm or at room temperature.

burger in a salad with caramelized onions, avocado, tomatoes, and thousand island dressing

This is a homemade black bean veggie burger served atop salad greens with the works: caramelized onions, roasted red peppers, avocado, tomatoes, and even tempeh bacon, if you like. It's an excellent way to enjoy a burger without the bun, and with some extra vegetables. Those watching their wheat intake will appreciate that this recipe is gluten-free. **Serves 4**

CARAMELIZED ONIONS

2 tablespoons olive oil

2 tablespoons vegan butter

3 pounds Spanish onions, sliced

1 teaspoon fine sea salt

1 tablespoon mirin

DRESSING

½ cup vegan mayonnaise

⅓ cup ketchup

3 tablespoons sweet relish or minced sweet pickles

2 tablespoons red wine vinegar

1 clove garlic, minced

1 teaspoon Dijon mustard

¾ teaspoon fine sea salt

½ teaspoon paprika

¼ teaspoon freshly ground black pepper

SALAD

1 large carrot, peeled

1 medium beet, peeled

6 to 8 cups mixed baby lettuces

Fine sea salt and freshly ground black pepper

ASSEMBLY

½ cup sliced store-bought roasted red peppers

4 Black Bean Veggie Burgers (recipe follows)

1 avocado, peeled, pitted, and diced

2 ripe tomatoes, cut into wedges (optional)

Maple Tempeh Bacon (page 25), coarsely crumbled (optional)

Caramelized Onions: Heat the oil and vegan butter in a large, heavy skillet over medium heat. Add the onions and salt. Cook, stirring often, until golden brown, about 1 hour. Add the mirin and cook until the onions are brown, about 15 minutes.

Dressing: Whisk all the ingredients in a medium bowl to blend.

Salad: Cut the carrot and the beet with a mandoline into long, thin curly shoestrings, or use a vegetable peeler to cut them into long shavings. Toss the carrot, beet, and mixed baby lettuces in a large bowl with enough dressing to coat lightly. Season the salad to taste with salt and pepper.

Assembly: Mound the salad in the center of each of 4 plates. Spoon some of the caramelized onions and all of the roasted peppers over the burger patties and arrange a smothered patty on each plate with the salad. Reserve any remaining caramelized onions for another use. Scatter the avocado, tomatoes, and tempeh bacon, if using, over the salad and serve.

Black Bean Veggie Burgers

While I use these homemade veggie burgers in my Burger in a Salad recipe, they're also delicious served in a hearty whole-grain bun with all your favorite burger fixings. My family members enjoy customizing their own burgers, so I set out an assortment of toppings and let everyone stack their own. Thinly sliced red onions, sliced tomatoes, mashed avocado, vegan cheese slices, stone-ground mustard, and vegan mayonnaise are must-haves at our house. Be sure to begin preparing this recipe ahead of time; the burgers need to chill for at least 2 hours before they're cooked. **Makes 12 patties**

3½ tablespoons neutral cooking oil, plus more as needed

1 cup finely diced onion

4 teaspoons minced garlic

2 cups finely diced peeled yams

⅔ cup finely diced peeled carrots

½ cup finely diced celery

2½ teaspoons fine sea salt

2 teaspoons finely diced jalapeño chile

2½ teaspoons ground cumin

1 teaspoon freshly ground black pepper

1 teaspoon paprika

⅔ cup fresh corn kernels, or frozen corn kernels, thawed

½ cup finely diced red bell pepper

½ cup corn flour (not cornmeal)

4 cups cooked short-grain brown rice (page 180)

2 cups rinsed and drained canned black beans

¼ cup minced fresh parsley

3 tablespoons powdered egg replacer

Line a baking sheet with parchment paper.

Heat 1½ tablespoons of the oil in a large, heavy sauté pan over medium heat. Add the onion and sauté until translucent, about 5 minutes. Add the garlic and sauté until fragrant, about 30 seconds. Add the yams, carrots, and celery. Sprinkle with 1 teaspoon of the salt and sauté until the vegetables are just tender, about 10 minutes. Add the jalapeño, the remaining 1½ teaspoons salt, the cumin, black pepper, and paprika and cook for 1 minute. Add the corn and bell pepper and sauté until they become slightly tender, about 2 minutes.

Transfer the mixture to a large bowl and stir in the corn flour. Add the rice, beans, and parsley. Using your hands, mix thoroughly.

Place half of the burger mixture in a food processor and pulse until it is finely chopped and slightly mushy. Return the pulsed burger mixture to the remaining burger mixture. Sprinkle the egg replacer over the burger mixture, and using your hands, mix to blend very well.

Form the burger mixture into twelve 3½-inch patties that are ½ to ¾ inch thick. Place the patties on the prepared baking sheet, then cover and refrigerate for at least 2 hours or overnight. Alternatively, you can store them in an airtight container and freeze; thaw before using.

Heat the remaining 2 tablespoons oil on a flat griddle pan over medium heat. Working in batches and adding more oil as needed for each batch, cook the patties until they are browned on both sides and cooked through, about 3 minutes per side.

Leafy Greens and Lettuce Greens

Leafy Greens, pound for pound, supply more vitamins than red meat. Varieties include collard, mustard, dandelion, or turnip greens; spinach; kale; chard; and cabbages. Leafy greens are distinguished from lettuce greens in that leafy greens tend to be sturdier and heartier, and they're often cooked rather than eaten raw, although there is some overlap between the two categories. Leafy greens are nutrient-dense, packed with iron, calcium, vitamin C, vitamin K, and folic acid; they are low in fat and calories, high in fiber, and rich in phytochemicals, meaning that many leafy greens are considered superfoods. You'll find a trio of greens—collards, kale, and green chard—in my Leafy Green Trio Hot Sauté (page 206). Collard greens and kale are especially versatile, as they are delicious eaten raw or cooked; I use raw collard greens in my Living Wrap (page 67) and raw kale in my Harvest Kale Salad (page 115).

Lettuce Greens are generally tender green leaves that are eaten raw. But in some cases, lettuce greens are interchangeable with leafy greens; spinach, watercress, and arugula are three examples. I love watercress raw in a salad but also love to steam it, as you will find in my One-Pot Vegetables (page 145). Among the lettuce greens that are only eaten raw is romaine. It has crisp, almost crunchy leaves, and it holds up well to any thick salad dressing, such as in my Southwestern Salad (page 112). Bibb and butter lettuces have soft, elegant leaves that perfectly suit My Niçoise (page 126). Mixed baby lettuces, sometimes called mesclun, are popular and widely available; keep a mix on hand, and you'll be able to throw together a quick salad at any time.

Roasted Vegetable Chop with Tarragon Vinaigrette

The roasted vegetables prepared for this salad would also make a great side dish on their own, served either warm or at room temperature. Feel free to decide which vegetables to roast, making this salad a delicious way to use what you have on hand or what is in season. I also call for sunflower seeds, which add a little bit of protein and crunch to the salad, but you could substitute nuts, if you like. This salad pairs well with soup—especially the Tomato-Lemon Rice Soup (page 93) and the California-Style Gazpacho (page 97). **Serves 4**

ROASTED VEGETABLES

2 tablespoons olive oil

½ teaspoon fine sea salt, plus more to taste

¼ teaspoon freshly ground black pepper, plus more to taste

1 small cauliflower, cut into florets

1 red bell pepper, cut into ½-inch-wide strips

1 medium carrot, peeled and cut into ½-inch-thick quarter-moons

1 bunch asparagus, ends trimmed

2 zucchini, cut into 1-inch-wide half-moons

½ teaspoon chopped fresh dill

VINAIGRETTE

1 large shallot, chopped (about ¼ cup)

¼ cup red wine vinegar

1 tablespoon Dijon mustard

1 teaspoon fine sea salt, plus more to taste

¼ teaspoon freshly ground black pepper, plus more to taste

¼ cup plus 2 tablespoons extra-virgin olive oil

2 tablespoons fresh tarragon leaves

ASSEMBLY

6 cups lightly packed mixed baby lettuces (about 3 ounces)

1 head oak leaf or red leaf butter lettuce, torn into large bite-size pieces

Fine sea salt and freshly ground black pepper

Sunflower seeds, for garnish

Roasted Vegetables: Preheat the oven to 475°F. Whisk the oil, the ½ teaspoon salt, and the ¼ teaspoon black pepper in a large bowl to blend. Add the cauliflower, bell pepper, and carrot and toss to coat. Arrange the vegetables evenly over a large, heavy rimmed baking sheet. Add the asparagus and zucchini to the bowl and toss to coat; set aside. Roast the vegetables that are on the baking sheet for 10 minutes. Stir the roasted vegetables, then add the asparagus and zucchini and nestle them among the roasted vegetables. Reserve the bowl to use again later. Continue to roast until the vegetables are tender, but not mushy, about 10 minutes.

Return the vegetables to the reserved bowl and toss them with the dill. Season the vegetables to taste with salt and pepper.

Vinaigrette: Blend the shallot, vinegar, mustard, the 1 teaspoon salt, and the ¼ teaspoon pepper in a blender until smooth. With the blender on high speed, add the oil slowly in a steady stream, blending well. Add the tarragon leaves and blend until they appear as green specks. Season the vinaigrette to taste with salt and pepper.

Assembly: Toss all of the lettuces in a large bowl with enough vinaigrette to coat. Season the lettuces to taste with salt and pepper. Mound the lettuces on a serving platter. Toss the roasted vegetables with enough of the remaining dressing to coat. Mound the roasted vegetables over the lettuces. Sprinkle with sunflower seeds and serve immediately.

Choosing fruits and vegetables that are grown organically in pesticide-free soil is the best thing you can do for yourself and your family. Imagine holding an apple in your hand and spraying it with bug killer—who would want to eat that apple? We don't see the pesticides, but that doesn't mean they aren't there.

I'm lucky to live in an area that allows me to buy organic easily: I shop at a farmers' market and live near some of the best natural foods stores in the country. I strongly believe in the power of purchasing organically grown foods. My dollars go toward supporting small family farms and keeping chemicals off my plate, out of my body, and out of the environment.

organic produce: The Dirty Dozen and the clean 15

The common belief that organic food is too expensive is a mind-set that's worth challenging. If you buy food in bulk when it's available, shop at farmers' markets and independent food stands, and eat food that's in season, you can likely keep the cost of organic produce within reach of your budget. When comparing conventionally grown produce to organic, it also makes sense to consider the hidden costs of conventional farming: It's hard to fathom the long-term impact of toxic chemicals on human health and the health of the planet.

According to the Environmental Working Group (whose mission it is to use the power of public information to protect public health and the environment), the foods they call the "Dirty Dozen" are the most pesticide-laden among conventionally grown fruits and vegetables. What they call the "Clean 15" are foods that won't harm you if you buy the conventionally grown versions.

THE DIRTY DOZEN

Apples	Cucumbers	Potatoes
Bell peppers	Grapes	Snap Peas-imported
Celery	Nectarines-imported	Spinach
Cherry tomatoes	Peaches	Strawberries

THE CLEAN 15

Asparagus	Eggplant	Papayas
Avocados	Grapefruit	Pineapples
Cabbage	Kiwifruit	Sweet corn
Cantaloupe	Mangoes	Sweet peas-frozen
Cauliflower	Onions	Sweet potatoes

Keep this list in mind as you shop, and don't let a lack of organic options be a reason for not eating your vegetables: If organics aren't available or within your budget, look for the Clean 15 first. It's also helpful to shop where you can get to know your local farmers and their growing methods, whether at markets or farm stands.

My Niçoise

Depending on how strict you are, a Niçoise salad without tuna can still be called a Niçoise. This traditional salad has always been vegetable-based, with interesting flavors and textures coming from thin green beans, olives, and tomatoes, among the many other ingredients. I like to toss the components together in a bowl, combining the flavors and textures, rather than arranging some elements separately on a platter, as is done for a composed salad. Instead of tuna, I use homemade Peppercorn-Crusted Tofu Chèvre (page 110). **Serves 4**

8 ounces slender green beans (such as haricots verts), trimmed

4 medium red-skinned potatoes (about 1 pound total), cut into ½-inch-thick wedges

VINAIGRETTE
¼ cup fresh lemon juice

1 small shallot, minced (about 2 tablespoons)

2 teaspoons Dijon mustard

2 teaspoons minced fresh thyme

¾ teaspoon fine sea salt

¼ teaspoon freshly ground black pepper

½ cup extra-virgin olive oil

SALAD
1 large head butter lettuce, leaves separated and larger leaves torn in half

3 ripe tomatoes, cut into wedges, or 10 to 12 cherry tomatoes, halved

Fine sea salt and freshly ground black pepper

1 log Peppercorn-Crusted Tofu Chèvre (page 110), sliced into rounds

⅓ cup Niçoise olives or kalamata olives

2 tablespoons capers, drained

1½ tablespoons minced fresh flat-leaf parsley

Cook the green beans in a large pot of boiling salted water until they are crisp-tender, about 4 minutes. Drain and submerge the green beans in a bowl of ice water just until they are cold. Drain the green beans again and pat dry. Set aside.

Place the potatoes in a steamer basket set in a saucepan filled with 1 inch of simmering water. Cover and steam until they are just tender and still hold their shape, about 8 minutes. Set aside to cool completely.

Vinaigrette: While the vegetables are cooling, whisk the lemon juice, shallot, mustard, thyme, salt, and pepper in a medium bowl to blend. Gradually whisk in the oil to blend well.

Salad: Arrange the lettuce on a serving platter or in a large shallow salad bowl. Place the green beans, potatoes, and tomatoes in a large bowl. Toss with enough of the vinaigrette to coat, then season to taste with salt and pepper. Spoon the beans, potatoes, and tomatoes atop the lettuce. Arrange the tofu cheese slices amid the vegetables. Sprinkle the olives, capers, and parsley over the salad. Spoon more vinaigrette over the salad and serve immediately.

watercress and butter lettuce salad with israeli couscous, orange-basil tempeh, and sweet miso dressing

This recipe is a good example of how to elevate a leafy-green salad to entrée status through the incorporation of plant proteins and healthy grains. The Orange-Basil Tempeh (recipe follows) could easily be served on its own as a traditional entrée. Israeli couscous is similar to traditional couscous, but it's much larger, with nearly pearl-size grains. While either type of couscous will work well in this salad, if you can find Israeli (sometimes called Mediterranean) couscous, it will add a wonderful texture and heft to the dish. (If using traditional couscous, follow the cooking instructions on the package.) **Serves 4**

COUSCOUS

1 cup Israeli couscous

1 teaspoon neutral cooking oil

DRESSING

¼ cup brown rice vinegar

3 tablespoons yellow or white miso

2 tablespoons fresh lemon juice

1 tablespoon agave nectar

1 tablespoon chopped fresh dill

2 cloves garlic, minced

½ teaspoon fine sea salt, plus more to taste

¼ teaspoon freshly ground black pepper, plus more to taste

½ cup extra-virgin olive oil

SALAD

2 tomatoes, seeded and cut into ½-inch pieces

2 celery stalks, finely diced

½ orange bell pepper, finely diced

⅓ cup finely chopped fresh flat-leaf parsley

⅓ cup finely diced red onion (from ½ small onion)

2 scallions, finely chopped

Fine sea salt and freshly ground black pepper

1 large head red leaf butter lettuce or green butter lettuce, torn into large bite-size pieces

1 bunch watercress, trimmed (about 3 cups)

Orange-Basil Tempeh (recipe follows), at room temperature

½ cup Roasted Pistachios (page 55)

Israeli Couscous: Bring a pot of salted water to a boil over high heat. Add the couscous and boil just as you would for pasta, stirring occasionally, until the couscous is plump and tender, but not mushy, about 7 minutes. Drain the couscous in a colander (be sure to use one with small holes so that the couscous doesn't fall through). Transfer the couscous to a large baking sheet and toss with the 1 teaspoon oil to coat (this will prevent the couscous balls from sticking together). Spread the couscous in a single layer and set aside to cool completely.

Dressing: Blend the vinegar, miso, lemon juice, agave nectar, dill, garlic, the ½ teaspoon salt, and the ¼ teaspoon pepper in a blender until smooth. With the blender on high speed, add the oil slowly in a steady stream, blending well. Season the dressing to taste with salt and pepper.

Salad: Toss the couscous, tomatoes, celery, bell pepper, parsley, red onion, and scallions in a large bowl with enough of the dressing to coat lightly. Season the couscous mixture to taste with salt and pepper.

Toss the lettuce and watercress in a large bowl with enough of the remaining dressing to coat and season to taste with salt and pepper. Mound the lettuces on a serving platter, then spoon the couscous mixture on top of the lettuces. Arrange the tempeh over the couscous, then sprinkle with the roasted pistachios and serve.

orange-basil tempeh

Marinate the tempeh at least an hour and up to overnight. This is a good do-ahead step, either the day before or the first thing you do when you start to prep the meal. The longer the tempeh marinates, the deeper flavor it will have. **Serves 4**

¼ cup fresh orange juice

3 tablespoons finely chopped fresh basil

2 tablespoons agave nectar

2 tablespoons tamari

1 tablespoon minced garlic

1 tablespoon extra-virgin olive oil

Zest of 1 orange (about 2 teaspoons)

1 (8-ounce) package grain-based tempeh, halved horizontally, then cut into ½-inch cubes

Whisk the orange juice, basil, agave nectar, tamari, garlic, oil, and zest in a 9- to 10-inch sauté pan to blend. Add the tempeh and turn to coat. Arrange the tempeh in the pan so it is in a single layer and submerged in the marinade. Set aside to marinate for at least 1 hour or cover and refrigerate overnight.

Set the sauté pan over medium-low heat. Cover and cook until the tempeh is hot and the marinade has reduced, about 15 minutes. Serve the tempeh warm or at room temperature.

Grecian Goddess Salad with Quinoa Tabbouleh and Lemon Vinaigrette

Tabbouleh is a Middle Eastern grain-based dish, traditionally made with bulgur wheat and loaded with fresh green herbs and lemon. I've taken this basic formula and amped it up with the use of quinoa, a superfood rich in protein (it has more than any other grain), fiber, and whole-grain goodness. Quinoa is actually a seed, which was originally cultivated in the Andes Mountains of South America and has gained popularity in the United States as we learn more about its nutritional value. This salad is vibrant and green, and it is a perfect companion for the Edamame and Spinach Hummus with Endive Spears (page 44). I like to serve this salad with spears of endive, which are fantastic for scooping both the salad and the hummus in one delicious bite. **Serves 4**

LEMON VINAIGRETTE

¼ cup fresh lemon juice

2 tablespoons olive oil

1 tablespoon walnut oil or avocado oil

1 garlic clove, minced

¼ teaspoon fine sea salt

⅛ teaspoon ground white pepper

SALAD

8 cups lightly packed mixed baby lettuces (about 4 ounces)

2 Persian cucumbers, peeled, seeded, and cut into half-moons

1 red bell pepper, diced

Fine sea salt and freshly ground black pepper

4 cups Quinoa Tabbouleh (recipe follows)

½ cup sunflower sprouts

Edamame and Spinach Hummus with Endive Spears (page 44)

Vinaigrette: Mix all of the ingredients in a medium bowl with a fork or a whisk until they are well blended. It will make about ½ cup.

Salad: Toss the lettuces, cucumbers, and bell pepper with enough of the vinaigrette to coat. Season the salad to taste with salt and pepper. Mound the salad on a large platter. Spoon the tabbouleh over the salad and garnish with the sunflower sprouts. Serve with the hummus and endive spears.

quinoa tabbouleh

Serves 4

1 cup quinoa

1⅔ cups water

1¼ teaspoons fine sea salt

1½ cups finely chopped fresh curly parsley

3 plum tomatoes, seeded and diced

4 scallions, diced

½ cup finely chopped fresh mint

¼ cup extra-virgin olive oil

2 tablespoons fresh lemon juice

2 teaspoons finely chopped fresh dill

1 teaspoon minced garlic

½ teaspoon freshly ground black pepper

2 Belgian endives (red and green), spears separated

Rinse the quinoa well in a fine-meshed strainer under cold running water. Drain well. Bring the water to a boil in a heavy saucepan over high heat. Add ½ teaspoon of the salt and the rinsed quinoa. Return the water to a boil, then decrease the heat to medium-low. Cover and simmer until the quinoa is tender and the liquid has been absorbed, about 20 minutes. Fluff the quinoa with a fork and transfer it to a large bowl to cool to room temperature.

Toss the cooled quinoa with the parsley, tomatoes, scallions, and mint. Whisk the olive oil, lemon juice, dill, garlic, pepper, and the remaining ¾ teaspoon salt in a small bowl to blend. Pour the dressing over the quinoa mixture and toss to coat.

Serve the quinoa with the endive spears for dipping.

mixed oak and green leaf salad with sesame-Hiziki croquettes, garbanzo beans, and Ginger-Tahini Dressing

The croquettes are delicious on their own, as is the salad. The salad served without the croquettes makes a great side dish or starter for many of my Simple Meals (page 139). The croquettes recipe is a great introduction to using sea vegetables: Hiziki is a mineral-rich sea vegetable harvested on the coast of Japan. Garbanzo beans, also known as chickpeas, are available canned or dried. For the sake of convenience, I tend to use canned garbanzo beans at home, but if you are a purist at heart, you could certainly cook your own. **Serves 4**

DRESSING

½ cup roasted tahini

⅓ cup water

¼ cup fresh lemon juice

2 scallions, minced

3 tablespoons minced peeled fresh ginger

2 tablespoons tamari

½ teaspoon fine sea salt, plus more to taste

¼ teaspoon freshly ground white pepper, plus more to taste

SALAD

1 head oak leaf lettuce, torn into large bite-size pieces

1 head green leaf lettuce, torn into large bite-size pieces

Fine sea salt and freshly ground black pepper

ASSEMBLY

1 (15-ounce) can garbanzo beans, drained, rinsed, and patted dry

1 medium beet, peeled and cut into matchstick-size strips or grated

12 Sesame-Hiziki Croquettes (recipe follows)

¼ cup sunflower seeds

Dressing: Combine the tahini, water, lemon juice, scallions, ginger, tamari, the ½ teaspoon salt, and the ¼ teaspoon pepper in a blender and blend until smooth and creamy. Season the dressing to taste with salt and pepper.

Salad: Toss the lettuces in a large bowl with enough of the dressing to coat. Season to taste with salt and pepper.

Assembly: Mound the salad on plates or a large platter. Scatter the garbanzo beans over. Top with the beet strips and serve the croquettes alongside. Garnish with the sunflower seeds and serve immediately.

sesame-HIZIKI croquettes
If the mixture seems dry, add a little more water. When cooked, the croquettes should be crispy on the outside and moist on the inside. This recipe makes 24 croquettes, but only 12 are needed for this salad. The remaining croquettes can easily be frozen for later use. When you're ready to use them, allow them to defrost and follow the frying instructions below.

Makes about 24 croquettes

3 tablespoons dried hiziki

2½ cups water, plus more to soak the hiziki

1 cup millet

1¾ teaspoons fine sea salt

1 tablespoon toasted sesame oil

1 large carrot, peeled and shredded (about 1¾ cups)

6 scallions, minced

3 cloves garlic, minced

½ cup roasted tahini

1 tablespoon tamari

1½ teaspoons ground cumin

⅛ teaspoon ground white pepper

⅓ cup minced fresh curly or flat-leaf parsley

2 tablespoons brown sesame seeds

1 cup drained canned garbanzo beans, rinsed and patted dry

3 tablespoons corn flour (not cornmeal) or whole-wheat flour

About 6 tablespoons high-heat neutral cooking oil

Place the hiziki in a bowl and add enough cold water to fully cover the hiziki. Set aside until it is hydrated and softened, about 15 minutes. Strain the hiziki from the soaking liquid, and discard the soaking liquid.

Combine 2 cups of the fresh water, the millet, and ½ teaspoon of the salt in a heavy saucepan and bring to a boil over high heat. Decrease the heat to low. Cover and simmer without stirring until the millet is fluffy and the water is absorbed, about 25 minutes.

Meanwhile, heat the sesame oil in a heavy sauté pan over medium heat. Add the hiziki and sauté until tender, about 5 minutes. Add the carrot, scallions, and garlic and sauté until tender, about 5 minutes. Add the remaining ½ cup water, the tahini, tamari, cumin, and white pepper. Decrease the heat to low and cook until the mixture thickens slightly, about 2 minutes. Remove the pan from

the heat and mix in the parsley, brown sesame seeds, and the remaining 1¼ teaspoons salt. Set aside to cool.

Blend the garbanzo beans in a food processor until they are chopped as finely as possible and will clump together when pressed in your hand. Stir the mashed garbanzo beans and corn flour into the cooled millet, add the hiziki-vegetable mixture to blend well. Using 2 tablespoons of the croquette mixture for each, form the mixture into about 1½-inch disks.

Heat 3 tablespoons of the cooking oil in a large, heavy frying pan over medium heat. Working in batches and adding more oil as needed for each batch, fry the croquettes until they are crisp and golden brown on the outside and hot in the center, about 2½ minutes per side. Transfer the croquettes to paper towels to drain the excess oil. Serve warm.

There is a very simple and reliable formula for making vinaigrette, which you can then dress up with a wide variety of herbs, spices, mustards, fine sea salt, and black pepper. As a general rule, you should aim to have a ratio of one part acid (good-quality vinegar like balsamic, apple cider, red wine, raspberry, or brown rice or white rice vinegar, and/or citrus juice) to three parts good-quality oil (extra-virgin olive oil, or any other you might have on hand). Citrus juice is a nice component to add to vinaigrettes: Often it enhances the vinegar with its bright, fresh flavor rather than replacing it altogether, although a simple dressing of olive oil and lemon juice drizzled over a leafy green salad can be very satisfying.

formula for vinaigrette

Keep in mind that oil and vinegar will start to separate as soon as you stop blending or whisking them. The best way to combine oil and vinegar is in a blender. If you don't have a blender, simply whisk them together in a glass bowl just before using. If you make enough dressing to save, cover tightly and refrigerate it for up to 7 days. Before using, be sure to take the dressing out of the fridge and allow it to warm up, rewhisking it just before tossing your salad. (I sometimes store dressings in a glass jar so they can simply be shaken before using.) Follow the formula, and you'll have a delicious vinaigrette in minutes.

good fats

While we've all been conditioned to fear fat, good fats are a vital component of a healthy diet. When consumed in moderation, good fats can actually help to improve your overall health. There are two broad categories of fats: saturated and unsaturated. As a general rule, good fats tend to be unsaturated, although coconut oil is a notable exception (see below). Among the unsaturated fats, there are monounsaturated and polyunsaturated fats. Both types of fat help to lower total cholesterol, but only monounsaturated fats help to lower LDL (bad cholesterol) while increasing HDL (good cholesterol).

AVOCADOS are a true wonder in terms of nutritional value: They're packed with nutrients and vitamins such as fiber, vitamin E, B vitamins, and folic acid—and they contain more potassium than bananas. Avocados are rich in monounsaturated fats, and they're cholesterol-free. The balance of vitamins and essential fatty acids in avocados has been linked to lowering cholesterol, as well as reducing the risk of stroke and improving the appearance of skin and hair. Avocados have even been shown to help the body better absorb nutrients from other foods. It's no wonder that some people call mashed avocados the perfect baby food. Avocados also happen to be a favorite of grown-ups, and they play a critical role in many of my recipes. Be sure to seek out avocados that are slightly soft to the touch, and heavy for their size.

COCONUT OIL is a saturated fat, but recent research into the benefits of coconut oil suggests that this good fat might even be considered a super-food. Coconut oil contains an optimal blend of fatty acids, which are said to have antimicrobial, antioxidant, antifungal, and antibacterial properties. As with any fat, coconut oil should be used in moderation. There is a subtle difference between refined and unrefined, and I alternate between

the two. I like to incorporate it in small quantities where I can, such as in my Super Hippie Granola (page 5). Look for it at your natural foods store.

NUTS AND SEEDS can have an important role in a healthy, plant-based diet: They are one of the best plant sources of protein; they are rich in fiber, phytonutrients, and antioxidants such as vitamin E and selenium; and they have a variety of B vitamins. Although the fat content can be high in some nuts, these fats are monounsaturated or polyunsaturated with rich omega-3 fatty acids and, when consumed in moderation, have been shown to lower LDL cholesterol. You'll

find an assortment of nuts and seeds throughout this book; use them as ingredients, snacks, and nutrition-boosting garnishes, too.

OLIVE OIL is rich in monounsaturated fats and is by far the healthiest cooking oil—and the one I use most often. Olive oil can be found in both extra-virgin and virgin forms, both of which are less refined than other grades of olive oil, making them the richest in heart-healthy fats. Look for expeller-pressed oils, as this designation denotes oils that have been extracted by pressing, rather than by chemical methods.

ann's favorite salad with crumbled maple tempeh bacon and balsamic vinaigrette

This salad is a great way to use up the odds and ends that inevitably accumulate when you cook at home. I love texture in my salads, so using up the last bits of carrots, celery, and cucumber is a refreshing addition. This recipe is going to require you to make Maple Tempeh Bacon (page 25), but it will be totally worth it once you taste the smoky, flavorful crunch that these little bacon-like crumbles bring to the salad. My signature dressing is a balsamic vinaigrette—a flavorful and versatile choice that complements a wide variety of vegetables. Feel free to use mine, or use my basic formula for vinaigrette (page 135) and your favorite ingredients to come up with a signature salad dressing of your own. **Serves 4**

BALSAMIC VINAIGRETTE

¼ cup balsamic vinegar

2 teaspoons Dijon mustard

1 teaspoon pure maple syrup

2 cloves garlic, minced

½ teaspoon fine sea salt

¼ teaspoon freshly ground black pepper

¾ cup extra-virgin olive oil

SALAD

8 cups of whatever salad greens you have (such as romaine, red leaf, or mixed baby lettuces)

1 carrot, peeled and cut into thin quarter-moon pieces

1 celery stalk, cut into ¼-inch dice

1 small cucumber, cut into thin quarter-moon pieces

1 tomato, coarsely chopped

1 avocado, peeled, seeded, and diced

2 radishes, cut into thin quarter-moon pieces

½ cup torn dried dulse pieces (see page 198; optional)

½ cup coarsely chopped fresh dill or parsley, or any fresh herbs (optional)

10 to 15 pieces Maple Tempeh Bacon (page 25), crumbled with your hands

Vinaigrette: Place all the ingredients except the oil in a blender and mix together on medium-high speed. Decrease the blender speed to the lowest setting and slowly add the oil to the vinegar mixture, blending until the mixture is emulsified. This makes almost 1 cup.

Salad: Toss all the ingredients in a large bowl with enough vinaigrette to coat. Refrigerate any remaining vinaigrette for another use. Serve.

simple meals

simple meals

One of the questions I hear most from non-vegans is "What do you eat for dinner if you don't have meat?" It's a fair question, considering that many people can't imagine the answer. When I say that I eat grains, vegetables, and plant proteins, it sounds a little unfamiliar—and maybe even like a lot of work to people who are more comfortable roasting meat than soaking beans. In fact, I have a repertoire of simple meals that I can pull together any night of the week from the items I keep in my pantry and refrigerator. As a working mother, I know firsthand the value of a recipe that can be made quickly.

While I enjoy experimenting with more time-consuming recipes and more exotic ingredients at my restaurants, at home, my philosophy is to eat simply. Home is where you're most in charge of what your family eats, so it's critical to keep it nourishing and healthful—maybe even making up for some at-school or at-work dietary indiscretions. But given the time constraints and demands of modern life, it's also critical to keep things easy. Go ahead and save the more complicated meals for when you entertain or when you go out to eat. For family suppers, you'll want recipes that are easy to shop for and simple to prepare, with results that will appeal to everyone around your table.

What you'll find in this chapter are simple meals for everyday cooking. Some are vegan takes on classic comfort foods, like Lasagna Rolls with Tofu Ricotta and Everyday Tomato Sauce (page 166) and Lentil Loaf with Savory Gluten-Free Gravy (page 156), while others draw on enticing global flavors, such as Sichuan Noodles with Hot Spicy Peanut Sauce (page 147) and One-Pot Vegetables and Tofu with Sesame Rice (page 145). What they all share is that they're simple in execution and ready to be rotated into your weeknight routine.

While these recipes are intended to be the meal's centerpiece, I've made notes throughout to suggest salads, soups, or simple sides that would be ideal complements to the full meal. Read on for over a dozen flavorful, healthful, and simple plant-based meals, deliciously answering the question of what the vegan family eats for dinner.

pinto bean enchiladas

This is a standout recipe that I've been making since I started cooking. Although it requires some advance preparation—as you must prepare the beans from scratch—the actual assembly and cooking time is minimal, and the payoff is well worth the planning. The main reason why the beans must be prepared from scratch is that rather than relying upon loads of cheese to bind the enchiladas, this recipe creates a sauce from the beans' cooking liquid, which is thickened with flour and then poured over the bean-filled tortillas. Although the bulk of the recipe is cheese-free, if you would like to add shreds of your favorite vegan cheese, feel free to dust the top with a layer and broil for the last few minutes of cooking.
Serves 4 to 6 (makes 12 enchiladas)

BEANS AND STOCK
About 9 cups water

1½ cups dried pinto beans

1 (6 by 2-inch) piece dried kombu

ENCHILADA SAUCE
2 tablespoons neutral cooking oil

1 onion, finely chopped

6 cloves garlic, minced

2 teaspoons cayenne pepper

2 teaspoons ground coriander

1 teaspoon ground cumin

¼ cup whole-wheat pastry flour

2 tablespoons tamari

1½ tablespoons umeboshi paste

Fine sea salt

ENCHILADAS
¼ cup neutral cooking oil, plus more as needed

12 fresh corn tortillas

Fine sea salt

Tofu Sour Cream (page 104)

¼ cup thinly sliced scallions

2 tablespoons chopped fresh cilantro

Beans and Stock: Combine 7 cups of the water, the beans, and kombu in a large, heavy saucepan and bring to a simmer over high heat. Decrease the heat to medium-low, then cover and simmer gently until the beans and kombu are tender, about 1½ hours. Drain the beans, reserving the bean stock. You should have about 3 cups of stock. Return the beans and kombu to the pan and mash with a potato masher until some bits of beans still remain and the kombu is completely mashed. Set the bean mixture aside. Add enough of the remaining 2 cups water to the bean stock to equal 5 cups total, then set the stock aside.

Enchilada Sauce: Heat the 2 tablespoons oil in a large, heavy saucepan over medium-high heat. Add the onion and garlic and sauté until the onion is tender and becoming golden, about 8 minutes. Stir in the cayenne pepper, coriander, and cumin. Stir in the flour. Add the reserved bean stock, whisking constantly to blend. Whisk in the tamari and umeboshi. Simmer gently, whisking occasionally, until the sauce thickens and the flavors blend, about 10 minutes. Season the sauce to taste with salt. Set the sauce aside.

Enchiladas: Preheat the oven to 350°F. Spoon 2 cups of the sauce over the bottom of a 13 by 9 by 2-inch baking dish.

Heat the ¼ cup oil in a large skillet over medium-high heat. Using tongs, fry the tortillas, one at a time, in the oil until the tortillas begin to crisp slightly but are still very pliable, about 20 seconds per side. Lay the fried tortillas on paper towels to absorb the excess oil. Add more oil to the pan as needed when frying the tortillas.

Stir ¾ cup of the sauce into the mashed beans, then season the beans to taste with salt.

Working with 1 tortilla at a time, lay a tortilla on the work surface. Spoon a generous 3 tablespoons of the bean mixture in a log shape up the center of the tortilla, and roll up the tortilla like a cigar. (Each enchilada will be about 1 inch in diameter.) Repeat with the remaining tortillas and bean mixture, placing the enchiladas seam-side-down in the prepared baking dish.

Spoon the remaining sauce over the enchiladas. Bake until the sauce bubbles and the enchiladas are heated through, about 30 minutes. Top with the tofu sour cream and sprinkle with the scallions and cilantro.

Do-Ahead Tip: To make these enchiladas ahead, reserve all of the sauce. Roll up the enchiladas, and place them in a dish without any sauce. (Keeping the sauce separate ensures that the enchiladas don't become soggy.) The enchiladas and the sauce can be stored separately, covered and refrigerated, for up to 2 days. When you're ready to bake and serve the enchiladas, pour about 2 cups of the sauce into the baking dish under the enchiladas, then pour the rest of the sauce all over the enchiladas and bake as directed.

one-pot vegetables and tofu with sesame rice

This recipe is the embodiment of simplicity, as it is a one-pot meal comprised of colorful vegetables cooked in a fragrant stock. If you have an attractive skillet, use it here for a beautiful stovetop-to-table dish that invites family-style dining. In addition, this recipe allows for a great deal of flexibility, feel free to include any vegetables you might have on hand. The vegetables are arranged individually, and their juices are enhanced by the sweet mirin; even my kids were arguing over who got to finish the last of this delicious stock. The easy cooking method and easy cleanup make this recipe truly family-friendly. **Serves 4**

1 medium onion

1 large head broccoli, stems removed and florets cut into bite-size pieces (about 2 cups)

½ small butternut squash (about 1¼ pounds), peeled and cut into ½-inch cubes

2 medium carrots, peeled and roll-cut (see page 174)

¼ head green cabbage, cored and sliced into ½-inch pieces

8 ounces sugar snap peas, trimmed

3 ounces small fresh shiitake mushrooms, stemmed

¼ teaspoon fine sea salt

1 (5-inch) piece fresh ginger, peeled

⅔ cup mirin

¼ cup plus 2 tablespoons tamari

1 (14-ounce) container water-packed firm tofu, drained and cut into ¾-inch cubes

½ bunch watercress, stems removed (about 1½ cups)

Sesame Rice (recipe follows), or soba or udon noodles, cooked according to the package instructions

2 scallions, thinly sliced

1 nori sheet, cut into thin strips

Quarter the onion through the stem end, then place the whole cut onion in the middle of a large cast-iron skillet, doing your best to keep the onion together. Arrange the broccoli, squash, carrots, cabbage, sugar snap peas, and mushrooms in clusters around the onion, keeping each vegetable separate from the other and arranging the vegetables so that the colors are balanced and attractive. Add just enough water to cover the bottom of the skillet (about 1 cup). Sprinkle the ¼ teaspoon salt evenly over the vegetables. Cover and turn the heat to high. Bring the vegetables to a boil, then decrease the heat to medium-low and simmer until the squash is crisp-tender, about 12 minutes.

Using a Microplane grater, grate the ginger over a paper towel or sheet of cheesecloth, then squeeze the pulp to extract 2 teaspoons of ginger juice into a small bowl. Mix in the mirin and tamari. Add the tofu and toss to coat.

Spoon the tofu mixture over the vegetables and simmer uncovered until the tofu is hot, about 5 minutes. Add the watercress and simmer until it wilts, about 2 minutes. Remove the skillet from the heat and set it on a trivet in the middle of the dining table.

Divide the rice among dinner plates or bowls and have each person pick out their vegetables, using chopsticks to place them atop the rice. With a wide spoon, spoon some of the stock over the top of the vegetables on each plate. Serve the sliced scallions and strips of nori alongside to sprinkle on top of the vegetables.

sesame rice

Serves 4

1 tablespoon toasted sesame oil

4 cloves garlic, minced

4 cups cooked Short-Grain Brown Rice (page 181)

¼ cup sesame seeds, toasted

Heat the oil in a large, heavy saucepan over medium heat. Add the garlic and sauté until fragrant, about 30 seconds. Stir in the rice and sesame seeds and cook just until heated through, about 3 minutes.

I call for freshly squeezed ginger juice in several recipes. Besides the Arame Strudel (page 195), you'll see this spicy-sweet ingredient in my Ginger Miso Soup (page 98), as well as in my Ginger-Apple Smoothie (page 13). Making your own ginger juice at home is easy—no need to run over to your local juice bar. Instead, make sure you have the correct grater: Reach for a Microplane grater, or a grater made especially for ginger, which you'll find in a kitchen supply store. Ginger graters are inexpensive and can be used to finely grate other ingredients, too—such as citrus zest. Follow the

homemade ginger juice

directions I've given in each of these recipes, and I promise you'll have this fragrant and golden juice at your fingertips and in your recipes in no time.

sichuan noodles with hot spicy peanut sauce

When I lived in New York, I fell in love with the multitude of noodles that were available throughout the city from various ethnic restaurants. After moving to Los Angeles, I went on a date and expressed a yen for Sichuan noodles; he obliged and we went to a restaurant called Sichuan Café. As fate would have it, I located my first restaurant in that very same space. While I love these noodles plain with just the sauce, I've extended the recipe to include instructions for adding a few fresh vegetables to the dish.

Serves 4 to 6

SAUCE

¼ cup minced peeled fresh ginger

6 cloves garlic

½ cup tamari

½ cup toasted sesame oil

¼ cup agave nectar

¼ cup brown rice vinegar

¼ cup smooth peanut butter

¼ cup tahini

1 teaspoon crushed red pepper

NOODLES

1 tablespoon toasted sesame oil

1 pound dried whole-grain udon noodles

3 tablespoons chopped shelled roasted peanuts

3 scallions, sliced diagonally

1½ tablespoons toasted sesame seeds

Sauce: Mince the ginger and garlic together in a blender. Add the tamari, sesame oil, agave nectar, vinegar, peanut butter, tahini, and crushed red pepper. Blend until the mixture is smooth and creamy.

Noodles: Bring a large pot of salted water to a boil. Add the sesame oil, then add the noodles and cook, stirring often, until they are al dente, about 7 minutes. Drain the noodles in a colander, then transfer the noodles to a large bowl. While the noodles are still hot, toss them with enough of the sauce to coat. Divide the noodles among bowls. Sprinkle with the peanuts, scallions, and sesame seeds and serve.

Variation: Although I love this dish with just the noodles and the creamy sauce, adding vegetables brings more texture, color, and nutrition to the recipe. Heat 2 teaspoons toasted sesame oil in a wok or a large frying pan over medium heat. Add 3 baby bok choy (leaves separated, and larger leaves halved lengthwise); 1 red bell pepper, thinly sliced; and 1 yellow bell pepper, thinly sliced. Stir-fry until the vegetables are crisp-tender, about 2 minutes. Stir the vegetables into the noodles right before the sauce is added.

a south american stew: vegan-style, stuffed in a whole kabocha squash

I was testing recipes for a *Vegetarian Times* article, and I hosted a dinner party to get some feedback on a few of the dishes I had created. This dish was a true revelation for me. My guests had a wide range of culinary inclinations—from fast-food junkies to genuine foodies—but every person at the table raved over this hearty and satisfying stew. It was a profound moment for me, as I realized that everyone is hungry for nourishing whole foods. **Serves 6 to 8**

8 dried pitted apricots, coarsely chopped

6 dried pitted prunes, coarsely chopped

1½ cups warm water

1 large kabocha squash (about 5½ pounds)

About 3 tablespoons olive oil

1 medium yellow onion, finely chopped

2 cloves garlic, minced

1 (14.5-ounce) can whole tomatoes with juices, tomatoes coarsely chopped

½ (6-ounce) can tomato paste

2 Yukon Gold potatoes (about 8 ounces), peeled and cut into ¾-inch dice

1 sweet potato (about 8 ounces), peeled and cut into ¾-inch dice

1 small red bell pepper, cut into ½-inch dice

½ cup fresh corn kernels, or frozen corn kernels, thawed

1 (15-ounce) can kidney beans, drained and rinsed

1 tablespoon mirin

1½ teaspoons fine sea salt, plus more to taste

1 teaspoon freshly ground black pepper

Soak the apricots and prunes in a small bowl with the 1½ cups warm water until tender, at least 2 hours or, if you can, overnight, as this will allow the soaking water to become really sweet, almost syruplike. Drain, reserving the fruit and the soaking liquid separately.

Preheat the oven to 350°F, and lightly coat a large, heavy rimmed baking sheet with olive oil. Scrub the outside of the kabocha squash. Using a sharp heavy pointed knife, cut a circular opening (about 3 to 4 inches in diameter) in the top of the squash. Reserve the top. Scoop out

the seeds and fiber and discard. Douse your hands with about 1 tablespoon of the oil, set the squash bowl and lid on the oiled baking sheet, and rub the oil on your hands all over the skin of the squash. This helps prevent the outside of the squash from getting too dry. Set the squash aside while you prepare the stew.

Heat the remaining 2 tablespoons oil in a heavy pot over medium heat. Add the onion and garlic and sauté until tender, about 3 minutes. Add the tomatoes and their juices and the tomato paste, and stir until the paste

dissolves and the mixture simmers, about 3 minutes. Add the Yukon Gold potatoes, the sweet potato, and the reserved soaking liquid from the dried fruit. Bring to a simmer, then reduce the heat to medium-low. Cover the pot and simmer gently until the Yukon potatoes are almost tender, about 12 minutes. Add the red bell pepper, corn kernels, and soaked apricots and prunes and simmer, uncovered, until the peppers begin to soften, about 3 minutes. Add the beans, mirin, the 1½ teaspoons salt, and the pepper. Cover and simmer until the Yukon potatoes are tender, but not falling apart (they won't soften very much when baked in the squash), about 5 minutes.

Carefully ladle the stew into the hollowed-out squash, then place the squash lid on top. Reserve any remaining stew that won't fit into the squash and keep it warm to serve with the squash.

Bake until the squash flesh is tender and a fork can pierce through the squash easily, about 1 hour and 15 minutes (the baking time will depend on the size of the squash). Another good way to tell if the squash is done is to lift the lid and poke the squash flesh around the opening to see if it is tender.

Place the squash on a serving platter. Remove the squash lid, and starting at the top of the squash, cut the squash into 1½-inch-wide wedges. The squash will fan open like a lotus flower with each piece, and the stew will pool over the squash wedges. Serve a wedge of squash with a large spoonful of the stew to each person.

cutting techniques

GRATING is a quick way to turn solid ingredients into tiny shreds. Graters come in all sizes and shapes for a variety of uses. For fresh ginger, use a paring knife to peel it if desired (there's no need to peel ginger if you're just making ginger juice, see page 146), and then grate with a ginger grater, or any handheld grater with fine holes, such as a Microplane. As you get toward the end of the ginger, be careful to keep your knuckles and fingers out of the way so you don't shred them.

Baked penne and cauliflower with cheesy sauce

Any small pasta such as corkscrews, fusilli, rigatoni, or macaroni will work in place of the penne; I've found that gluten-free pasta in smaller shapes like these holds up well, so feel free to try it. The sauce makes about 4¾ cups; I reserve ¾ cup of the sauce to spread over the top instead of a layer of grated nondairy cheese. It makes a nice, thick, creamy top layer that when broiled gets crusty on the edges.

Serves 6 to 8

3 tablespoons plus 1 teaspoon vegan butter

1 (1½- to 1¾-pound) head cauliflower, cored and cut into 1-inch florets

¼ cup nutritional yeast

1 small onion, finely chopped

3 cloves garlic, minced

1 (12-ounce) can diced stewed tomatoes, drained

2 teaspoons Dijon mustard

2 teaspoons fine sea salt

1 teaspoon paprika

½ teaspoon ground white pepper

2 cups unsweetened soy milk or rice milk

¼ cup Cashew Cream (page 83)

8 ounces Daiya shredded nondairy cheddar-style cheese

12 ounces penne or any small tube- or cylindrical-shaped pasta

Preheat the oven to 375°F. Coat an 11 by 9 by 2-inch baking dish with 1 teaspoon of the vegan butter.

Cook the cauliflower in a large pot of boiling salted water until it is crisp-tender, about 5 minutes. Using a large strainer spoon, remove the cauliflower from the pot of water and transfer it to a bowl. Reserve the pot of water.

Cook the nutritional yeast in a heavy saucepan over medium-low heat, stirring constantly, until it is golden brown, about 2 minutes. Add the remaining 3 tablespoons vegan butter and stir until it's melted and the mixture is foamy. Add the onion, garlic, and steamed cauliflower and sauté until the onion starts to soften, about 5 minutes. Add the tomatoes and cook for 2 minutes to blend the flavors. Whisk in the mustard, salt, paprika, and white pepper. Whisk in the milk, cashew cream, and cheese.

Simmer until the cheese melts and the mixture thickens slightly, about 2 minutes, stirring as it cooks to make sure the cheese doesn't stick to the bottom of the pot.

Return the reserved pot of water to a boil over high heat. Add the pasta and cook, stirring occasionally, until it is tender but still firm to the bite, about 7 minutes. Drain.

Transfer the pasta to the prepared baking dish. Stir in the cauliflower-cheesy sauce, reserving about ¾ cup. Pour the reserved cheese sauce over the top of the combined pasta and cauliflower-cheesy sauce. Cover and bake until heated through, about 25 minutes.

Uncover and bake for another 10 minutes, or until the top browns a bit. If you'd like the top to brown more, place it under the broiler until it browns to your liking.

Variation: For a crisp, golden brown bread crumb topping, toss some fresh bread crumbs with some melted vegan butter, then sprinkle them over the pasta before baking.

Do-Ahead Tip: The dish can be assembled a few hours before baking and kept covered at room temperature. When ready to serve, bake as directed.

Seitan (pronounced *say-tan*) is a versatile ingredient used in vegetarian and vegan cooking. It's high in protein and has a chewy, meaty texture. Seitan is often referred to as "wheat meat" because it's made from wheat gluten.

what is seitan?

What I like about the Field Roast sausages I use in the bangers and mash recipe (page 162) is that they incorporate vegetables and herbs into their seitan base, with results that are softer in texture and more sausage-like than wheat-meat-like. I don't use much seitan in my home cooking, but I still think it is an important product that folks should know about and consider using in their vegan home cooking. Seitan can be found in the refrigerated section of your natural foods store, usually near the tofu.

vegetables

Vegetables are at the very core of a vegan diet; they supply the full spectrum of vitamins and minerals we need to live and grow in good health. Although there are many products on the market now that offer substitutes for meat and dairy, veganism is a *plant*-based diet for a reason: Eating a diet rich in vegetables helps to lower cholesterol, it improves circulation, and it provides your body with the natural variety of vitamins and minerals it needs to perform at its very best.

GROUND VEGETABLES are round-shaped vegetables that grow on the top layer of soil and are high in vitamins and minerals, including the antioxidant beta-carotene. Consider cauliflower, broccoli, summer and winter squashes, cucumbers, celery, and so many more that you'll find throughout this book. Yellow squash rounds out the Boiled Vegetable Salad with Umeboshi-Scallion Dressing (page 204), for instance, and asparagus spears crown my Sesame-Shiitake Tofu Frittata (page 17).

ROOT VEGETABLES grow underground, as their name suggests. They are complex carbohydrates, and a good source of vitamins and minerals. Root vegetables require a greater effort by the body to digest; therefore, they improve digestion by bringing more blood into the abdominal region, promoting warmth. That may be why we think of many root vegetables, like potatoes, for instance, as comfort foods. Among the long list of roots are such common ingredients as carrots, onions, beets, and radishes. Some lesser-used but no less satisfying root vegetables include turnips, rutabagas, parsnips, jicama, fennel, burdock, and celeriac. You'll find all of these used in this book; my Nishime-Style Root Vegetables (page 197) is one delicious example of cooking with root vegetables.

Lentil Loaf with savory gluten-free gravy

As I've become more aware of the need to limit my wheat consumption over the years, I've looked for ways to modify some of my favorite recipes to make them gluten-free. This lentil loaf is a perennial favorite at my restaurants, and I have made some minor modifications to make a gluten-free version that is both substantial and satisfying. This is a great recipe to make when you have a little extra time on your hands and want something to really impress your friends and family. Although it has a few more steps than most of my Simple Meals, it is well worth the time and effort. (For more on gluten-free cooking, see page 161.)
Serves 8

1 small butternut squash (about 2 pounds), peeled, seeded, and cut into 1- to 2-inch chunks

3½ tablespoons olive oil

1¼ teaspoons fine sea salt

5 cups water

1 cup dried green lentils

1 cup millet

1 large onion, diced

3 cloves garlic, minced

2 celery stalks, diced

1 medium carrot, peeled and diced

2½ tablespoons chopped fresh rosemary

1½ tablespoons chopped fresh thyme

1½ teaspoons chopped fresh oregano

1 cup gluten-free rolled oats

¾ cup minced fresh parsley

½ cup whole almonds, finely chopped

¼ cup white miso paste, diluted in 3 tablespoons water

Savory Gluten-Free Gravy (recipe follows)

To roast the squash, preheat the oven to 375°F. Line a large, heavy baking sheet with parchment paper. Toss the squash in a bowl with 2 tablespoons of the oil and ½ teaspoon of the salt to coat. Arrange the squash evenly over the prepared baking sheet. Bake until the squash is very tender, about 50 minutes. While the squash is still hot, transfer it to a food processor and purée until it is smooth and creamy. Maintain the oven temperature.

Meanwhile, to cook the lentils and millet, bring the 5 cups water to a boil in a heavy saucepan over high heat. Add the lentils and cook for 5 minutes. Add the millet and ¼ teaspoon of the salt. Decrease the heat to medium-low. Cover and simmer until the lentils and millet are tender and the liquid is absorbed, about 30 minutes.

Heat 1 tablespoon of the oil in a heavy wide pot or large frying pan over medium-high heat. Add the onion and garlic and sauté until fragrant, about 30 seconds. Add the celery, carrot, rosemary, thyme, and oregano, and sauté until the vegetables are crisp-tender, about 9 minutes.

Combine the cooked lentils and millet, sautéed vegetables, oats, parsley, almonds, miso, and the remaining ½ teaspoon salt in a large bowl. Mix in the puréed squash.

Coat an 8½-inch square baking dish with the remaining 1½ teaspoons oil. Transfer the mixture to the dish, spreading evenly. Bake until the loaf is heated through and golden brown around the edges, about 45 minutes.

Cut the loaf into squares and transfer it to plates. Spoon the gravy over and serve.

savory Gluten-Free Gravy

Makes 4 cups

½ cup nutritional yeast

¼ cup gluten-free flour (such as Bob's Red Mill)

⅓ cup olive oil

½ cup finely chopped onion

2 teaspoons minced garlic

2 teaspoons chopped fresh thyme, or 1 teaspoon dried

2 teaspoons chopped fresh sage, or 1 teaspoon dried

1 tablespoon ground flaxseeds (optional)

4 cups water

¼ cup tamari

¾ teaspoon freshly ground black pepper

Stir the nutritional yeast and flour in a heavy skillet over medium heat for 5 minutes, or until pale golden and fragrant. Set aside.

Heat the oil in a large, heavy saucepan over medium heat. Add the onion and sauté until tender and beginning to brown, about 8 minutes. Add the garlic, thyme, and sage, and sauté for 30 seconds, or until fragrant. Whisk in the flour mixture and ground flaxseeds. Whisk in the water, tamari, and pepper. Bring the gravy to a simmer over medium-high heat, whisking frequently. Continue simmering until the gravy is thick and creamy.

The gravy will keep for 2 days, covered and refrigerated. To rewarm, bring the gravy to a simmer in a saucepan over medium heat, stirring occasionally.

pecan- and cornmeal-crusted tempeh with coconut–sweet potato purée

This is a dish that makes me nostalgic for my childhood in Memphis, Tennessee. Flavors like pecans, sweet potatoes, and cornmeal help define Southern cuisine, and I love to incorporate them into my food now to bring a little bit of the South to southern California. One tip for making the potato purée as luxurious as possible: Be sure to purée the shredded coconut until it disappears into the sweet potatoes. Although the recipe calls for sweet potatoes, garnet yams would be a perfectly acceptable substitute. **Serves 4**

TEMPEH

½ cup tamari

¼ cup water

2 tablespoons minced garlic

2 tablespoons minced peeled fresh ginger

2 tablespoons pure maple syrup

2 teaspoons dried thyme

2 teaspoons toasted sesame oil

⅛ teaspoon cayenne pepper

2 (8-ounce) square packages grain-based tempeh, cut horizontally in half, then cut diagonally into 8 triangles

1 cup pecans

½ cup cornmeal

½ teaspoon fine sea salt

Pinch of ground white pepper

½ cup spelt flour

½ cup unsweetened soy milk

High-heat neutral cooking oil, for deep-frying

SWEET POTATOES

5 small beige-colored sweet potatoes (about 1½ pounds total), peeled and cut into about ¾-inch pieces

1 cup unsweetened coconut milk, warmed

¼ cup shredded unsweetened dried coconut, toasted

Sea salt and ground white pepper

Tempeh: Whisk the tamari, water, garlic, ginger, maple syrup, thyme, sesame oil, and cayenne in a heavy 12-inch frying pan. Add the tempeh pieces so that they are in a single layer. Bring to a boil over high heat, then decrease the heat to medium-low and simmer gently for 10 minutes, turning the tempeh slices over after the first 5 minutes. Remove the pan from the heat and set it aside until the mixture is cool, about 25 minutes.

Using the pulse button, finely chop the pecans in a food processor until they are as broken down as possible without turning them into a paste. (If you overprocess the nuts, their high oil content will turn them into a paste, so be careful not to do that.) Add the cornmeal and pulse until the mixture has a nice even texture without any large chunks of pecans. Add the salt and white pepper.

Place the spelt flour, soy milk, and cornmeal-pecan mixture in 3 separate pie plates. Working with 1 piece of cooled tempeh at a time, coat the tempeh triangles in the spelt flour, then dunk them in the soy milk, and finally, roll them in the cornmeal-pecan mixture to coat completely.

Pour enough oil into a large, heavy frying pan to reach a depth of 2 inches. Heat the oil over medium heat until it reaches 350°F on a deep-fry thermometer. Working in batches, fry the breaded tempeh triangles until they are crisp and golden brown, about 2 minutes per side. Transfer to paper towels to drain the excess oil.

Sweet Potatoes: Place the sweet potatoes in a large saucepan of water. Bring the water to a boil over high heat and cook the potatoes until they are tender, about 30 minutes. Drain well.

Place the sweet potatoes in a food processor or blender. With the machine running, add the coconut milk and the toasted shredded coconut and blend until the purée is as smooth as possible. Stop the machine and scrape down the sides of the bowl occasionally. Season to taste with salt and white pepper.

To Serve: Spoon the sweet potatoes onto plates and place the tempeh alongside.

Gluten-free foods have been gaining in popularity in recent years, as the incidence of gluten allergies and intolerance is on the rise, as is the number of people diagnosed with celiac disease, an autoimmune disorder caused by a reaction to the gluten in wheat. Although I don't have a gluten allergy or celiac disease, I have noticed a profound improvement in the way I feel after having made the decision to reduce the amount of wheat and gluten in my diet. Ever since I made that connection, I have sought out ways to adapt my favorite recipes to make them gluten-free.

It's not always easy, but it has gotten easier. There are many products on the market now that cater to the gluten-free diet, including gluten-free cake mixes, crackers, and cereals. More restaurants are including gluten-free items on their menus as well. What makes removing gluten from the diet difficult is that grains are used in the preparation of so many foods that it's easy to eat gluten without even realizing it, whether you're eating packaged foods or dining at restaurants that aren't yet

going gluten-free

onboard. Even when cooking at home, you need to be aware that gluten can show up in some unlikely places—tamari or veggie burgers, for example.

So just exactly what is gluten? It's a special type of protein that is commonly found in wheat, rye, and barley—flours that are predominant in our American diet. Luckily, not all foods from the grain family contain gluten. Rice, corn, buckwheat, millet, amaranth, quinoa, and teff are gluten-free. At one time, oats were thought to contain some gluten, but it's now clear that oats processed in machines that also processed wheat were cross-contaminated with gluten—causing very real allergic reactions for those who were the most sensitive to wheat. Read the label carefully to make sure the oats you're buying are gluten-free, and contact the manufacturer to ask if necessary; those who have reactions to gluten know that a single exposure can cause severe symptoms.

It's no question for those with allergies or celiac disease: Staying on a strict gluten-free diet is worth the effort. But even for those of you with milder sensitivities, avoiding gluten can dramatically improve your health and energy.

Bangers and Mash: Apple Sage Field Roast Grain Sausage with Mashed Potatoes and Celeriac Root

When my friend Scott had me over for lunch one day, he offered me a vegan sausage with mustard to accompany the beautiful salad he had made. I politely declined as I have never found faux sausages appealing. He insisted I try a bite, and I am so glad I was adventurous that day. I fell in love with this brand of grain-based links; I brought some home and started experimenting with how could I make it interesting for my family. Bangers and Mash is British pub food at its finest. This is a fantastic meal for cold winter nights, or when you have a hungry group to feed. Using the field roast sausages makes this so simple to prepare, but if you want to take the time, serving it with the gluten-free gravy from the Lentil Loaf (page 157) makes this dish out of this world. **Serves 4**

2 tablespoons olive oil

2 large Spanish onions, halved and thinly sliced

2 large red onions, halved and thinly sliced

3 cloves garlic, minced

½ teaspoon fine sea salt

¼ teaspoon freshly ground black pepper

1 tablespoon mirin

1 tablespoon tamari

4 fully cooked vegan apple-sage sausages (Field Roast brand), split lengthwise

Mashed Potatoes and Celeriac (recipe follows)

Savory Gluten-Free Gravy (page 157; optional)

Stone-ground mustard or Dijon mustard (optional)

Heat 1 tablespoon of the oil in a large, heavy frying pan over medium-high heat. Add the onions, garlic, salt, and pepper, and cook, stirring constantly, until the onions are almost tender, about 5 minutes. Stir in the mirin and tamari and cook, scraping the browned bits off the bottom of the pan, until the onions are pale golden brown, about 20 minutes.

Just before serving, heat the remaining 1 tablespoon oil in another large, heavy frying pan over medium-high heat. Add the sausages and cook until they are browned on both sides and heated through, about 1½ minutes per side.

Spoon the mashed potatoes and celeriac in the middle of each plate and top with a sausage and onions. Spoon the gravy over and serve with the mustard, if desired.

Mashed Potatoes and Celeriac Root

Serves 4

2 small heads celeriac (about 11 ounces total), peeled and cut into ½-inch dice

2 large russet potatoes or Yukon Gold potatoes (about 2 pounds total), peeled and cut into 1-inch chunks

3 tablespoons vegan butter

About ⅔ cup nondairy milk, warmed

2 teaspoons chopped fresh rosemary

2 teaspoons snipped fresh chives

Fine sea salt and freshly ground black pepper

Boil the celeriac in a large saucepan of salted water for 5 minutes. Add the potatoes and boil until the vegetables are tender, about 20 minutes longer. Drain well.

Return the potatoes and celeriac to the saucepan. Stir over medium-high heat until dry, about 2 minutes. Remove from the heat. Add the butter and mash until the vegetables are smooth. Add enough of the milk to moisten. Stir in 1 teaspoon of the rosemary and all of the chives. Season the mash to taste with salt and pepper.

Transfer the mash to a serving dish. Sprinkle with the remaining 1 teaspoon rosemary and serve immediately.

maple-Dijon Tempeh and vegetable stew

This is a lovely winter's stew that uses a variety of delicious colorful vegetables. The marinade for the tempeh does double-duty in this recipe, as it's later added to the vegetable stew to give it its rich flavor. This stew can be served over a simple whole-grain dish, like brown rice or quinoa. **Serves 4**

TEMPEH

⅓ cup tamari

¼ cup water

3 tablespoons pure maple syrup

2 tablespoons Dijon mustard

2 tablespoons minced garlic

2 tablespoons minced peeled fresh ginger

2 tablespoons chopped fresh thyme

4 teaspoons chopped fresh rosemary

2 teaspoons toasted sesame oil

1 teaspoon freshly ground black pepper

1 (8-ounce) package grain-based tempeh, cut into ½-inch cubes

STEW

2 tablespoons olive oil

1 large Spanish onion, diced

3 garlic cloves, minced

4 small purple potatoes (about 24 ounces total), peeled and cut into 1-inch cubes

2 large garnet yams (about 18 ounces total), peeled and cut into 1-inch cubes

2 medium carrots, peeled, roll-cut (see page 174)

2 parsnips, peeled, roll-cut (see page 174)

2 celery stalks, thickly sliced

1 fennel bulb, diced

2½ cups water, plus more as needed

Freshly ground black pepper

Tempeh: Whisk the tamari, water, maple syrup, mustard, garlic, ginger, thyme, rosemary, sesame oil, and black pepper in a medium bowl to blend. Add the tempeh and toss to coat. Cover and marinate at room temperature, tossing occasionally, for at least 30 minutes, or cover and refrigerate up to overnight.

Stew: Heat the oil in a large, heavy pot over medium-high heat. Add the onion and garlic and sauté until the onion is tender, about 4 minutes. Add the potatoes, yams, carrots, parsnips, celery, and fennel. Cook until the vegetables release their juices, about 5 minutes. Add the 2½ cups water, the marinated tempeh, and the marinade. Decrease the heat to medium-low.

Cover and simmer gently, stirring gently and occasionally, until the vegetables become tender, about 25 minutes. Add more water to create enough sauce to coat the vegetables, if necessary. Season to taste with pepper.

Quality pots and pans are a substantial investment, but one that will pay you back with many years of sturdy service. If you take care of them, they will last for a lifetime—perhaps longer, as is evidenced by the colander that was passed on to me by my grandmother. The best-quality stainless steel pots will often have bottoms lined with either aluminum or copper to conduct heat, and the heavy gauge of the stainless steel itself will help to hold the heat and cook your food at an even and consistent temperature.

Cast iron and enameled cast iron are other types of pots well worth the investment. These pots, the best of

pots and pans

which are made by Le Creuset and Staub, are the gold-medal winners in the area of slow-cooking, a technique favored in many of the recipes in this book.

While all cooks want to use pots and pans with a high-heat capacity, there are some environmental factors to consider as well. Materials with high thermal conductivity—including stainless steel, cast iron, and copper—not only heat up faster, thereby requiring less gas or electricity to cook your food, but also distribute heat more evenly. Heavier pots contain more metal than thinner ones, so they hold heat better, which is great for cooking grains and vegetables.

Although these can be expensive items, they don't have to break the bank. It helps to build your collection one piece at a time. Department stores will periodically put high-quality pots and pans on sale, and there are many places online to look for great deals too.

Lasagna Rolls with Tofu Ricotta and Everyday Tomato Sauce

This is a fun way to serve lasagna: Instead of the traditional layering, you top the individual noodles with a vegan ricotta cheese and vegetable mixture and roll it up. My tofu ricotta cheese is a blend of tofu, miso, and tahini, which creates a creamy consistency that easily spreads. The tomato sauce takes no more than 10 minutes to make; if there is any left over, use it the next day over rice or noodles. **Serves 6 (makes 12 rolls)**

2½ tablespoons olive oil

2 onions, thinly sliced

6 cloves garlic, minced

2 tablespoons chopped fresh basil

1 teaspoon fine sea salt

½ teaspoon freshly ground black pepper

3 medium carrots, peeled and cut into ¼-inch pieces

2 zucchini, cut into ¼-inch pieces

1 head broccoli, stems removed and florets finely chopped

2 cups Tofu Ricotta Cheese (recipe follows)

12 eggless lasagna noodles

3 cups Everyday Tomato Sauce (recipe follows)

Preheat the oven to 350°F.

Heat 1 tablespoon of the oil in a large, heavy frying pan over medium-high heat. Add the onions, garlic, basil, salt, and pepper. Sauté until the onions are tender, about 10 minutes. Add the carrots, zucchini, and broccoli and sauté until the carrots are crisp-tender, about 12 minutes. Let cool completely. Mix the vegetable mixture into the tofu ricotta cheese.

Cook the noodles in a large pot of boiling salted water, stirring often, until tender, about 10 minutes. Drain and rinse the noodles, then toss them with 1 tablespoon of the remaining oil to prevent the noodles from sticking together.

Coat a 13 by 9 by 2-inch baking dish with the remaining 1½ teaspoons oil. Spread 1 cup of the tomato sauce on the bottom of the dish. Using a spatula, spread about ½ cup of the vegetable mixture over each lasagna sheet, leaving about ½ inch of each end uncovered. Roll up each sheet tightly and place it seam-side-down in the baking dish. Pour the remaining 2 cups tomato sauce over the lasagna rolls.

Cover the dish with aluminum foil. Bake until the sauce bubbles, about 55 minutes. Remove the foil and continue baking for 15 minutes.

Using a spatula, spread about ½ cup of the vegetable mixture over each lasagna sheet, leaving about ½ inch of each end uncovered. Roll up each sheet tightly and place it seam-side-down in the baking dish.

TOFU RICOTTA CHEESE

When blended, the tofu gives this vegan cheese a creamy consistency that resembles ricotta. This recipe is borrowed from my first book, *The Real Food Daily Cookbook*—when you have a good recipe, why change it? **Makes about 3 cups**

1 (14-ounce) container water-packed firm tofu, drained and cut into quarters

⅔ cup yellow miso

⅔ cup water

½ cup tahini

¼ cup olive oil

5 large garlic cloves

1½ teaspoons dried basil

1½ teaspoons dried oregano

¾ teaspoon sea salt

Blend all the ingredients in a food processor until smooth.

The cheese will keep for 2 days, covered and refrigerated.

EVERYDAY TOMATO SAUCE

This is a perfect, simple tomato sauce. The key is to use canned crushed tomatoes, easily found in a grocery or natural foods store. Eden and Glen Muir are my favorite brands because they are organic. **Makes about 4 cups**

¼ cup extra-virgin olive oil

4 shallots, thinly sliced

3 cloves garlic, minced

½ teaspoon fine sea salt

1 (28-ounce) can crushed tomatoes

1 cup water

2 tablespoons chopped fresh basil

1 teaspoon chopped fresh oregano

Heat the olive oil in a heavy saucepan over medium-high heat. Add the shallots, garlic, and salt and sauté until fragrant, about 20 seconds. Stir in the tomatoes and the 1 cup water. Bring to a gentle simmer, then decrease the heat to low and simmer gently, stirring occasionally, for 20 minutes, to allow the flavors to blend. Stir in the basil and oregano. Remove from the heat.

plant proteins

Real food pantry

Plant proteins are an essential component of a healthful meatless diet, and well worth adding to any diet. They bring complex carbohydrates, fiber, texture, and flavor to the plate. Plant proteins are satisfying and hearty, lending heft to salads, soups, and side dishes. Read on for more about such plant proteins as beans and soy products, and remember that nuts are rich in protein, too.

DRIED BEANS, PEAS, AND LENTILS ARE COLLECTIVELY CALLED LEGUMES. Beans are high in complex carbohydrates, fiber, iron, and folic acid; they have more protein than any other vegetable food. There are many high-quality, organic canned beans available, but if you have the time, it's worthwhile to prepare dried beans from scratch. Although it requires lengthy soaking (which just means planning ahead), making your own beans allows you to control the amount of salt you use, and eliminates the need for any stabilizers or preservatives.

For a long time I didn't eat beans—no particular reason, they just fell out of favor with me. When I reintroduced them to my diet, I fell in love with them all over again; it was like I was reunited with an old friend. They are so satisfying because they are simple and accessible: It doesn't take much to make them flavorful.

You'll find beans throughout my book, starring in such soups as Adzuki Bean Soup (page 90) or Black-Eyed Pea and Red Pepper Soup (page 101); in heartier dishes like my Pinto Bean Enchiladas (page 142) and South American Stew (page 148); and married with vegetables in the Cool French Lentil and Fennel Salad (page 190).

SOYBEANS are higher in fat and protein than any other bean; they are also the most difficult to digest due to an enzyme called the trypsin inhibitor. Soaking, cooking, and fermenting soybeans destroys their trypsin inhibitor, which is why soybeans are available as the following products:

EDAMAME are young, green soybeans in the pod that are picked before they ripen (and before the trypsin inhibitor is fully engaged). They can be found in the freezer section, and purchased both in and out of their shells. When you're cooking for kids, I recommend buying edamame in the shell and boiling them in salted water. Even young children seem to enjoy peeling and eating them.

TEMPEH is a fermented soybean cake; it's higher in protein, dietary fiber, and vitamins than tofu. It also has a firmer texture and stronger flavor. Tempeh is a great choice for people who have difficulty digesting plant-based high-protein foods like beans or tofu. Try it in my Maple-Dijon Tempeh and Vegetable Stew (page 164); in my Watercress and Butter Lettuce Salad with Israeli Couscous, Orange-Basil Tempeh, and Sweet Miso Dressing (page 128); and, of course, in my Maple Tempeh Bacon (page 25).

TOFU OR BEAN CURD is made by coagulating soy milk, and then pressing the resulting curds into blocks. Tofu has very little flavor or smell on its own, so it can be used either in savory or sweet dishes, and is often seasoned or marinated to suit the dish.

Tofu has gotten a bad reputation over the decades for being at the center of some very drab vegetarian cooking, but I can assure you that it is a highly versatile ingredient that can be quite tasty. You'll see by trying it in my Tofu Scramble with Caramelized Onion and Sun-Dried Tomatoes (page 22), using it as a base for my creamy Chipotle Ranch Dressing (page 112), creating a Tofu Chèvre (page 109), or baking my delicious Chocolate Silk Pie with Cashew Crust (page 237).

Red Bean and Seasoned Tempeh Chili with Double-corn Jalapeño Corn Bread

Growing up, I loved chili and corn bread. My favorite bowls of chili were found in small-town restaurants and roadside diners. Once I became vegetarian, replacing the meat wasn't difficult; it was the luscious, almost creamy texture that was hard to re-create. This recipe is the answer to how to take one of my favorite dishes from childhood, and make it vegan. The addition of beer is an optional adult spin; it can easily be replaced with either vegetable stock or water. The touch of maple syrup darkens the tomato juices, giving them a rich brown color and deeper flavor. **Serves 6 to 8**

2 tablespoons olive oil

1 onion, finely diced

2 medium carrots, peeled and cut into ½-inch dice

1 tablespoon plus 2 teaspoons minced garlic

2 celery stalks, cut into ½-inch dice

1 red bell pepper, cut into ½-inch dice

1 small jalapeño chile, minced

1 (15-ounce) can red kidney beans, with liquid

1 (14½-ounce) can whole tomatoes, with juices, puréed

2 cups water

2 teaspoons dried oregano

2 teaspoons ground cumin

1½ teaspoons chili powder

1¼ teaspoons fine sea salt

2 (8-ounce) packages tempeh

1 teaspoon crushed red pepper

1 (12-ounce) bottle pale ale beer

2 teaspoons pure maple syrup

½ cup finely chopped fresh cilantro

Heat 1 tablespoon of the oil in a heavy pot over medium heat. Add the onion, carrots, and 1 tablespoon of the garlic and sauté until the onion is tender, about 5 minutes. Add the celery, red bell pepper, and jalapeño chile. Sauté until the bell pepper is crisp-tender, about 5 minutes. Add the canned beans and their liquid, puréed tomatoes, water, oregano, cumin, 1 teaspoon of the chili powder, and 1 teaspoon of the salt. Cover and simmer, stirring occasionally, until the vegetables are tender and the flavors blend, about 15 minutes.

Meanwhile, using a food processor fitted with the grater attachment, or a cheese grater, grate the tempeh. Toss the grated tempeh in a medium bowl with the remaining 2 teaspoons garlic, ½ teaspoon chili powder, ¼ teaspoon salt, and the crushed red pepper.

Heat the remaining 1 tablespoon oil in a large, heavy sauté pan over medium-high heat. Add the tempeh mixture and sauté until golden brown, about 8 minutes. Add the beer and stir to scrape up any bits from the bottom of the pan.

Stir the tempeh mixture into the chili beans. Add the maple syrup. Bring to a simmer over medium heat. Decrease the heat to medium-low and simmer gently, uncovered and stirring occasionally, until the mixture thickens and the flavors blend, about 1 hour. Stir in the cilantro. Ladle into individual bowls and serve with large pieces of Double-Corn Jalapeño Corn Bread.

The chili can be made 2 days ahead. Let cool, then cover and refrigerate. It will thicken overnight, so add a little water to it while rewarming it in a saucepan over medium-low heat.

DOUBLE-CORN JALAPEÑO CORN BREAD
Every chili needs a partner in corn bread. This one is quick and easy—it's my basic go-to corn bread recipe spiced with jalapeños and enhanced by fresh corn kernels. If you don't eat it all at the first serving, make sure you refrigerate it, as it doesn't keep long. **Serves 6 to 8**

1½ teaspoons plus ¾ cup neutral cooking oil

3 cups yellow cornmeal

1 cup whole-wheat pastry flour or all-purpose flour

3½ teaspoons baking powder

½ teaspoon fine sea salt

1½ cups water

8 ounces vacuum-packed soft silken tofu (such as Mori-Nu)

¾ cup pure maple syrup

1½ cups fresh corn kernels, or frozen corn kernels, thawed

2 tablespoons minced jalapeño chiles

Preheat the oven to 350°F. Coat a 9 by 9-inch square nonstick metal baking pan with 1½ teaspoons of the oil.

Sift the cornmeal, flour, baking powder, and salt into a large bowl. Set aside.

Blend the water, tofu, maple syrup, and the remaining ¾ cup oil in a blender until smooth. Stir the tofu mixture into the cornmeal mixture to blend. Fold in the corn kernels and jalapeño chiles. Transfer the batter to the prepared pan.

Bake for 40 to 45 minutes, until the corn bread is pale golden and cracked on top, and a toothpick inserted into the center of the bread comes out clean. Cut the bread into squares and serve warm.

CUTTING TECHNIQUES

ROLL CUTS are excellent for hard, long vegetables like carrots, daikon, and parsnips. Place the vegetable on the cutting board at an angle and make a diagonal cut to remove the first piece. Roll the vegetable halfway over (180 degrees) and slice through on the same diagonal. Repeat for the rest of the vegetable.

κung pαo τofu and vegetables

Prepare steamed brown rice to serve as a simple backdrop for the plentiful flavors in this spicy Asian-inspired dish. If you think you'd like it even hotter, try adding more crushed red pepper. **Serves 4**

TOFU

3 tablespoons tamari

⅓ cup water

3 tablespoons pure maple syrup

1½ tablespoons toasted sesame oil

1 tablespoon minced garlic

1 tablespoon minced peeled fresh ginger

1 teaspoon chili powder

1 teaspoon paprika

¾ teaspoon crushed red pepper

½ teaspoon fine sea salt

1 (14-ounce) container extra-firm tofu, drained and cut into ¾-inch cubes

STIR-FRY

2 tablespoons coconut oil

1 yellow onion, cut into 1-inch dice

½ head broccoli, trimmed into large florets

1 red bell pepper, cut into ¾-inch dice

1 large carrot, peeled and cut into thick half-moons

5 ounces sugar snap peas, trimmed

1½ tablespoons arrowroot, dissolved in 3 tablespoons water

½ cup shelled roasted peanuts

Cooked Short-Grain Brown Rice (page 180)

Tofu: Whisk the tamari, water, maple syrup, garlic, ginger, chili powder, paprika, crushed red pepper, and salt in a shallow casserole dish to blend. Add the tofu cubes and toss gently to coat. Let marinate for at least 30 minutes at room temperature, or cover and refrigerate up to overnight.

Stir-Fry: Heat the coconut oil in a large, heavy wok or sauté pan over medium-high heat. Add the onion, broccoli, bell pepper, carrot, and snap peas to the wok and stir-fry until the vegetables are crisp-tender, about 2 minutes. Stir in the tofu and its marinade. Drizzle the arrowroot mixture over the tofu mixture and stir-fry until the sauce simmers and thickens slightly and the tofu is heated through, about 3 minutes. Stir in ¼ cup of the peanuts.

To Serve: Transfer the stir-fry to a platter and sprinkle with the remaining ¼ cup peanuts. Serve with the rice.

super vegetable
Dinner smoothie

When the day is long and I've spent many hours in the kitchen cooking for others, sometimes I just don't feel like eating much. I know I don't really want to skip a meal, as I don't want to find myself rummaging through my fridge at midnight, eating all the wrong things. I want nutrients and I want flavor, but I'm just too tired to chew. It's on nights like these that I'll whip up this one-blender wonder, which I call my Super Vegetable Dinner Smoothie. **Serves 1**

6 ounces unsweetened coconut water (not coconut milk)

4 kale leaves, stemmed and coarsely chopped

1 small cucumber, peeled and coarsely chopped

1 celery stalk, coarsely chopped

½ medium carrot, peeled and shaved with a potato peeler

½ red bell pepper, coarsely chopped

½ avocado, peeled and pitted

¼ cup dried dulse (see page 198)

2 tablespoons fresh lemon juice

1 tablespoon chopped fresh cilantro

1 tablespoon white or yellow miso

1 clove garlic, chopped

Blend all of the ingredients together in a high-powered blender on high speed until smooth. The mixture should have body and a beautiful light to medium green color.

Variations: Be imaginative when making your own dinner smoothies: Explore which textures and flavors work best for your palate and appetite. Here are a few substitutions and alternative ingredients to try, based on much experimentation. You could add one or more of these ingredients to the mix, or leave out any one or two ingredients from the recipe. The important part is that it tastes good to you.

- Lettuce, collard greens, green chard, or watercress, instead of kale
- Zucchini instead of celery
- Fresh orange or lime juice instead of lemon juice
- Fresh dill, basil, or your favorite herb instead of cilantro
- Pinch of sea salt instead of miso
- One-half to one whole cored peeled apple
- Soaked flaxseeds (page 11) or soaked almonds (page 11)
- Grated peeled fresh ginger
- Pinch of cayenne
- Pinch of ground cumin
- Shredded peeled raw beets

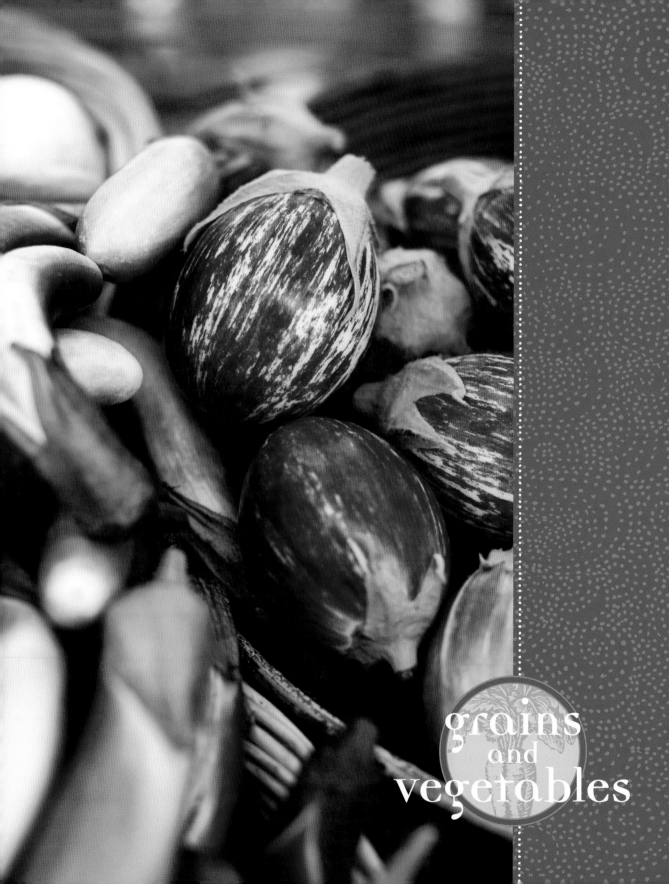

grains
and
vegetables

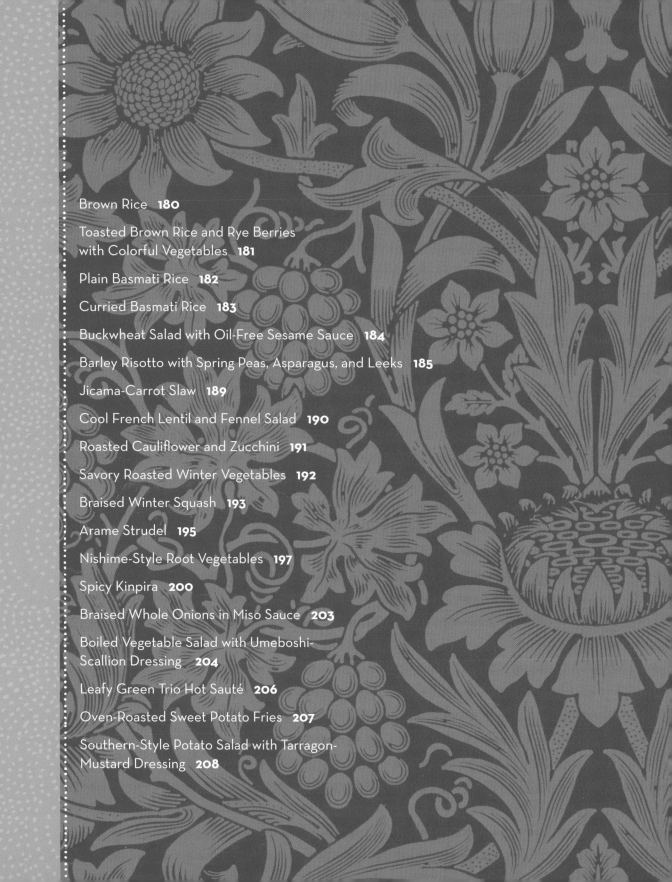

grains and vegetables

Your mother always told you to eat your vegetables, and she was right, of course. It's no secret that vegetables are the key to good health: They contain a wide variety of vitamins, minerals, and other plant compounds known to offer disease-reducing benefits. Vegetables are low in fat and calories, which means you can eat a lot of them without overdoing it. They're a good source of dietary fiber, which makes you feel fuller for longer.

Vegetables are also one of the strongest connections between consumers and farmers. When you hold a vegetable in your hand, you might not know exactly who grew it—but you know it came from the earth, and you know that it's a whole food. Cooking vegetables is a creative endeavor, with the varied, bright, and fresh colors and flavors of each season's best produce. The right cutting and cooking techniques also help to make each ingredient shine. You'll find inspiration in several of my favorite vegetable dishes, such as Roasted Cauliflower and Zucchini (page 191), Braised Winter Squash (page 193), and my down-home Leafy Green Trio Hot Sauté (page 206).

I'm here not only to back up your mother on the topic of vegetables, but also to add whole grains to your must-eat list. Eating vegetables goes hand in hand with eating whole grains—sometimes in the same bite, as I love to add vegetables to my whole-grain dishes to give them more color and texture. The most important thing to understand about grains is the difference between their whole and processed forms. There has been much hype aimed at convincing the public that we can get our daily servings of whole grains from a box of cereal or from fortified breads. While one can get a little in the way of whole grains from these foods, in my view, they're too processed to be considered wholesome.

Much more healthful and satisfying options include bowls of whole grains like Curried Basmati Rice (page 183) and Buckwheat Salad with Oil-Free Sesame Sauce (page 184). With the recipes in this chapter as your guide, whole grains are easily made into delicious and nutritious additions to your meal.

Brown Rice

This recipe shows you how to cook a basic pot of brown rice. You may use any variety of brown rice, including short-grain, long-grain, or medium-grain, often called golden rose. You might also experiment with some of the exotic Asian rice like Bhutanese, brown Kalijira, Forbidden, or Jade Pearl, which can be found at natural foods stores and gourmet foods shops. Their names alone make me want to cook a pot of rice daily. **Serves 4 to 6 (makes about 6 cups)**

2 cups brown rice, rinsed well

3½ cups water

¼ teaspoon sea salt

Combine the rice, water, and salt in a large, heavy saucepan. Bring to a boil, then decrease the heat to low. Cover and simmer gently, without stirring, for 35 minutes, or until the rice is tender and the liquid is absorbed. Remove from the heat. Let stand, covered, for 5 minutes. Uncover and fluff the rice with a fork. Cover and let stand for 5 minutes longer. Fluff the rice again and serve.

Toasted Brown Rice and Rye Berries with Colorful Vegetables

As much as I love a simple bowl of brown rice, I also enjoy taking my rice to the next level by combining it with other grains, and adding bits of vegetables, spices, and herbs. Adding rye berries (or wheat berries, which work equally well) lends a bit of a surprise, as they are chewier than rice. These berries are the whole grain before it's processed into flour; rye and wheat berries have almost been forgotten as most people settle for bread over whole grains. Toasting the grains before steaming creates a nutty aroma and a fluffy texture. **Serves 4 to 6 (makes about 7⅓ cups)**

1½ cups short-grain brown rice, rinsed well

½ cup rye berries or wheat berries, rinsed well

3½ cups water

¼ teaspoon plus ⅛ teaspoon fine sea salt

1 teaspoon olive oil

1 clove garlic, minced

1 medium carrot, peeled and finely diced

1 celery stalk, finely diced

Kernels from 2 ears of corn, or ½ cup frozen corn kernels

1 tablespoon minced fresh dill

Heat a large (9½- to 10½-inch) cast-iron skillet over medium-low heat to allow the skillet to get hot, but not smoking, about 2 minutes. Add the rice and rye berries. Using a long-handled rice paddle or a square-tipped wooden spoon, move the grains around in the skillet as they cook, until the rice eventually turns a warm golden color and the rye berries are lightly browned (they will already be a darker brown color than the rice), about 12 minutes.

Meanwhile, combine the water and ¼ teaspoon of the salt in a large, heavy saucepan and bring to a boil over high heat. Lower the heat to a simmer, then slowly add the toasted rice and rye berries. Cover and simmer gently, without stirring, for 35 minutes, or until the grains are tender and the liquid is absorbed. Remove the pan

from the heat. Let stand, covered, for 5 minutes. Uncover and fluff the rice with a fork. Cover and let stand for 5 minutes longer.

Heat the oil in a heavy sauté pan over medium heat. Add the garlic and cook until it is warm and fragrant, about 20 seconds. Add the carrot, celery, corn, and the remaining ⅛ teaspoon salt and sauté until the vegetables are tender, about 3 minutes.

Transfer the cooked grains to a serving bowl and add the vegetables and dill. Fluff the rice with a fork, gently mixing in the vegetables and dill, and serve.

plain basmati rice

My Tomato-Lemon Rice Soup (page 93) calls for fragrant rice such as basmati, and the recipe below details the perfect way to cook it. I like to use less water than many whole-grain recipes call for, and I prefer to boil the water first and then add the grain to assure a light, fluffy texture. Jasmine rice is another fragrant variety that could easily be used in place of basmati. It, too, is sold as brown or white rice. If eating brown rice is a new experience for you or your family, you'll find that starting with these lighter grains can ease you into enjoying whole grains. **Serves 4 (makes about 4 cups)**

3½ cups water

2 cups brown basmati rice, rinsed well

¼ teaspoon fine sea salt

Bring the water to a boil in a large, heavy saucepan over high heat. Add the rice and salt, then return the water to a boil. Decrease the heat to low, cover, and simmer gently for about 35 minutes, or until the rice is tender and all the liquid is absorbed. Fluff the rice with a fork and serve.

curried Basmati Rice

Once again, this is a dressed-up alternative to plain and simple rice. Here, I add a warm mix of spices to basmati rice, showcasing its Indian heritage. **Serves 4 to 6 (makes about 5½ cups)**

1 tablespoon olive oil or neutral cooking oil

2 cloves garlic, minced

½ teaspoon curry powder

¼ teaspoon ground cumin

1 small onion, diced

½ teaspoon fine sea salt

2 cups brown basmati rice, rinsed well

3½ cups water

1 cinnamon stick

1 cup frozen green peas, thawed, or shelled fresh green peas

Heat the oil in a large, heavy saucepan over medium-high heat until it becomes hot. Add the garlic, curry, and cumin and sauté for a few seconds, or until fragrant. Add the onion and ¼ teaspoon of the salt, then decrease the heat to low and cook, stirring occasionally, for 5 minutes, or until the onion is translucent. Add the rice and toss until the rice is coated with the oil and spices. Add the water, cinnamon stick, and the remaining ¼ teaspoon salt.

Bring to a boil over high heat, then decrease the heat to low, cover, and simmer gently for about 30 minutes, or until the rice is tender and all the liquid is absorbed. Scatter the peas over the rice, then cover again and allow the peas to steam for 2 minutes. Transfer the mixture to a serving dish and remove the cinnamon stick. Using a fork, gently fluff the rice to loosen the grains and mix in the peas. Serve.

buckwheat salad with oil-free sesame sauce

Buckwheat groats are the hulled, crushed kernels of buckwheat seeds; they have a slight green hue to them, and a fresh, grassy flavor. Once buckwheat groats are preroasted, they are called "kasha," and have a deeper, nuttier flavor. This recipe calls for the addition of Sweet Mustard Tempeh (page 116); you could substitute either the Maple Tempeh Bacon (page 25) or the Tamari Pan-Roasted Pepitas (page 54), if you like. The sesame sauce is quick to make, and it brings some of my favorite flavors together. Spoon a little sauce over each serving, or go ahead and dress the whole dish with it. **Serves 4 to 6**

SAUCE

⅓ cup sesame seeds

¼ cup water

2 tablespoons mirin

2 tablespoons rice vinegar

1 tablespoon umeboshi vinegar

2 teaspoons tamari

SALAD

1¾ cups water

1 cup buckwheat groats

½ teaspoon fine sea salt

2 small Persian cucumbers, quartered lengthwise, then diced into ⅛-inch-thick pieces

4 radishes, quartered, then thinly diced

½ cup sauerkraut, drained and coarsely chopped

Sweet Mustard Tempeh (page 116)

Sauce: Place the sesame seeds in a fine-meshed strainer and rinse them under cold running water. Set aside to drain well.

Blend the water, mirin, vinegars, and tamari in a blender until well blended. Add the sesame seeds and pulse just until the seeds break up but are still visible. Set aside.

Salad: Bring the water to a boil in a heavy saucepan over high heat. Add the buckwheat and salt and return to a boil. Cover and simmer over medium-low heat until all the water is absorbed and the buckwheat is tender, about 20 minutes. Fluff with a fork, then transfer the buckwheat to a baking sheet to cool.

Add the cucumbers, radishes, sauerkraut, and tempeh to the buckwheat. Spoon the salad onto plates. Drizzle a spoonful of the sesame sauce over each serving.

Barley Risotto with Spring Peas, Asparagus, and Leeks

Barley is a whole grain that comes in two forms; be sure to choose the pearled barley over the hulled. Consider soaking the barley overnight so that the grain will be soft when you cook it. Like any good risotto, this dish requires attention during cooking, and it's best served immediately, when it's soft and creamy. If you have leftovers, they're great for making into risotto cakes. **Serves 4 to 6**

¼ cup olive oil

2 leeks (white and pale green parts only), finely diced

2 teaspoons fine sea salt

1½ cups pearl barley

¾ cup dry white wine

About 5½ cups hot water

¼ cup finely chopped fresh parsley

1 tablespoon freshly grated lemon zest (from 2 lemons)

1 teaspoon freshly ground black pepper

6 ounces thin asparagus, tough ends trimmed and stalks cut diagonally into 1½-inch pieces

10 ounces frozen peas, thawed, or 1½ cups shelled fresh peas

Heat the olive oil in a large, heavy saucepan over medium heat. Add the leeks and sprinkle with 1 teaspoon of the salt. Sauté until the leeks are tender, about 6 minutes. Add the barley and stir to coat the barley with the leeks and oil. Add the wine and simmer over medium heat, stirring constantly, until most of the wine has been absorbed, about 3 minutes. Using a small ladle, add the hot water, about 2 ladlefuls at a time, and stir almost constantly between additions, waiting for the water to be absorbed before adding more. After the barley has cooked for 25 minutes, stir in the parsley, lemon zest, pepper, and the remaining 1 teaspoon salt. Continue cooking and adding the water, stirring almost constantly, until the barley is tender but still firm, about 20 minutes longer.

Meanwhile, cook the asparagus in a large pot of boiling salted water until al dente, about 1 minute. Using a slotted spoon, remove the asparagus from the boiling water and transfer the pieces to a bowl of ice water to cool. Repeat with the peas.

Stir the asparagus and peas into the finished risotto and cook just until they are heated through. Serve immediately.

whole grains

As the health benefits of choosing whole grains over highly processed grains have hit the mainstream, we're now more aware than ever that whole grains are a very important part of any diet. By definition, whole grains have not been refined, and therefore their bran, which contains fiber, B vitamins, and trace minerals, is intact. It's no wonder that whole grains have been important staple foods for most cultures since ancient times.

In our modern world, most whole grains are processed into flour. (For more on whole-grain flours, see page 220.) However, it is more nutritious—and simpler—to eat them in their original state. I use cooked whole grains in several of my recipes, from the brown rice in my Tomato-Lemon Rice Soup (page 93) to the millet in my Lentil Loaf with Savory Gluten-Free Gravy (page 156) to making a tabbouleh with quinoa in my Grecian Goddess Salad (page 130). Below are some of my favorite go-to whole grains; these four are gluten-free, and one of them is always on my table.

Basmati rice is a variety of long-grain rice grown in India and Pakistan. While it is available in white and brown varieties, I urge you to seek out and purchase brown basmati, as it retains its exterior hull, providing greater nutrition and fiber. Basmati rice is known for its aromatic fragrance and delicate flavor, which is why I love using it. It's also gluten-free. On page 182, you'll find instructions for cooking basmati rice, plus a simple recipe for Curried Basmati Rice.

BROWN RICE, whether long-grain or short-grain, is the most balanced of all the whole grains and is also gluten-free. Brown rice is my go-to whole-grain dish, and I'm not alone. In some parts of the world, the verb *to eat* literally means "to eat rice"— rice supplies as much as half of the daily calories for half of the world's population. When you're preparing rice, it makes nutritional sense to *always* choose brown rice: The process that produces brown rice removes only the outermost layer of the rice kernel and is the least damaging to its nutritional value. The conversion of brown rice into white rice destroys most of the vitamins and minerals and all of the dietary fiber and essential fatty acids. In fact, fully milled and polished white rice is required to be enriched with vitamins B1 and B3 and iron to give it some nutritional value. You'll find brown rice in many recipes throughout this book, including my Black Bean Veggie Burgers (page 118).

MILLET is a small non-glutinous grain (or seed) that has a sweet, nutty flavor; it's one of the oldest foods known to humans, and it has been used in Africa and India as a staple food for thousands of years. If millet looks like birdseed to you, that's because it often is the main ingredient in such mixes. The fact that millet is used to feed livestock makes it another example of the wisdom in eating lower on the food chain: Millet contains protein and fiber; several B-complex vitamins; and such minerals as magnesium, manganese, and phosphorus, among others. Millet can be steamed and served as you would rice, made into a breakfast porridge, or used as an ingredient in breads. I use it in my Sesame-Hiziki Croquettes (page 134), among other recipes.

QUINOA is another seed that is usually considered a grain. It has a mild nutty flavor and a light, fluffy texture but retains a slight crunch even when steamed. A good source of protein, quinoa is also rich in vitamins, minerals, and fiber. Quinoa originated in the Andes thousands of years ago; the Incas, who held the crop to be sacred, referred to quinoa as the mother grain. Quinoa is gluten-free and can be served steamed as an alternative to rice.

jicama-carrot slaw

"Quick, easy, cheap"—those are three words you sometimes want to hear in your kitchen, and they describe this fresh slaw perfectly. **Serves 6 to 8 (makes about 4 cups)**

Juice of 1 lime (about 2 tablespoons)

1 tablespoon agave nectar or pure maple syrup

1 tablespoon apple cider vinegar

½ teaspoon fine sea salt

⅛ teaspoon chili powder

1 (1½-pound) head jicama, peeled and coarsely shredded (about 4 cups)

1 medium carrot, peeled and coarsely shredded (about ¼ cup)

½ small white onion, finely diced (about ½ cup)

3 tablespoons minced fresh cilantro

Whisk the lime juice, agave nectar, vinegar, salt, and chili powder in a large bowl to blend. Add the jicama, carrot, onion, and cilantro and toss to coat with the dressing. Cover and refrigerate until cold, tossing occasionally, about 1 hour.

Pictured (left) with Southern-Style Potato Salad with Tarragon-Mustard Dressing, page 208.

cool french lentil and fennel salad

For this recipe, make sure to finely dice the vegetables so that their size is uniform with the lentils. The best, most delicate lentils are the peppery French green lentils; both their color and their flavor make them special. Lentils require no soaking and they cook quickly, making them less time-consuming to prepare than most dried legumes. **Serves 4 to 6 (makes about 6 cups)**

3 cups water

1 cup dried French lentils, sorted and rinsed

1 bay leaf

3 tablespoons olive oil

2 tablespoons red wine vinegar

2 cloves garlic, minced

2 teaspoons Dijon mustard

½ teaspoon dried dill

1 small white onion, finely diced (about ½ cup)

3 celery stalks, finely diced (about 1 cup)

1 cucumber, peeled, seeded, and finely diced (about 1 cup)

½ cup fresh or frozen corn kernels, lightly steamed, then cooled

⅓ cup finely diced fennel

Fine sea salt and freshly ground black pepper

Combine the water, lentils, and bay leaf in a large, heavy saucepan and bring to a boil over high heat. Decrease the heat to medium-low, then cover and simmer, stirring occasionally, for 20 minutes, or until the lentils are tender. Drain, remove the bay leaf, and let the lentils cool completely.

Whisk the oil, vinegar, garlic, mustard, and dill in a large bowl to blend. Add the cooled lentils, the onion, celery, cucumber, corn, and fennel. Toss to combine. Season to taste with salt and pepper and serve.

Roasted cauliflower and zucchini

Roasting is so easy—and it yields juicy vegetables that keep their shape and vibrant color. While imparting a slightly smoky sweetness to vegetables, roasting also concentrates their wonderful flavors. Cauliflower is one of my all-time favorite vegetables, and I find that everyone else likes it, too. This is an easy and accessible dish to make year-round. **Serves 4 to 6**

1 head cauliflower, cut into medium florets

3 zucchini, quartered lengthwise and cut into 3- to 4-inch lengths

2 tablespoons olive oil

1 teaspoon fine sea salt

¼ teaspoon freshly ground black pepper

Preheat the oven to 400°F. Lightly oil a large, heavy rimmed baking sheet.

Place the cauliflower and zucchini on the baking sheet, then drizzle the 2 tablespoons oil over the vegetables and roll the vegetables on the sheet until they are well coated with the oil. Sprinkle with the salt and pepper.

Bake for 15 to 20 minutes, until the vegetables are tender and beginning to brown.

savory roasted winter vegetables

I prefer cutting the vegetables for this recipe into large pieces, so that you can really experience the soft, warm, perfectly roasted essence of each one. To make this dish during the warmer months, use spring or summer vegetables, instead. **Serves 4 to 6**

¼ cup olive oil

2 teaspoons balsamic vinegar

4 cloves garlic, minced

1 tablespoon chopped fresh thyme

2 teaspoons minced fresh rosemary

1½ teaspoons fine sea salt

½ teaspoon freshly ground black pepper

½ kabocha squash (about 1¾ pounds), or 1 small butternut squash, peeled, halved, seeded, and cut into 1-inch chunks

2 small yams (red-skinned sweet potatoes; about 14 ounces total), peeled and cut lengthwise into 1-inch pieces

3 medium carrots (about 10 ounces total), peeled and cut into 1-inch rounds

2 large parsnips (about 8 ounces total), peeled and cut into 1-inch rounds

12 ounces Brussels sprouts, ends trimmed and sprouts halved

1 red onion, cut into ½-inch-thick rounds

Preheat the oven to 400°F. Line 2 large, heavy rimmed baking sheets with parchment paper.

Whisk the oil, vinegar, garlic, herbs, salt, and pepper in a large bowl to blend. Add the squash, yams, carrots, parsnips, Brussels sprouts, and onion. Toss to coat. Arrange the vegetable mixture evenly over the prepared baking sheets.

Roast, stirring every 20 minutes, for 45 minutes, or until the vegetables are tender and beginning to brown.

Transfer the roasted vegetables to a platter and serve.

Braised winter squash

This dish is a perfect example of how naturally sweet orange squashes can be. Any of the many winter squashes, such as acorn, delicata, Hubbard, kabocha, or Red Kuri, can stand in for the most popular winter squash of all: the butternut. **Serves 4**

2 (2-pound) butternut squash (or acorn or kabocha squash)

2 tablespoons olive oil

1 tablespoon minced garlic

1½ teaspoons minced peeled fresh ginger

¼ cup water

1 tablespoon mirin

1 teaspoon tamari

Fine sea salt and freshly ground black pepper

Halve the squash, scoop out the seeds, then cut each squash crosswise into 1-inch half-moons. Turn the half-moon segment on its side, and slice away the skin with a sharp knife.

Heat the oil in a large, heavy skillet over medium heat. Add the garlic and ginger and sauté until the garlic and ginger become tender, about 1 minute. Add the squash pieces, water, mirin, and tamari. When the liquid comes to a boil, turn the heat to medium-low, cover, and cook, turning the squash pieces after 10 minutes, until the squash is nearing tender but still quite firm, about 15 minutes total.

Uncover the pan and increase the heat to medium. Simmer, turning the squash pieces occasionally, until the liquid evaporates and the squash begins to caramelize, about 10 minutes. Season to taste with salt and pepper.

Arame strudel

This dish is the perfect way to introduce your family and friends to sea vegetables. Arame is a mild-tasting sea vegetable: Combining it with a flaky crust makes for a perfect union. Simply roll out the dough like you would a piecrust. **Serves 4 to 6**

ARAME FILLING
1 cup dried arame
(about ¾ ounce)

1 (2-inch) piece fresh
ginger, peeled

2 teaspoons sesame oil

1 small onion, cut in half
and thinly sliced

1 small carrot, peeled and cut
into matchstick-size strips

1 clove garlic, minced

2 tablespoons brown rice syrup

1 tablespoon mirin

1 tablespoon tamari

PASTRY
¾ cup unbleached white flour

¾ cup whole-wheat pastry flour

1 teaspoon fine sea salt

¼ cup neutral cooking oil

¼ cup ice-cold water

About 1 tablespoon mirin

Arame: Soak the arame in a bowl of water (enough to fully cover the arame) until it is rehydrated and becomes tender, about 15 minutes. Strain the arame from the soaking liquid, and reserve both the arame and the soaking liquid separately.

Meanwhile, using a Microplane or ginger grater, grate the ginger over a bowl lined with cheesecloth or a paper towel. Gather the edges of the cloth and squeeze the ginger pulp to extract 1 tablespoon of ginger juice into a small bowl. Discard the pulp. Set aside the juice.

Combine the sesame oil, onion, carrot, and garlic in a heavy sauté pan over medium heat and sauté until the onion is almost tender, about 3 minutes. Stir the arame into the onion and carrot. Decrease the heat to medium-low. Cover and cook, stirring occasionally, until the onion is translucent and the carrot and arame are tender, about 15 minutes. If the mixture looks too dry, add a splash of the reserved arame soaking liquid. (The vegetables should release enough juices on their own.)

Stir in the brown rice syrup, mirin, tamari, and the ginger juice. Cook uncovered until the excess liquid evaporates, but the mixture is still very moist, about 5 minutes. Set aside to cool completely.

Pastry: Mix both flours and salt in a medium bowl to blend. Using a fork, stir the oil into the flour mixture to form a crumbly meal. Add the ice-cold water and stir until the dough begins to form and clump together. Gather the dough into a mound, then flatten the dough into a disk that is about 7 inches in diameter. Wrap the dough with plastic wrap and refrigerate for 30 minutes.

Assembly: Preheat the oven to 375°F. Roll out the dough on a lightly floured work surface to a 12-inch round with a thickness of about ⅛ inch.

Spread the cooled arame mixture on the dough, forming an even layer and keeping the outer 1 inch of the dough uncovered. Roll the dough up into a long log that resembles a jelly roll. As you roll the dough, roll it just tight enough to allow all of the arame mixture to stay packed in, but not too tight. Fold in the end pieces. The strudel will be about 8 inches long and 3 inches wide. Transfer the strudel to the prepared baking sheet and brush the pastry with the mirin.

Bake until the strudel is golden brown and cooked through, about 50 minutes. Let the strudel cool slightly, then cut it crosswise into 1-inch-wide slices and serve.

carbohydrates: The good and the Bad

Don't be swayed by fad diets that come and go in cycles, declaring all carbohydrates unhealthy. A healthy diet must consist mostly of whole, unrefined complex carbohydrates. That's right: Carbs are good for you. But, if you take whole wheat berries (or any other plant food) and send them off to a refining factory to strip away all the fiber and nutrition, breaking down the complex carbohydrates into simple sugar molecules, then you have a fattening food that will spike your blood sugar level and wreak havoc on your overall heath. And that's where carbs get their bad reputation—it's the simple carbs that so many people are addicted to, and that offer so little for your body. That's why the recipes in this book, the tenets of macrobiotic cooking, and the recommendations of any sensible eating program limit or restrict refined white flours and sugary foods.

I find it helpful to think of food in its whole form rather than in terms of protein, fat, and carbs; the latter is a reductionist scientific method of analyzing the nutritional content of food. If you are a regular person like me who wants to enjoy good food and not become an expert in biochemistry, then it's easier to just learn what food looks like when it's in the garden or on the farm, and learn to discern if it has been refined in a factory someplace before it got to your plate. If you can do that, you'll make smart, nutritionally sound food choices.

nishime-style root vegetables

This was one of the first dishes that I mastered early in my cooking career, and I am still eating it all these years later. Nishime-style cooking (as well as kinpira-style cooking—see the next recipe) is Japanese country cooking at its best: Nishime uses a slow-cooking method to allow the vegetables to sweat and then to cook in their own juices, which renders them soft and sweet. Layer the vegetables beginning with what cooks the least amount of time on the bottom of the pot, and trust that you'll need very little water. The end result is a pot of slow-cooking vegetables that produce a strong, calm energy. **Serves 6**

1 (6- by 1-inch) strip kombu

1 medium yellow onion

½ kabocha squash (about 1¼ pounds), peeled, seeded, and cut into 2- to 3-inch pieces

2 medium carrots (about 6 ounces total), peeled and roll-cut into 1-inch pieces (see page 174)

2 medium parsnips (about 8 ounces total), peeled and roll-cut into 1-inch pieces (see page 174)

2 small turnips, or 1 large turnip (about 12 ounces total), peeled and cut into 1-inch-thick wedges

2 small rutabagas, or 1 large rutabaga (about 1 pound total), peeled and cut into 1½-inch pieces

3 tablespoons tamari

Place the kombu strip in a heavy 3½-quart pot and add just enough water to cover the kombu (about ¾ cup). Let soak for 20 minutes.

Meanwhile, peel the skin off of the onion, then score the onion into 4 sections, keeping the onion attached at the root end. Set the onion atop the kombu in the middle of the pot. Surround the onion with the squash pieces. Top with the carrots, then the parsnips, turnips, and rutabagas. The heaviest vegetables go on the top. (I never do believe it, but I do it, and it always works.)

Bring the vegetables to a boil over high heat, then reduce the heat to medium-low. Cover the pot and simmer until the vegetables are tender, about 45 minutes.

Transfer the vegetables to a serving platter, leaving the kombu in the pot. Stir the tamari into the cooking liquid, then pour the liquid over the vegetables. Cut the kombu into matchstick-size strips and garnish the vegetables with the kombu.

sea vegetables

Real Food Pantry

Sea vegetables (or, technically speaking, marine algae) tend to be some of the most underappreciated and underused vegetables in our country; they're very popular in Japan and Korea, and certain other coastal areas around the world. Perhaps sea vegetables' more common name—seaweed—hasn't been the best sales pitch for them stateside. But as a group, sea vegetables are among the most nutritious foods on earth. They are full of vitamins and minerals as well as a wide range of important amino acids. The following are some of my favorite sea vegetables; they are available from most natural foods stores.

AGAR-AGAR is an odorless, tasteless sea vegetable that is the vegan alternative to gelatin. I use it in my Kanten with Apricots, Figs, and Hazelnuts (page 235), to make my version of a healthy whipped cream (page 233), and in my Vegan Cashew Cheese (page 57).

ARAME is a spaghetti-like, dark brown sea vegetable that's rich in iron, calcium, and other minerals. I feature it in my Arame Strudel (page 195).

DULSE is deep red in color and is one of the few sea vegetables that does not have to be cooked. It's chewy and can be eaten as a snack or tossed into salads and soups. I use it in my Super Vegetable Dinner Smoothie (page 176).

HIZIKI is a wiry, noodle-shaped blue-black sea vegetable that has a strong, nutty aroma. It's used in the croquettes for my Mixed Oak and Green Leaf Salad with Sesame-Hiziki Croquettes, Garbanzo Beans, and Ginger-Tahini Dressing (page 133).

KOMBU is a wide, thick dark green sea vegetable. When added to the cooking water for beans, kombu helps break down naturally occurring gases. In addition to cooking beans with kombu, I use it in my Kombu Dashi (page 99), a Japanese-style seaweed stock.

NORI are thin black or dark purple sheets of dried seaweed. When roasted, nori turns green. You may recognize nori as the wrapper commonly found around sushi; I use it in my Umeboshi Rice Balls (page 50), and I show you how to make your own toasted nori on page 50.

spicy kinpira

Kinpira is a style of slowly sautéing root vegetables. Burdock—often called "gobo"—is a long, thin brown-black root vegetable that has strong medicinal qualities thought to strengthen and purify the blood. Like the Nishime-Style Root Vegetables (see page 197), this is a dish that aims to strengthen and increase your vitality. I like to kick it up by adding a little heat from the crushed red peppers. This unusual dish is wonderful served with rice or noodles. **Serves 4 to 6**

2 large carrots, or 3 medium carrots (about 10 ounces total)

1 large burdock root, or 2 medium roots (about 6 ounces total)

1 tablespoon toasted sesame oil

½ teaspoon crushed red pepper

2 tablespoons water, plus more as needed

2 tablespoons tamari or shoyu

Peel the carrots, then cut them into long matchstick-size strips. You can cut them with a chef's knife, but using a julienne vegetable peeler, a mandoline, or a vegetable slicer makes this easier to do. Repeat with the burdock root, soaking the strips in a bowl of cold water as you cut them (burdock oxidizes and discolors quickly). If the water discolors, drain the water and cover the burdock strips with fresh cold water.

Heat the oil in a heavy frying pan over medium heat. Add the crushed red pepper, and using a chopstick or a wooden spoon, stir the flakes. Drain the water from the burdock and add the burdock. Sauté for 3 minutes, then add the carrots and sauté for 2 minutes.

Add the 2 tablespoons fresh water and the tamari and bring the mixture to a boil. Decrease the heat to medium-low. Cover and simmer gently, stirring occasionally, until the vegetables are crisp-tender and the liquid is absorbed, about 5 minutes. As the mixture cooks, the burdock and carrots will sweat and release enough liquid to steam themselves. If there is not enough liquid, add a tablespoon or more of water.

CUTTING TECHNIQUES

MATCHSTICK CUTS begin with cutting long vegetables into uniformly thin, diagonal slices. Next, stack the slices about 4 high, and cut into long, thin strips, forming matchstick-like pieces. The more you use this cut, the better you'll be at getting the final results to be as thin as you'd like.

I n short, *macrobiotics* means "big life." The macrobiotic way is eating a simple and balanced diet and living in harmony with nature and your surroundings. Balance is the fundamental idea—balance as the key to happiness, health, and longevity. As such, macrobiotics translates into a well-balanced grain-and-vegetable diet, high in fiber, low in fat, and rich in plant-based protein; it sometimes includes fish. Macrobiotics emphasizes eating a variety of seasonal organic foods that are close to their whole, fresh, natural state.

An integral part of the macrobiotic theory is the Far Eastern concept of yin and yang. Yin and yang are opposite yet complementary forces that govern all life and can be found in all things. Macrobiotics groups food in terms of yin and yang, according to the five tastes (sour, sweet, salty, hot/pungent, and bitter) and the effects each has on the body. (To read more about macrobiotics, turn to some of the books I reference in the Sources section on page 244.)

A quick course in macrobiotics

Learning about macrobiotics was a powerful education for me because I learned how foods impact my energy and mood. I learned about the concept of balance, not only on my plate, but in the larger context of life. Most importantly, studying macrobiotics was how I learned to cook. I have a great affinity for these foods and cooking methods. Eating rice and incorporating the many interesting, unusual, and delicious condiments used in macrobiotic cooking has always agreed with me (you can read more about some of my favorite Asian ingredients on page 68).

Macrobiotics has often gotten a bad rap: People think it's a diet prescribed to sick people, or that people who eat this way are dietary zealots. Contrary to rumors that you'll spend all day in your kitchen, once you get into the swing of cooking macrobiotically, it can be relatively simple. Macrobiotics employs various cooking methods, such as the ones used in this book: sautéing, roasting, toasting, baking, frying, and incorporates some raw foods, too. Whether or not you become macrobiotic, I encourage you to include some of the amazing health-supportive dishes from this book in your repertoire.

Braised whole onions in miso sauce

This is a beautiful dish to serve, so be sure to arrange the onions on a pretty serving platter. The miso lends a slightly salty flavor to the sweetness of the slow-cooking onions. It doesn't matter what size the onions are—any from small to medium will work well—just make sure to select onions of the same size, so they will cook evenly. **Serves 6**

7 medium yellow onions (about 9 ounces each)

2 teaspoons toasted sesame oil

3 cups water, plus 4 tablespoons

6 tablespoons golden miso

1 tablespoon arrowroot

2 tablespoons finely chopped fresh parsley

Remove the skins from the onions and cut off the ends. Make 6 to 8 shallow cuts in each onion. It will look like it is sectioned, but it isn't, because the cuts you make are shallow.

Select a shallow pot that will hold the onions snugly in a single layer, such as a 10½-inch 5-quart pot. Add the oil to the pot and arrange the onions in the pot so that they are cut-side-up and tightly packed, which will help them stay in place. Add enough cold water to come 1 inch up the sides of the onions (about 3 cups).

Whisk the miso and 3 tablespoons of the water in a small bowl to blend well. Spoon the miso mixture over the onions.

Cover the pot and bring the liquid to a boil over high heat. Decrease the heat to medium-low and simmer until the onions are cooked all the way through and they are tender and a bit translucent, about 1 hour. Using a slotted spoon, carefully remove the onions from the pot so they stay intact and place them on a platter.

Bring the braising liquid to a boil over high heat. Whisk the arrowroot with the remaining 1 tablespoon water in a small bowl to dissolve the arrowroot. Drizzle the arrowroot mixture into the braising liquid in the pot and simmer, whisking constantly, until the sauce thickens slightly and reduces to 1¾ cups, about 12 minutes. Pour the sauce over the onions. Garnish with parsley and serve.

Boiled vegetable salad with umeboshi-scallion Dressing

Don't let the title fool you: It's important to cook each vegetable separately in boiling water just long enough to reach their peak tenderness and flavor. I've chosen my favorite vegetables; feel free to incorporate any combination of seasonal vegetables that you especially like. The quick and easy dressing adds a depth of flavor and color; it incorporates umeboshi, which can't be topped for its clean, light, and refreshing flavor. I prefer to make this dressing with the umeboshi paste; however, you can substitute umeboshi vinegar for the paste and water. Simply sprinkle with vinegar to taste. **Serves 4**

VEGETABLES
½ head cauliflower, trimmed into florets (about 1½ cups)

6 red or tricolored radishes, trimmed

1½ celery stalks, cut diagonally into ¼-inch-thick slices (about 1 cup)

1 yellow squash, cut into ¼-inch-thick half-moons (about 1 cup)

½ head broccoli, trimmed into florets (about 1½ cups)

2 medium carrots, peeled and roll-cut into 1-inch pieces (about 1 cup; see page 174)

DRESSING
½ cup water

1½ tablespoons umeboshi paste

3 scallions, thinly sliced diagonally

3 tablespoons sesame seeds, toasted

Vegetables: Bring a large saucepan of lightly salted water to a boil over high heat. Working with 1 vegetable at a time, cook the vegetables in the order listed until their colors brighten and they are just tender, about 2 minutes for each vegetable. After each vegetable is cooked, immediately submerge it in a large bowl of ice water to stop it from cooking, then drain it well and pat dry with a clean kitchen towel. Quarter the larger radishes or cut the smaller radishes in half.

Dressing: Whisk the ½ cup water with the umeboshi paste in a small bowl to blend. Stir in the scallions and 2 tablespoons of the sesame seeds.

Assembly: Gently toss the vegetables in a large bowl with enough of the dressing to coat. Garnish with the remaining 1 tablespoon sesame seeds and serve.

Leafy Green Trio Hot Sauté

This dish has soul: It's enhanced with red bell peppers, crushed red pepper, lots of garlic, and a splash of vinegar. It's a fun way to offer leafy greens to people—and to get them coming back for more. **Serves 4 to 6**

3 tablespoons olive oil

3 tablespoons minced garlic

¼ teaspoon crushed red pepper

½ teaspoon smoked paprika

1 bunch kale (about 8 ounces), stemmed and cut into 2-inch-thick strips

1 bunch collard greens (about 8 ounces), stemmed and cut into 2-inch strips

1 small bunch green chard (about 8 ounces), stemmed and cut into 2-inch strips

1 small red bell pepper, diced

Fine sea salt and freshly ground black pepper

2 tablespoons apple cider vinegar

Heat the oil in a large, heavy skillet or a large wok over medium heat. Add the garlic and crushed red pepper and sauté just until fragrant, about 30 seconds. Stir in the paprika. Add the kale, collards, chard, and red bell pepper and sauté until the greens wilt and become tender, about 12 minutes. Remove from the heat. Season the greens mixture to taste with salt and pepper.

Transfer the greens mixture to a bowl. Drizzle with the vinegar and serve.

oven-roasted sweet potato fries

Bright orange "sweet potato" fries—usually made with garnet yams—have become popular at restaurants, and even some fast-food places. I was under the impression that the finer restaurants were hand-making these delicious fries. To my great disappointment, I learned that these orange jewels were coming in the back door of kitchens in frozen bags. From that day on, I've made my own at home and found that they are such a quick and easy dish to put together that I hardly ever order them when I am eating out. My kids love these, and I'm betting yours will, too. Serve the fries with or without ketchup. **Serves 4**

4 medium garnet yams
(about 1¾ pounds total)

2½ tablespoons high-heat
neutral cooking oil

1 teaspoon fine sea salt

1 teaspoon paprika

½ teaspoon garlic powder

¼ teaspoon freshly
ground black pepper

Preheat the oven to 425°F. Line 3 large, heavy baking sheets with parchment paper.

Peel the yams, then slice them lengthwise into ½-inch-thick slabs. Cut the slabs lengthwise into ½-inch-thick strips.

Stir the oil, salt, paprika, garlic powder, and pepper in a large bowl to blend. Add the sweet potatoes and toss to coat. Arrange the sweet potatoes in a single layer on the prepared baking sheets, being sure not to overcrowd them.

Bake, turning the potatoes occasionally, until the sweet potatoes are tender and golden brown, about 25 minutes. Let cool for 5 minutes before serving.

southern-style potato salad with tarragon-mustard dressing

Southerners are very particular about their potato salad, and every region prides itself on thinking theirs is the best. What makes this one stand out so much is the aromatic tarragon in the dressing, and the use of mustard instead of mayonnaise, giving it a nice bit of pungent flavor. Adding diced celery gives the salad an appealingly crunchy texture, while tahini adds creaminess. **Serves 6 (makes about 10 cups)**

3¼ pounds medium red-skinned potatoes

1 medium red onion, minced (about 1 cup)

1 cup chopped celery

3 tablespoons minced fresh parsley

2 tablespoons minced fresh tarragon

1 tablespoon minced fresh dill

½ cup extra-virgin olive oil

½ cup fresh lemon juice

3 tablespoons raw tahini

1 tablespoon Dijon mustard

1 tablespoon minced garlic

1 teaspoon hot sauce (such as Tabasco)

Fine sea salt and freshly ground black pepper

Place the potatoes in a large pot of salted water and bring to a boil over high heat (this will take about 30 minutes). Decrease the heat to medium and simmer until the potatoes are just tender and a knife can easily glide through a potato without the potato falling apart, about 8 minutes longer.

Drain the potatoes in a colander, then rinse them with cold water. Drain the potatoes well and pat them dry with a clean kitchen towel. Transfer the potatoes to a baking sheet and set aside until they have cooled to room temperature.

When the potatoes are cool, halve them lengthwise, then cut them crosswise into about ¼-inch-thick slices. Combine the potatoes, onion, celery, parsley, tarragon, and dill in a large bowl.

Whisk the oil, lemon juice, tahini, mustard, garlic, and hot sauce in a small bowl to blend. Pour the dressing over the potatoes and gently toss to coat. Season to taste with salt and pepper. Serve at room temperature, or cover and refrigerate until ready to serve.

desserts

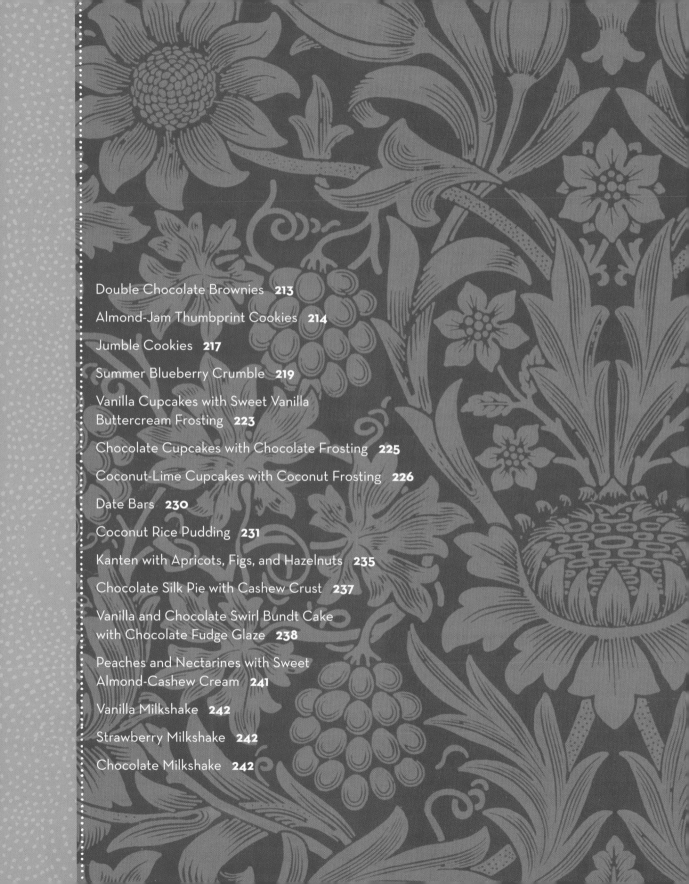

We all love desserts. I think it's the sublime trio of sweeteners, flours, and fats—the way they converge in a dish is something we don't want to live without, nor should we have to. Desserts are celebratory, bringing together family and friends for special occasions. They are teatime treats and after-dinner indulgences. It's no wonder so many happy memories surround the eating of sweets. As with anything consumed more for pleasure than for nutrition, we do need to eat sweets in moderation. And it's important to bake those desserts with more wholesome sweeteners, flours, and fats whenever possible.

Admittedly, it's a process to retrain a palate that craves white sugar and white flour. I know this firsthand, as I grew up addicted to white sugar. My shift was a rather long one, but that doesn't mean yours will be. After a decade of embracing a diet where I used only natural sweeteners, I have finally found a balance between wanting sweets and wanting to avoid them. Now I can indulge every so often without going back to constant sugar cravings.

These days, I'm especially interested in creating more wholesome desserts for my children—desserts that will sweeten the special moments without spoiling developing taste buds. What I offer in this chapter are vegan baked goods that are delicious and satisfying without the use of butter or eggs. Most of these recipes are also made with more healthful alternatives to white granulated sugar and white flour. Using wholesome alternatives to traditional ingredients means incorporating more whole foods into your diet without having to go too far out of your culinary comfort zone. White sugar can be replaced with maple syrup or maple sugar (for more sugar alternatives, see page 228), white flour can be replaced with a variety of whole-grain flours (see page 220), and butter and eggs can often be replaced with good-quality neutral cooking oil (see page 136). While I prefer more wholesome alternatives, I do use organic cane sugar in some once-in-a-while desserts, and I use a little unbleached white flour for the lightness it lends special-occasion sweets—you'll find both ingredients in my cupcakes, for instance. The beauty of using more healthful ingredients on a daily basis is that occasional indulgences won't matter as much.

The following are my favorite cookies, cupcakes, pies, cakes, and more. These recipes are tried and true from years of experience in creating my own healthful, nutritious, and delicious treats—ones that are sure to satisfy any sweet tooth. In fact, these desserts taste so similar to their traditional counterparts that I often hear "I can't believe there's no dairy!" and "Are you sure you don't use eggs in this?" I guarantee that if you follow the recipes in this chapter, you'll be hooked on better-quality desserts, from Summer Blueberry Crumble (page 219), made with oat flour, to old-fashioned Date Bars (page 230), made with maple syrup.

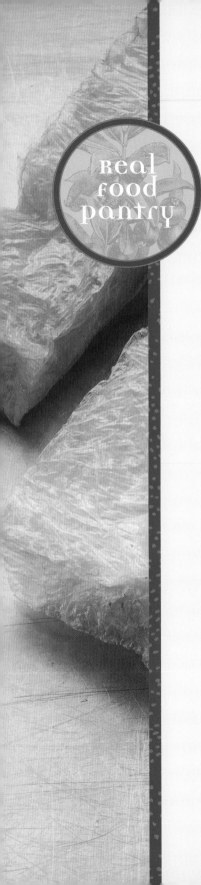

unusual baking ingredients

Vegan baking takes a few unique ingredients to get the desired results without using dairy, eggs, or gelatin. Look for these special ingredients at your local natural foods store.

AGAR is a sea vegetable that can replace gelatin in vegetarian and vegan cooking. Since gelatin is made from the bones of an animal, it's not considered vegetarian (nor is it considered appetizing by anyone who stops to think about it). Using a clear gelatinous sea vegetable is a much better choice in my world. Available at most natural foods stores, agar is sold as dried flakes or bars, or in powdered form. When I started cooking, the bars were popular, but these days, I prefer the flakes—they are widely available and dissolve easily. You'll need agar to make my delicious Jell-O-like Kanten with Apricots, Figs, and Hazelnuts (page 235).

ARROWROOT is the dried and powdered root of the West Indian arrowroot, an ancient crop whose culinary history dates back to Napoleonic times. Arrowroot is a healthy alternative to cornstarch: It thickens sauces without making them cloudy, and it is unaffected by acidity or freezing. Available in the spice aisle of most grocery stores, arrowroot is best used by mixing it with cold water before adding it to a recipe. I use it to thicken the berry juices in my Summer Blueberry Crumble (page 219).

XANTHAN GUM is a natural thickener, emulsifier, and stabilizer often used in gluten-free baking to replicate the binding and leavening properties supplied by the gluten in wheat. Xanthan gum is derived primarily from cornstarch; I only use it when baking with gluten-free flours. I've tried making my Coconut-Lime Cupcakes with Coconut Frosting (page 226) without it, and the cupcakes do not hold together as well when the flour mix is made without xanthan gum.

Double chocolate Brownies

These brownies are thick and cakey with a crumbly texture; they're studded with enough chocolate chips to satisfy any chocolate-lover. Try adding a cup of your favorite chopped nuts, if you like. Although I prefer the subtle sweetness of maple sugar, I've included the measurements for organic cane sugar too.
Makes 12 brownies

1½ cups unbleached white flour

1 cup maple sugar, or 1½ cups organic cane sugar

1 cup unsweetened cocoa powder

½ teaspoon baking soda

½ teaspoon fine sea salt

1 cup plus 2 tablespoons neutral cooking oil (see page 224)

¾ cup agave nectar

1 tablespoon vanilla extract

1 ⅛ teaspoons apple cider vinegar

½ cup boiling water

1¾ cups semisweet chocolate chips

Preheat the oven to 350°F. Lightly oil a 9 by 9 by 2-inch square nonstick baking pan or glass baking dish.

Sift the flour, maple sugar, cocoa powder, baking soda, and salt into a large bowl; discard any large grains of maple sugar that remain in the strainer. Whisk the oil, agave nectar, vanilla, and vinegar in a medium bowl to blend. Whisk the oil mixture into the flour mixture until well blended. Scrape the sides of the bowl, then continue mixing for 30 seconds. Carefully whisk in the boiling water. Stir in the chocolate chips.

Transfer the batter to the prepared baking pan, spreading evenly. Bake until a toothpick comes out with moist crumbs attached, about 45 minutes.

Store the brownies in an airtight container at room temperature for up to 2 days.

almond-jam thumbprint cookies

These little gems are moist and not too sweet, with just the right amount of crunchiness. They will impress anyone from grown-ups at a dinner party to kids at snack time. I find that a food processor does the best job of pulsing the almonds into a fine flour. Use your favorite jam or jelly; it's also fun to use more than one type of jam in a single batch, to mix up both the flavors and the colors. **Makes about 36 cookies**

2½ cups raw whole almonds

1½ cups oat flour

1 cup whole-wheat pastry flour or barley flour

½ teaspoon baking soda

½ teaspoon fine sea salt

1 cup pure maple syrup

¼ cup apple juice

¼ cup neutral cooking oil

2 teaspoons almond extract

About ¾ cup raspberry preserves, apricot preserves, or apple butter

Preheat the oven to 325°F. Line 2 heavy baking sheets with parchment paper.

Pulse the almonds in a food processor until they form a fine flour with some small speckles of nuts still visible. You'll want to leave some small bits of the almonds to lend a nice crunchy texture to the cookies.

Stir the ground almonds, oat flour, pastry flour, baking soda, and salt in a large bowl to blend. Whisk the maple syrup, apple juice, oil, and almond extract in a medium

bowl to blend. Stir the wet ingredients into the flour mixture until blended.

Using a 1-ounce ice cream scoop (about 2 tablespoons), scoop the dough in mounds onto the prepared baking sheets, spacing 1 inch apart. (If you don't have an ice cream scoop, just roll 2 tablespoons of dough into a ball for each cookie.) Using the end of a wooden spoon, make an indentation about ½ inch in diameter that goes to the bottom of the cookie, but not through the bottom. Spoon the preserves into a pastry bag or a small resealable plastic bag. If you're using a plastic bag, use scissors to cut 1 bottom corner off the bag. Pipe the preserves into each indentation, mounding them just above the top of the cookie. The jam will melt down as the cookies bake, so be sure to mound it up a bit when filling the indentations.

Bake the cookies until they puff and become pale golden on the top and bottom, about 25 minutes. Transfer the baking sheets to cooling racks and let cool.

The cookies will keep for 2 days, stored in an airtight container at room temperature.

butter and shortening Replacements

Baking without butter is simply unimaginable to many. In the past, vegans depended on margarine (some brands contain dairy, and some don't). Once we learned that trans fats clog arteries more than butter, margarine's popularity plummeted. Today, many tub margarines are made without trans fats; be sure to read the labels.

I like using a combination of vegan fats for enriching both sweets and savories. When a vegetable oil won't lend a recipe the right texture and taste, I reach for vegan butter sticks, vegan shortening, or a combination of the two. While there are probably other brands worth trying, my personal favorites are made by Earth Balance. Today's butter substitutes are far more evolved than the margarine of old; not only are these all-natural and free of trans fats and cholesterol, but they also include a blend of canola, soybean, palm fruit, and olive oils—vegetable oils that have actually been shown to have some powerful health benefits.

Earth Balance Vegan Buttery Sticks taste and act like real butter, so bakers will love substituting them for butter in conventional recipes; you can also use the buttery sticks to spread on toast or to sauté vegetables. With one hundred calories and eleven grams of fat per tablespoon, they're definitely not diet food.

Vegan shortening is an emulsion of natural oils. Because it doesn't offer the same appealing flavor of the buttery sticks, it's a product that is best used only for baking. Although incredibly rich, shortening is worth trying for certain special-occasion desserts. It adds stability to buttercream frostings, which is why I use it in all my cupcake frosting recipes. My cooking has come a long way from the days when my grandmother kept a jar of shortening next to her stove.

jumble cookies

Thought of as the precursor to sugar cookies, jumble cookies were once favored by travelers for their long shelf life. They're thought to have first reached North America on the *Mayflower*. What began as a hard spiced cookie (or "biscuit"), sometimes rolled and twisted before being boiled and baked, has evolved over time—and the meaning of the name seems to have changed right along with the ingredients. Today jumble cookies are popular because you can throw in lots of ingredients like chocolate, dried fruit, nuts, and seeds. I add barley malt as well as maple sugar to strengthen the crispy texture of these thick cookies.

Makes 24 cookies

2½ cups unbleached white flour

3 cups old-fashioned rolled oats

2 teaspoons ground cinnamon

1½ teaspoons baking soda

½ teaspoon fine sea salt

12 ounces vegan butter (such as Earth Balance)

1 cup maple sugar, or 1½ cups organic cane sugar

1 cup barley malt

1½ tablespoons pure maple syrup

1½ tablespoons vanilla extract

3 cups semisweet chocolate chips

2 cups pecans, very coarsely chopped

Preheat the oven to 325°F. Line 2 heavy baking sheets with parchment paper.

Stir the flour, oats, cinnamon, baking soda, and salt in a medium bowl to blend. Using a stand mixer fitted with the paddle attachment, beat the vegan butter and maple sugar in the mixer bowl on medium-high speed until fluffy, about 8 minutes. (Alternatively, a handheld mixer can be used, but the mixing times will be longer.) A fluffy batter is a must for these cookies: They need air, which creates a great texture in the cookie.

Mix in the barley malt, maple syrup, and vanilla, beating until fluffy, about 4 minutes. Add the flour mixture and beat just until blended. Stir in the chocolate chips and pecans. If desired, store the dough in an airtight container and freeze for up to 2 months, then thaw before continuing.

Using an ice cream scoop, scoop about ⅓ cup of the dough for each cookie onto the prepared baking sheets, forming 6 mounds on each baking sheet and spacing the mounds evenly apart.

Bake until the cookies puff and become pale golden on the top and bottom, about 20 minutes. Transfer the baking sheets to cooling racks and let cool for 10 minutes. Using a metal spatula, transfer the cookies directly to the racks and let cool. Repeat with the remaining cookie dough.

Store the cookies in an airtight container at room temperature for up to 2 days.

summer
blueberry crumble

This is one of my all-time favorite summer fruit desserts: The bubbly sweet burst of the blueberries with the oat flour is delicious. I often made it back when I cooked for people in their homes, and I had fans requesting this dessert year-round. I like to use oat flour because of its subtle sweetness, as well as its added texture and visual impact. This recipe offers the choice of using either oil or melted vegan butter. Taking that extra step to melt the butter really makes a difference in terms of adding crispness to the crumbly topping. Try this recipe using other summer berries like strawberries or blackberries. **Serves 8**

FILLING

5 cups (about 1½ pounds) fresh blueberries

½ cup pure maple syrup

¼ teaspoon fine sea salt

1 teaspoon arrowroot powder, dissolved in 2 tablespoons of water

TOPPING

1⅓ cups old-fashioned rolled oats

⅔ cup whole pecans

⅓ cup neutral cooking oil or vegan butter

⅓ cup pure maple syrup

¾ teaspoon vanilla extract

¼ teaspoon fine sea salt

Preheat the oven to 350°F. Lightly oil a 9 by 9 by 2-inch square baking dish.

Filling: Combine 4 cups of the blueberries, the maple syrup, and the salt in a large, heavy saucepan over medium-high heat and cook, stirring occasionally, until the berries burst and their juices are released, about 5 minutes. Decrease the heat to medium-low and slowly stir in the arrowroot mixture. Bring the blueberry mixture to a gentle simmer. Remove the pan from the heat and stir in the remaining 1 cup blueberries. Spoon the blueberry mixture into the prepared baking dish.

Topping: Blend the oats in a food processor to a coarse flour with some bits of oats still visible. Add the pecans and pulse just until the pecans are coarsely chopped. Transfer the oat mixture to a large bowl. Using a fork, mix in the oil, then mix in the maple syrup, vanilla, and salt. The oat mixture will look wet.

To Finish: Sprinkle the oat mixture over the blueberry mixture. Bake until the blueberry mixture bubbles and the topping is toasted and golden brown, about 25 minutes. Let cool slightly and serve warm.

flours

Just as there are many interesting and healthful alternatives to plain white sugar, there are also many flours worth exploring beyond the white all-purpose product that has become the default for bakers and cooks. At their core, flours are simply processed foods derived from whole grains and cereals. The degree to which these grains are milled or refined determines the nutritional content of the final product. Most traditional flours are highly processed and retain little of their original nutritional content. By learning to experiment with some alternative flours, you can enjoy making baked goods that taste delicious (in fact, you might come to prefer some of the heartier flavors of whole grains), while also sneaking in additional nutrients.

ALL-PURPOSE GLUTEN-FREE BAKING FLOUR is becoming more widely available as the demand for gluten-free foods continues to rise. This baking flour tends to include a combination of garbanzo bean flour, tapioca flour, white sorghum flour, potato starch, and fava bean flour, which allows it to act in a very similar way to traditional all-purpose flour. All-purpose gluten-free baking flour is more savory than sweet in flavor and often leaves a subtle aftertaste. It works well in my gluten-free Coconut-Lime Cupcakes with Coconut Frosting (page 226). I use other gluten-free flours, too, such as tapioca and brown rice flours in my Gluten- and Soy-Free Waffles (page 35), and garbanzo-fava flour in my Sesame-Shiitake Tofu Frittata (page 17).

BARLEY FLOUR is a fine powder made by grinding whole barley grain. It has a sweet, nutty flavor, and it's high in fiber, too. Along with many other flours, barley flour can be used to replace the wheat flour in baked goods for a more interesting taste and texture. I've found that barley flour and wheat flour are interchangeable in my recipes for Date Bars (page 230) and Almond-Jam Thumbprint Cookies (page 214).

BUCKWHEAT FLOUR, in spite of its name, isn't related to wheat. This has made it popular with those following a gluten-free diet. Buckwheat flour is a whole-grain flour, rich in fiber and protein; its earthy taste has made it popular—often mixed with other flours—for producing pancakes, blini, savory crepes, and soba noodles. Buckwheat flour makes my Blueberry Corn Pancakes (page 34) hearty and tasty.

CORN FLOUR is basically cornmeal processed to its finest texture, creating a flour. In fact, you can make your own corn flour simply by pulsing cornmeal at a high speed in a food processor. I like to use it for a subtle corn flavor and to keep things gluten-free I use it in my Black Bean Veggie Burgers (page 118).

OAT FLOUR is made from ground oats. This flour can be used in a wide variety of recipes, especially ones that are more rustic in texture. While oat flour can be purchased, you can make it at home in a few seconds, in the same way as the corn flour above—in your food processor. That's how I make my oat flour for the Summer Blueberry Crumble (page 219). I highly recommend making oat flour, as it allows more control over the texture of the final flour.

SPELT FLOUR is great for baking. I like its mellow, nutty, slightly sweet flavor, which is why I use it in my Nutty Raspberry Muffins (page 33). It's great in quick breads and in crusts for savory dishes: I substitute spelt flour in most recipes calling for whole-wheat flour, while light spelt flour can take the place of unbleached white flour. Spelt is an ancient grain that is a cousin of wheat. While it's not gluten-free, some people with a wheat intolerance can enjoy foods prepared with spelt.

UNBLEACHED WHITE FLOUR is a highly refined wheat flour with the bran and germ removed. It is not chemically bleached, and that's a good thing: The bleaching process eliminates the majority of nutrients in the flour. Unbleached white flour is very versatile; it can be used in nearly any baked good, as it provides unrivaled lightness and a tender crumb that is difficult to achieve using only alternative flours. This flour is interchangeable with unbleached all-purpose flour. I like using it in my Vanilla Cupcakes (page 223) and Chocolate Cupcakes (page 225), because they should be as light as possible, and in my Double Chocolate Brownies (page 212) and Vanilla and Chocolate Swirl Bundt Cake (page 238), as well.

WHOLE-WHEAT PASTRY FLOUR is made from wheat, naturally; "whole wheat" means that not all of the bran and germ have been removed, so the resulting flour is far more nutritious than white flour. Like other pastry flour, whole-wheat pastry flour has been milled down to a very fine powder, which gives baked goods a more delicate crumb. Whole-wheat pastry flour does tend to be heavier than its whiter cousin, but it will produce more delicate results than coarser whole-wheat flour.

cupcakes

Every sweet little cupcake deserves a fabulous frosting—namely, buttercream. Buttercream frosting is exactly what it sounds like: a thick, sweet icing made from butter and sugar. In order to mimic the texture and flavor of a classic buttercream, there are vegan alternatives to butter that can give you similar results to the original recipe, and with the added benefit of being both cholesterol-free and chock-full of omega fatty acids.

I like to use the Earth Balance brand of buttery sticks, as well as their natural shortening. I've found that combining vegan butter with vegetable shortening works better than vegan butter alone. Used together, they create an exceptional faux buttercream for cupcakes and cake icings. The following recipes are delicious reminders that you can have your cupcake and eat it, too.

vanilla cupcakes with sweet vanilla buttercream frosting

Makes 12 cupcakes

CUPCAKES

2½ cups unbleached white flour

1½ cups organic cane sugar

1½ teaspoons baking powder

1 teaspoon baking soda

½ teaspoon fine sea salt

1½ cups plain almond milk

2 teaspoons apple cider vinegar

1 cup neutral cooking oil

4 teaspoons vanilla extract

½ teaspoon almond extract

FROSTING

½ cup cold vegan butter (such as Earth Balance)

½ cup non-hydrogenated vegan shortening, at room temperature

2 cups (about 8 ounces) powdered sugar

1½ tablespoons vanilla extract

Cupcakes: Preheat the oven to 350°F. Line 12 standard muffin cups with paper liners.

Sift the flour, sugar, baking powder, baking soda, and salt into a large bowl and set aside. Mix the almond milk and cider vinegar in a medium bowl and set aside, stirring occasionally, for 5 minutes (the milk will thicken slightly). Mix in the oil, vanilla, and almond extract. Add to the flour mixture and mix just until blended.

Divide the batter equally among the prepared muffin cups and bake until a toothpick inserted into the center of a cupcake comes out clean, about 25 minutes. Transfer the pan to a cooling rack and let cool for 10 minutes. Remove the cupcakes from the pan and let the cupcakes cool completely.

Frosting: Fit a stand mixer with the paddle attachment. Beat the vegan butter and shortening in the mixer bowl on medium-high speed until the mixture is smooth and creamy. (Alternatively, a handheld mixer can be used, but

the mixing times will be longer.) Sift the powdered sugar into the butter mixture and beat on low speed to blend. Beat in the vanilla. Scrape the bowl and continue mixing on medium speed until the frosting is light and fluffy, about 4 minutes.

Transfer the frosting to a pastry bag fitted with a large star tip and pipe the frosting decoratively atop the cupcakes. Alternatively, the frosting can be spread decoratively over the cupcakes.

Store the cupcakes in an airtight container at room temperature for up to 3 days.

baking with oil

Many recipes in this chapter and throughout the book call for a neutral cooking oil. "Neutral" refers to the flavor profile of the oil. For desserts, you want to look for an oil that is mild enough that it will not interfere with the other flavors. Mostly, I recommend using monounsaturated oils, such as canola, grapeseed, safflower, and sunflower oil. See the Sources section (page 243) for more information on preferred brands.

CHOCOLATE CUPCAKES WITH CHOCOLATE FROSTING
Makes 12 cupcakes

CUPCAKES

2½ cups unbleached white flour

1½ cups organic cane sugar

½ cup unsweetened cocoa powder

1½ teaspoons baking powder

1 teaspoon baking soda

½ teaspoon fine sea salt

1½ cups plain or vanilla soy milk

2 teaspoons apple cider vinegar

1 cup neutral cooking oil

4 teaspoons vanilla extract

FROSTING

½ cup cold vegan butter (such as Earth Balance)

½ cup non-hydrogenated vegan shortening, at room temperature

2 cups (about 8 ounces) powdered sugar

¼ cup unsweetened cocoa powder

1 tablespoon vanilla extract

5 teaspoons plain or vanilla soy milk

Cupcakes: Preheat the oven to 350°F. Line 12 standard muffin cups with paper liners.

Sift the flour, sugar, cocoa, baking powder, baking soda, and salt into a large bowl and set aside. Mix the soy milk and cider vinegar in a medium bowl and set aside, stirring occasionally, for 5 minutes (the milk will thicken slightly). Mix in the oil and vanilla. Add to the flour mixture and stir just until blended.

Divide the batter equally among the prepared muffin cups and bake until a toothpick inserted into the center of a cupcake comes out clean, about 32 minutes. Transfer the pan to a cooling rack and let cool for 10 minutes. Remove the cupcakes from the pan and let the cupcakes cool completely.

Frosting: Fit a stand mixer with the paddle attachment. Beat the vegan butter and shortening in the mixer bowl on medium-high speed until the mixture is smooth and creamy. (Alternatively, a handheld mixer can be used, but the mixing times will be longer.) Sift the powdered sugar and cocoa powder into the butter mixture, then beat on low speed to blend. Beat in the vanilla. Scrape the bowl and continue mixing on medium speed, gradually adding the soy milk, until the frosting is light and fluffy, about 4 minutes.

Transfer the frosting to a pastry bag fitted with a large star tip and pipe the frosting decoratively atop the cupcakes. Alternatively, the frosting can be spread decoratively over the cupcakes.

Store the cupcakes in an airtight container at room emperature for up to 3 days.

coconut-lime cupcakes with coconut frosting

These cupcakes are made with gluten-free all-purpose baking flour, showing that delicious desserts can be adapted for a gluten-free diet. There are some slight differences in the behavior and taste of gluten-free flours; in this particular recipe, the coconut oil and milk complement the flour perfectly.

Makes 12 cupcakes

CUPCAKES

2½ cups all purpose gluten-free baking flour

1½ cups organic cane sugar

2 teaspoons xanthan gum

1½ teaspoons baking powder

1 teaspoon baking soda

½ teaspoon fine sea salt

1½ cups unsweetened light coconut milk

1 cup melted unrefined coconut oil, cooled (see page 6)

4 teaspoons vanilla extract

2 teaspoons freshly grated lime zest

FROSTING

½ cup shredded unsweetened dried coconut

¾ cup cold vegan butter (such as Earth Balance)

¼ cup non-hydrogenated vegan shortening, at room temperature

2½ cups (about 10 ounces) powdered sugar

1 tablespoon vanilla extract

Cupcakes: Preheat the oven to 350°F. Line 12 standard muffin cups with paper liners.

Sift the flour, sugar, xanthan gum, baking powder, baking soda, and salt into a large bowl and set aside. Mix the coconut milk, oil, vanilla, and lime zest in a medium bowl to blend. Add to the flour mixture and mix just until blended.

Divide the batter equally among the prepared muffin cups and bake until a toothpick inserted into the center of a cupcake comes out clean, about 30 minutes. Transfer the pan to a cooling rack and let cool for 10 minutes. Remove the cupcakes from the pan and let the cupcakes cool completely.

Frosting: Decrease the oven temperature to 300°F. Sprinkle ¼ cup of the coconut evenly over a heavy baking sheet and toast the coconut in the oven, stirring it occasionally to make sure it browns evenly, until it is golden brown, about 8 minutes.

Fit a stand mixer with the paddle attachment. Beat the vegan butter and shortening in the mixer bowl on medium-high speed until the mixture is smooth and creamy. (Alternatively, a handheld mixer can be used, but the mixing times will be longer.) Sift the powdered sugar into the butter mixture and beat on low speed to blend. Beat in the remaining ¼ cup untoasted coconut flakes and the vanilla. Scrape the bowl and continue mixing on medium speed until the frosting is light and fluffy, about 4 minutes.

Transfer the frosting to a pastry bag fitted with a large plain tip and pipe the frosting decoratively atop the cupcakes. Alternatively, the frosting can be spread decoratively over the cupcakes. Sprinkle with the toasted coconut.

Store the cupcakes in an airtight container at room temperature for up to 2 days.

Growing up, I thought Aunt Jemima had the exclusive rights to maple syrup. Little did I know that Aunt Jemima never got close to a maple tree—what I thought of as maple syrup was actually made of corn syrup, high-fructose corn syrup, and caramel color. When I went off to college in Vermont, and subsequently toured many a sugar shack, my mind and taste buds were enlightened to the naturally sweet and delicious flavor of pure maple syrup.

The tradition of tapping maple trees for their sap is older than our country. Early settlers from Europe first learned about maple syrup from Native Americans. Legend has it that the first accidental maple syrup maker was an Iroquois woman whose mate yanked his tomahawk from a tree. The weather had turned warm and the sap ran from the cut in the tree. Thinking

The Legend of Maple Syrup

it was water, she prepared a stew with it; the sweet flavor delighted those who ate it, and maple syrup was born. Native Americans were known to reduce sap until all the water evaporated, producing crystallized maple sugar, which they traded with early settlers.

During the early days of colonization, maple syrup was the main sweetener used, since sugar was prohibitively expensive. As sugar became cheaper to produce, it began to replace maple syrup as a relied-upon sweetener. In fact, maple syrup production is approximately one-fifth of what it was in the beginning of the twentieth century. Producing maple syrup is a laborious process: The sap, which is 98 percent water, has to be reduced slowly—it takes 40 to 50 gallons of sap to make 1 gallon of maple syrup.

The most common types of maple syrup are Grade A and Grade B. Grade A tends to be a lighter color with a more refined taste, perfect for pancakes and waffles. Grade B tends to be a darker, more viscous amber with a much more pronounced flavor. Because of the intensity of the flavor, Grade B tends to be used when a deeper flavor is desired, such as in baked goods.

The skinny on sweeteners

Desserts rely on sweeteners for flavor, moisture, and texture. I grew up on standard white table sugar and loved every empty calorie. It wasn't until later that I came to prefer alternative sweeteners, because they allowed me to enjoy eating desserts without suffering the inevitable sugar crash that followed. While some people notice it more than others, refined sugar spikes your blood sugar levels, releasing insulin in your body, which then causes blood sugar levels to plummet.

Besides the roller-coaster ride we experience as the body works so hard to stabilize its blood sugar level, white sugar is a highly processed food—exactly what those of us interested in good health are trying to avoid. In fact, the processing itself makes white sugar ethically unacceptable to many vegans, because bone char is used in the filtering of some cane sugar. (Vegans also typically avoid honey. Unlike white sugar, honey is minimally processed; whether or not you see it as acceptable in your own diet is a personal choice.)

The following is a guide to some of my favorite alternative sweeteners. There are times when white sugar has its place, even in a healthy diet, but it should be used in moderation. Incorporating alternative sweeteners can allow you to enjoy desserts more frequently, without over-indulging in refined sugar.

Agave nectar is derived from the agave, a large, spiky plant native to Mexico. Similar to honey in consistency, but milder in flavor, agave nectar has only recently come into wide use as a sweetener; it's long been used to produce tequila, however. Agave nectar has a low glycemic level, meaning it doesn't raise blood sugar levels as much as refined sugar. It has trace amounts of minerals, including calcium, potassium, magnesium, and iron. Pure, organic agave nectar is a good natural sweetener for beverages like my

Nondairy Milkshakes (page 242) and for tea. For baking, it's often used in combination with other sweeteners, as in my Double Chocolate Brownies (page 212). Agave nectar is also great for drizzling over hot breakfast cereals, such as Quick Oats and Quinoa Flakes (page 16).

Barley malt is a slowly digested sweetener made from sprouted barley. It is dark brown, thick, and sticky and possesses a strong malty flavor. It is about half as sweet as cane sugar. Barley malt is best used in combination with another sweetener; in my Jumble Cookies (page 217), for instance, I use it with maple sugar and maple syrup. Look for barley malt in natural foods stores.

Brown rice syrup, also best used in tandem with another sweetener, is a combination of barley malt and whole-grain brown rice, which is cooked until all the starch is converted to sugar. It has a unique caramel-like flavor, and a thick consistency similar to honey. Use it in my Super Hippie Granola (page 5) to help clump the ingredients together into delicious clusters. Brown rice syrup is considered to be one of the most healthful sweeteners in the natural foods industry, since it is produced from a whole-food source and is made up of simple sugars. It's available in natural foods stores.

Maple sugar is made by boiling maple syrup until all of the water has evaporated, leaving only the maple sugar crystals behind. Because maple syrup burns easily, this is a tricky process and can have a high price tag associated with it.

However, the health benefits and ease of substituting maple sugar crystals for refined white sugar make it worth the expense. Maple sugar is a perfect choice for those recipes that just don't work as well using a liquid sweetener; it's a key ingredient in Double Chocolate Brownies (page 212) and in my Jumble Cookies (page 217).

Maple syrup is a sweetener made from the sap of maple trees. In cooler climates, maple trees store sugar in their roots in the form of sap; in the spring, the sap rises and can be tapped and concentrated. Maple syrup, a good source of magnesium and zinc, is most popular as a topping for pancakes and waffles, but it's also a delicious natural sweetener that can be used in baking. Maple-based sweeteners are my favorites for using in desserts, as they are not only sweet enough to satisfy my cravings, but they also are metabolized at a slower rate than conventional white sugar, so they don't cause the dramatic spikes in blood sugar.

Organic cane sugar is made from the juice pressed from sun-ripened sugarcane, with the molasses removed; it tastes almost like white sugar but is less processed. Organic cane sugar is a delicious addition to sweets, but it should be used in moderation, as cane sugar can have dramatic effects on blood sugar, and on your metabolism, too. In several dessert recipes, I've included measurements for organic cane sugar as a substitute for my preferred sweetener. Because some cane sugars are processed with bone char, it's important to seek out brands that are vegan; see the Sources section (page 243) for some recommendations.

Date Bars

My version of date bars takes the classic components of this rustic favorite and refines it into an elegant treat. I prefer making my own oat flour for a texture that is somewhere between a fine flour and whole oats. Orange juice and zest enhance the natural sweetness of dates; nuts and coconut bring additional texture and flavor to the recipe, making this dessert stand apart from other bars. **Makes 18 to 24 bars**

2 cups old-fashioned rolled oats

1⅓ cups whole-wheat pastry flour or barley flour

⅔ cup shredded unsweetened dried coconut

⅔ cup walnuts, chopped

½ teaspoon plus ⅛ teaspoon fine sea salt

⅔ cup pure maple syrup

½ cup neutral cooking oil or melted vegan butter, cooled

2 teaspoons vanilla extract

16 Medjool dates, pitted

½ cup fresh orange juice or water

¾ teaspoon freshly grated orange zest

Preheat the oven to 350°F. Lightly oil a 13 by 9 by 2-inch baking dish. Blend the oats in a food processor until a coarse flour forms, but some oats still remain. Transfer the oat mixture to a large bowl. Mix in the pastry flour, coconut, walnuts, and ½ teaspoon of the salt.

Whisk the maple syrup, oil, and vanilla in a medium bowl to blend. Stir the maple syrup mixture into the flour mixture to blend. The mixture will be moist and sticky.

Blend the dates, orange juice, orange zest, and the remaining ⅛ teaspoon salt in a food processor until smooth (you do not have to clean out the food processor before using it to blend the dates).

Scatter half of the oat mixture over the bottom of the baking dish, then with your fingers wrapped with plastic wrap, press the oat mixture into the bottom of the baking dish to cover evenly. Spread all of the date purée over the oat mixture, smoothing evenly with a spatula. Sprinkle the remaining oat mixture over the date filling, then gently pat the topping.

Bake until the oat mixture is set and the topping is crisp and golden, about 40 minutes. Transfer the pan to a rack and let cool completely. Cut into squares and serve.

coconut rice pudding

This is a departure from the typical rice pudding, which tends to be very white and sticky. My version is beige in color because it's made with brown rice, which contributes nutritious benefits from whole grains to your dessert. I prefer using short-grain brown rice as the grains stay tender when cold, which makes the pudding creamier. **Serves 8**

½ cup dried currants

½ cup almonds, coarsely chopped

3 cups cold water

1 cup short-grain brown rice

1 cup homemade almond milk (see page 30) or store-bought

1 (14-ounce) can unsweetened light coconut milk

¾ cup pure maple syrup

½ teaspoon ground cinnamon

¼ teaspoon freshly grated orange zest

⅛ teaspoon freshly grated nutmeg

1 (2-inch) piece vanilla bean, split lengthwise

Soak the currants in a small bowl of warm water for 30 minutes. Drain and set the currants aside.

Preheat the oven to 350°F. Line a heavy rimmed baking sheet with parchment paper. Spread the almonds on the prepared baking sheet. Bake, stirring every 5 minutes, until the almonds turn golden.

Meanwhile, combine the 3 cups fresh cold water and the rice in a large, heavy saucepan. Bring the water to a boil over medium-high heat, then decrease the heat to low. Cover and simmer until the rice is tender and the water is absorbed, about 50 minutes.

Stir in the almond milk, coconut milk, maple syrup, cinnamon, orange zest, nutmeg, and currants. Scrape the seeds from the vanilla bean into the rice mixture, then add the bean. Bring to a simmer over medium-high heat.

Decrease the heat to medium-low and continue cooking uncovered, stirring often, until the mixture thickens slightly and resembles cooked oatmeal, about 35 minutes. Remove the vanilla bean. The pudding will continue to thicken as it cools.

Pour the hot pudding into a large bowl. Cover and refrigerate until the pudding is cold, at least 6 hours or up to 2 days.

Spoon the rice pudding into bowls. Garnish with the chopped almonds and serve.

Nondairy cream Replacements

Cooks count on heavy cream to add its silky texture to everything from puréed vegetable soups to cream pies. And then there is *whipped* cream—the crowning touch on a variety of sweet breakfast dishes and festive desserts. Fortunately, there are many times when a recipe that calls for heavy cream will work just as well with a dairy-free cream replacement. And whipped topping can be soy-based instead of cream-based, so you can make the switch without missing a thing.

NUT-BASED cream replacers can either be purchased at the store, such as MimicCreme, or be made from scratch at home, such as my Vegan Cashew Cream (page 83), which I use to top my Rich Dark Onion Soup (page 82). MimicCreme is a blend of almonds and cashews; it's available in both sweetened and unsweetened varieties, for use in either sweet or savory dishes. Nut-based creams don't whip: They are intended for use as a liquid ingredient and can be used in recipes that call for heavy cream, such as soups and even ganache.

SOY WHIPPED TOPPINGS from the store, such as the popular Soyatoo! brand, are available in the refrigerated section of most natural foods stores. These soy-based toppings can be purchased in either a pressurized can, for instant use, or in a box, which requires that you whip it at home. Either way, Soyatoo! makes a great addition to sweet treats: I've topped both my waffles (page 35) and my Chocolate Silk Pie (page 237) with it. You can also make a soy-based whipped topping from scratch at home; my recipe follows.

TOFU WHIPPED Cream

This is a recipe I have relied upon for years: I included it in my first book, *The Real Food Daily Cookbook*, and I love it so much that I had to include it again. It's a soy-based whipped topping that you can make at home, using all-natural ingredients. The recipe couldn't be simpler, although it does depend upon the use of agar to create the consistency one wants in a whipped cream. **Makes about 2 cups**

1 (12.3-ounce) container vacuum-packed extra-firm silken tofu (such as Mori-Nu)

¼ cup pure maple syrup

1 teaspoon vanilla extract

⅓ cup apple juice

1 tablespoon agar agar flakes

Pinch of salt

Blend the tofu, maple syrup, and vanilla in a food processor until smooth and creamy. Set aside.

Combine the juice, agar, and salt in a small, heavy saucepan. Bring to a simmer over high heat. Decrease the heat to medium-low. Cover and simmer, stirring frequently, for 15 minutes, or until the agar dissolves. Immediately blend the hot agar mixture into the tofu mixture. Transfer the tofu mixture to a bowl.

Cover and refrigerate for 1 hour, or until the mixture is set. Return the tofu mixture to the food processor and blend until it is smooth and creamy

The tofu whip will keep for 2 days, covered and refrigerated. Whisk before using.

κanten with apricots, figs, and Hazelnuts

Kanten (pronounced *can-tin*) is a jelled dessert (I call it a healthy Jell-O) made with agar instead of gelatin. It's a great way to prepare a light, refreshing fruit dessert that's not only free from animal products, but also from added sweeteners, flours, and fats. The variations are endless: Put together your choice of juices and assorted fresh and dried fruits. The key to using agar is to allow the agar flakes to soak in the juice for at least 15 minutes prior to turning on the heat. The rule of thumb is this: For every cup of liquid, use 1 tablespoon of agar flakes (for more on this ingredient, see page 213). **Serves 4 to 6**

1 cup dried apricots (about 6 ounces)

1 cup dried Calimyrna figs (about 6 ounces), stemmed

5 cups apricot nectar or apple juice

5 tablespoons plus 1 teaspoon agar flakes

⅛ teaspoon fine sea salt

1 teaspoon vanilla extract

1 cup hazelnuts, toasted and finely chopped

Place the dried apricots and figs in a medium bowl. Add enough boiling water to cover the fruit completely and soak until the fruit is tender, about 45 minutes. Drain the soaking liquid and cut the fruit into small bite-size pieces.

While the fruit is soaking, stir ½ cup of the apricot nectar and the agar flakes in a heavy saucepan and set aside for 15 minutes to allow the agar flakes to soften. Add the remaining 4½ cups of the apricot nectar and the salt to the agar mixture and bring to a simmer over high heat. Decrease the heat to medium-low. Cover and simmer, stirring frequently, for 15 minutes, or until the agar dissolves. Stir in the vanilla.

Transfer the kanten to a large bowl. Set aside, whisking occasionally, for 1 hour, or until the kanten is at room temperature and thickens, but is not set.

Spoon 2 cups of the thickened kanten into a blender and blend until the kanten is lighter in color and foamy. Return to the remaining kanten and gently stir in the apricots and figs. Spoon the kanten into a large glass bowl. Cover and refrigerate for 4 hours, or until the kanten is cold.

Spoon the kanten into small bowls. Garnish with the hazelnuts and serve.

Keep the kanten covered and refrigerate for up to 2 days.

Oftentimes, people considering a vegan diet worry that following through will mean giving up chocolate. The good news is that most types of high-quality chocolate are actually vegan: The best chocolate contains cocoa butter instead of dairy or hydrogenated fats.

is chocolate vegan?

In fact, there are many widely available brands of high-quality chocolate that not only skip the fillers, emulsifiers, and milks that many lower-quality products rely upon, but are specified as "vegan," meaning they also use vegan sugar and soy lecithin. There is a wide range of vegan chocolate available, from unsweetened to semisweet.

Despite its high fat and sugar content, chocolate can be good for you; in fact, it makes most superfoods lists. Chocolate contains flavonoids (the same good stuff in red wine and tea) and antioxidants. In fact, there is some evidence that very dark chocolate in small quantities is actually good for cardiovascular health: The darker it is, the less sugar it contains, and the more available its health benefits are. Chocolate also contains vitamin E, iron, copper, magnesium, and potassium.

chocolate silk pie with cashew crust

Calling all chocolate-lovers: This is a quick pie that you can put together at the last minute and pretend you've been baking all day. The filling has a nice silky texture like a pie made with eggs and dairy. The secret ingredient is tofu, but nobody will be able to tell. This pie is delicious proof that dairy-free desserts can taste just as good or even better than their more conventional counterparts. The crust can easily be made the day before. Use a traditional pie pan or a springform pan: either version works. **Serves 10 to 12**

CRUST
½ cup raw whole cashews

1 cup unbleached all-purpose flour

3 tablespoons neutral cooking oil

3 tablespoons pure maple syrup

½ teaspoon vanilla extract

¼ teaspoon fine sea salt

FILLING
1½ cups semisweet chocolate chips

1½ (12.3-ounce) vacuum-packed firm or extra-firm silken tofu (such as Mori-Nu)

¾ cup pure maple syrup

1½ teaspoons vanilla extract

¼ teaspoon fine sea salt

Soy whipped topping (such as Soyatoo!) or Tofu Whipped Cream (page 233)

Crust: Preheat the oven to 350°F. Lightly coat a 9-inch pie dish with oil. Pulse the cashews in a food processor until finely ground. Stir the ground cashews and the flour in a large bowl to blend. Whisk the oil, maple syrup, vanilla, and salt in a medium bowl to blend. Stir the oil mixture into the cashew-flour mixture to blend.

Press the mixture into the prepared pie dish. Bake until the crust is set and very pale golden around the edges, about 20 minutes. Let cool completely.

Filling: Decrease the oven temperature to 325°F. Stir the chocolate chips in a medium bowl set over a saucepan of simmering water until the chocolate is melted and smooth.

Purée the tofu, maple syrup, vanilla, and salt in a food processor until smooth. Blend in the melted chocolate. Scrape down the sides and bottom of the food processor bowl once or twice to make sure the mixture is well blended. Pour the chocolate mixture into the prebaked piecrust.

To Finish: Bake until the edges puff slightly and look dry but the rest of the filling is still glossy and jiggles, about 45 minutes. Don't worry that the filling is not set at this point, since it will become firm once it is cold.

Refrigerate the pie until it is cold, at least 3 hours or up to 2 days. Cut the pie into wedges and serve with soy whipped topping or tofu whipped cream.

vanilla and chocolate swirl bundt cake with chocolate fudge glaze

Bundt cakes are everyday cakes—easy to make (using just one pan) and delicious eaten as they are or dressed up with a simple glaze or icing. This swirled Bundt cake will satisfy both chocolate-lovers and those who favor vanilla: The two batters meet in the middle and bake, making for a pretty design when you cut and serve it. The addition of a quick chocolate glaze makes it that much more irresistible; to further embellish this cake, serve it with fresh berries or a dollop of nondairy ice cream. **Serves 12 to 16**

CAKE
Nonaerosol nonstick cooking spray

3½ cups unbleached white flour

2 teaspoons baking powder

2 teaspoons baking soda

1 teaspoon fine sea salt

1½ cups pure maple syrup

⅔ cup neutral cooking oil

1 tablespoon apple cider vinegar

1¾ cups plain or vanilla soy milk

1 tablespoon plus ½ teaspoon vanilla extract

⅓ cup unsweetened cocoa powder

2 tablespoons decaffeinated instant coffee powder

GLAZE
1 cup semisweet chocolate chips

2 tablespoons pure maple syrup

3 tablespoons rice milk

Cake: Position a rack in the center of the oven and preheat the oven to 325°F. Spray a 9- to 10-inch Bundt cake pan with nonaerosol nonstick cooking spray.

Whisk the flour, baking powder, baking soda, and salt in a large bowl to blend. Using a handheld electric mixer, beat the maple syrup, oil, vinegar, and 1½ cups of the soy milk in a large bowl to blend. Add the flour mixture and mix just until blended.

Transfer half of the batter to a second bowl. To the first bowl of batter, mix in 1 tablespoon of the vanilla. To the second bowl of batter, mix in the cocoa powder, coffee powder, the remaining ¼ cup soy milk, and the remaining ½ teaspoon vanilla.

Pour the chocolate batter into the prepared pan, then pour in the vanilla batter. Do not worry about mixing the 2 batters together to create a marble effect; as the cake bakes, the batters will blend together on their own to create a pretty design. Bake until a toothpick inserted near the center comes out with some crumbs attached, about 50 minutes.

Let the cake cool in the pan on a rack for 30 minutes, then invert the cake onto the rack and let cool completely. At this point, the cake can be made 1 day ahead and stored airtight at room temperature.

Glaze: Stir the chocolate chips in a medium bowl set over a saucepan of simmering water until the chocolate melts completely. Remove the bowl from over the saucepan. Stir in the maple syrup and rice milk. Drizzle the glaze over the cake and let stand until the glaze is set. The glaze looks best the day it is made, so plan to serve the cake the same day you glaze it.

Cut the cake into wedges and serve.

peaches and nectarines with sweet almond-cashew cream

This is a very satisfying and easily assembled dessert made with seasonal fresh fruit: In the summer, any stone fruit works well; in the winter, apples and pears make a nice combination. The nut cream was inspired by a recipe in *The Natural Gourmet* by Annemarie Colbin. I must have made almost every recipe in that book when I first started cooking; it is still a favorite of mine. Using the mirin is optional, but including it brings a rich sweetness and luster to the recipe, making the cream unique and sophisticated.
Serves 6

1 cup raw whole cashews

1 cup raw whole almonds

2 tablespoons pure maple syrup

1 tablespoon vanilla extract

About 1¾ cups plain almond milk or water

2 tablespoons mirin

5 ripe peaches, pitted

4 ripe nectarines, pitted

Place the cashews and almonds in a medium bowl. Add enough cold water to cover. Soak for 2 hours. Drain the soaking liquid.

Blend the cashews and almonds in a blender until finely ground. Add the maple syrup and vanilla. With the machine on low, gradually add enough almond milk to form a thick but pourable cream. Blend in the mirin.

Cut the peaches and nectarines into ¾-inch-thick wedges. Place the peaches and nectarines in individual bowls, then spoon the cream over and serve immediately.

nondairy milkshakes

With the right nondairy ice cream, deliciously creamy vegan milkshakes are easy to make. For the best results, the nondairy ice cream has to have the right consistency: It should be thick and creamy, without separating or becoming watery. I've tried every nondairy ice cream on the block, and I've found that the Tempt brand is great for making a long-lasting, thick shake. Don't let the fact that it is made from hemp seeds dissuade you—it is creamy and has the mouthfeel you want in an ice cream. My other favorites are Good Karma and So Delicious, both of which make terrific milkshakes too. **Each recipe makes 1 milkshake, enough to fill a 16-ounce glass**

vanilla milkshake

1½ cups vanilla hemp milk ice cream (¾ pint)

1 cup ice cubes

¾ cup vanilla hemp milk

2 tablespoons agave nectar

strawberry milkshake

1 cup vanilla hemp milk ice cream (½ pint)

¾ cup ice cubes

¾ cup vanilla hemp milk

1 small container (about 8 ounces) fresh strawberries, stemmed

2 tablespoons agave nectar

chocolate milkshake

1½ cups chocolate fudge hemp milk ice cream (¾ pint)

1 cup ice cubes

¾ cup vanilla hemp milk

2 tablespoons agave nectar

For each milkshake, place all the ingredients in a blender and blend on low speed for 30 seconds, or until the ice is coarsely crushed. Stop and allow the ingredients to settle, then blend on high speed for another 30 seconds, or until the mixture is thick and creamy.

Pour the milkshake into a tall glass and serve immediately, with a straw.

sources

natural foods companies

Bob's Red Mill (www.bobsredmill.com) *high quality and gluten-free flours*

Daiya (www.daiyafoods.com) *dairy-free cheese*

Eden Foods (www.edenfoods.com) *specializes in Japanese foods, grains and beans*

Essential Living Foods (www.essentiallivingfoods.com) *exotic superfoods*

Field Roast Sausage (www.fieldroast.com) *grain- and vegetable-based plant protein*

Florida Crystals (www.floridacrystals.com) *vegan sugar*

Follow Your Heart (www.followyourheart.com) *healthy fats and dairy-free cheese*

French Meadow Bakery (www.frenchmeadow.com) *organic breads*

Gold Mine Natural Foods (www.goldminenaturalfoods.com) *macrobiotic online store*

Good Karma Foods (www.goodkarmafoods.com) *first organic rice ice cream*

Living Harvest (www.livingharvest.com) *deliciously decadent hemp products*

Lotus Foods (www.lotusfoods.com) *a world of exotic rice*

Lundberg Family Farms (www.lundberg.com) *fine quality rice*

Sambazon (www.sambazon.com) *real deal acai*

Spectrum Natural Foods (www.spectrumorganics.com) *healthy oils*

Sunspire Natural Chocolates (www.sunspire.com) *truly inspired natural chocolates*

The Grain & Salt Society (www.celticseasalt.com) *quality sea salt*

Turtle Mountain (www.turtlemountain.com) *dairy-free indulgences*

KITCHEN TOOLS and SMALL WARES

Le Creuset (www.lecreuset.com) or Staub (www.staubusa.com) *top-of-the-line cookware*

Shun Knives (www.shunknives.org) *my favorite knives*

Vitamix (www.vitamix.com) *high-performance blenders*

EDUCATION

Food Matters by Mark Bittman (www.markbittman.com) *fantastic personal story on eating a mostly vegan diet*

Eating Animals by Jonathan Safran Foer (www.eatinganimals.com) *explores the stories we live by to justify how we eat*

Diet for a Small Planet by Frances Moore Lappé and *Hope's Edge: The Next Diet for a Small Planet* by Frances Moore Lappé and Anna Lappé (www.smallplanet.org) *social and personal significance in vegetarian eating*

Food Politics by Marion Nestle (www.foodpolitics.com) *informative Web site, too*

The Omnivore's Dilemma, In Defense of Food and *Food Rules* by Michael Pollan (www.michaelpollan.com) *a clear-headed examination of our national eating disorder*

Diet for a New America by John Robbins (www.johnrobbins.info) *a well-documented exposé of factory farms and how we eat*

Books by Michio Kushi (www.michiokushi.org) *a wide collection of books on macrobiotics*

The Real Food Daily Cookbook (www.realfood.com) *my first cookbook*

Veg News magazine (www.vegnews.com) *premiere lifestyle magazine*

Vegetarian Times magazine (www.vegetariantimes.com) *Their website has the world's largest collection of vegetarian recipes and I am proud to be their executive chef*

organizations and initiatives, *the titles say it all*

EcoLogo Program (www.ecologo.org)

Environmental Working Group (www.ewg.org)

Green Seal (www.greenseal.org)

Meat Free Monday (www.supportmfm.org)

Meatless Monday (www.meatlessmonday.com)

Physicians Committee for Responsible Medicine (www.pcrm.org)

The Good Life Center at Forest Farm (www.goodlife.org)

metric conversions and equivalents

APPROXIMATE METRIC EQUIVALENTS

Volume

¼ teaspoon	1 milliliter
½ teaspoon	2.5 milliliters
¾ teaspoon	4 milliliters
1 teaspoon	5 milliliters
1¼ teaspoons	6 milliliters
1½ teaspoons	7.5 milliliters
1¾ teaspoons	8.5 milliliters
2 teaspoons	10 milliliters
1 tablespoon (½ fluid ounce)	15 milliliters
2 tablespoons (1 fluid ounce)	30 milliliters
¼ cup	60 milliliters
⅓ cup	80 milliliters
½ cup (4 fluid ounces)	120 milliliters
⅔ cup	160 milliliters
¾ cup	180 milliliters
1 cup (8 fluid ounces)	240 milliliters
1¼ cups	300 milliliters
1½ cups (12 fluid ounces)	360 milliliters
1⅔ cups	400 milliliters
2 cups (1 pint)	460 milliliters
3 cups	700 milliliters
4 cups (1 quart)	0.95 liter
1 quart plus ¼ cup	1 liter
4 quarts (1 gallon)	3.8 liters

Weight

¼ ounce	7 grams
½ ounce	14 grams
¾ ounce	21 grams
1 ounce	28 grams
1¼ ounces	35 grams
1½ ounces	42.5 grams
1⅔ ounces	45 grams
2 ounces	57 grams
3 ounces	85 grams
4 ounces (¼ pound)	113 grams
5 ounces	142 grams
6 ounces	170 grams
7 ounces	198 grams
8 ounces (½ pound)	227 grams
16 ounces (1 pound)	454 grams
35.25 ounces (2.2 pounds)	1 kilogram

Length

⅛ inch	3 millimeters
¼ inch	6 millimeters
½ inch	1¼ centimeters
1 inch	2½ centimeters
2 inches	5 centimeters
2½ inches	6 centimeters
4 inches	10 centimeters
5 inches	13 centimeters
6 inches	15¼ centimeters
12 inches (1 foot)	30 centimeters

metric conversions and equivalents

COMMON INGREDIENTS AND THEIR APPROXIMATE EQUIVALENTS

1 cup uncooked brown rice = 185 grams

1 cup flour = 140 grams

1 stick vegan butter (4 ounces · ½ cup · 8 tablespoons)
= 110 grams

1 cup organic cane sugar or maple sugar, firmly packed
= 225 grams

METRIC CONVERSION FORMULAS

To Convert	Multiply
Ounces to grams	Ounces by 28.35
Pounds to kilograms	Pounds by .454
Teaspoons to milliliters	Teaspoons by 4.93
Tablespoons to milliliters	Tablespoons by 14.79
Fluid ounces to milliliters	Fluid ounces by 29.57
Cups to milliliters	Cups by 236.59
Cups to liters	Cups by .236
Pints to liters	Pints by .473
Quarts to liters	Quarts by .946
Gallons to liters	Gallons by 3.785
Inches to centimeters	Inches by 2.54

OVEN TEMPERATURES

To convert Fahrenheit to Celsius, subtract 32 from Fahrenheit, multiply the result by 5, then divide by 9.

Description	Fahrenheit	Celsius	British Gas Mark
Very cool	200°	95°	0
Very cool	225°	110°	¼
Very cool	250°	120°	½
Cool	275°	135°	1
Cool	300°	150°	2
Warm	325°	165°	3
Moderate	350°	175°	4
Moderately hot	375°	190°	5
Fairly hot	400°	200°	6
Hot	425°	220°	7
Very hot	450°	230°	8
Very hot	475°	245°	9

Information compiled from a variety of sources, including *Recipes into Type* by Joan Whitman and Dolores Simon (Newton, MA: Biscuit Books, 2000); *The New Food Lover's Companion* by Sharon Tyler Herbst (Hauppauge, NY: Barron's, 1995); and *Rosemary Brown's Big Kitchen Instruction Book* (Kansas City, MO: Andrews McMeel, 1998).

index

index

index

index

index

index

index

index

index

index